MONEY, MEDIA, AND THE GRASS ROOTS

Volume 164 Sage Library of Social Research

RECENT VOLUMES IN . . .
SAGE LIBRARY OF SOCIAL RESEARCH

MONEY, MEDIA, AND THE GRASS ROOTS

State Ballot Issues and the Electoral Process

Betty H. Zisk

Volume 164
SAGE LIBRARY OF
SOCIAL RESEARCH

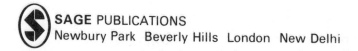

SAGE PUBLICATIONS
Newbury Park Beverly Hills London New Delhi

For information address:

SAGE Publications, Inc.
2111 West Hillcrest Drive
Newbury Park, California 91320

SAGE Publications Inc.  SAGE Publications Ltd.
275 South Beverly Drive   28 Banner Street
Beverly Hills   London EC1Y 8QE
California 90212   England

SAGE PUBLICATIONS India Pvt. Ltd.
M-32 Market
Greater Kailash I
New Delhi 110 048 India

Printed in the United States of America

Library of Congress Cataloging-in-Publication Data

Main entry under title:

Zisk, Betty H., 1930-
    Money, media, and the grass roots.

    (Sage library of social research ; v. 164)
    Bibliography: p.
    Includes index.
    1. Elections—United States—States—Case studies.
2. Voting—United States—States—Case studies.
3. Referendum—United States—States--Case studies.
4. Electioneering—United States—States—Case
studies.   5. Campaign funds—United States—States—
Case studies.   I. Title   II. Series.
JK1967.Z57   1986   324.973'0092'6   86-13035
ISBN 0-8039-2794-0
ISBN 0-8039-2795-9 (pbk.)

CONTENTS

ACKNOWLEDGMENTS

Help for a study seven years in the making was fortunately widely shared, generous, and (mostly) patient. Support at Boston University came from many sources, including a small grant for word processing from Dean Michael Mendillo; logistic help and moral support from Susan Fortini and Suzanne O'Connor; and finally, the enthusiasm and sound advice that only a theory-building colleague can give, from Professor Judith Gillespie. As always, I am grateful to my sons (to whom this work is dedicated) and to two loving friends, Leah Vetter and Michael Szczepkowski, simply for being "there" for me.

My parents, who introduced me to the wondrous world of Proposition 13, and all of those fellow volunteers in California and Massachusetts campaigns, 1964-1982, who shared the work, the agony, and occasionally the joy on open housing, the death penalty, and the bottle bill deserve mention. The Michigan and California officials who reminded me, in phone conversations, that some state workers are there to serve; the librarians at Boston University and UCLA who found facts and figures, fixed machines, and borrowed obscure reports for me; and finally, my two Sage editors, Lisa Freeman-Miller and Susan Loring—have all contributed in more ways than they know. It was Susan who suggested (quoting Montaigne) that the time had come to "abandon" my seven-year-old brainchild. And so, with thanks and with sole responsibility for errors of fact or interpretation, I leave the study, though not the lifetime role of participant in this maddening and exciting gift of the Progressives— Direct Democracy!

—Betty H. Zisk

TO Jonathan, Stephen, and Matthew Zisk—
sons, friends, and sometime fellow-activists

1

INTRODUCTION

This is a comparative study of the campaigns and outcomes on major ballot questions in four states, over a period of seven years—1976 to 1982. It encompasses an in-depth look at expenditures, advertising, grass-roots activity, and voting behavior, in Massachusetts, Michigan, Oregon, and California, on 72 controversies that include almost every major issue of our time. Among these issues are taxes, economic regulation, the environment, the nuclear freeze, and crime control proposals, as well as many less prominent topics like self-service gas, parklands development, and the never-ending argument about fluoridation.

Some of these campaigns were born of citizen wrath at government, at criminals, perhaps at their own helplessness. Some featured colorful or charismatic figures (Cesar Chavez, Jerry Falwell, Tom Hayden) or bizarre campaign techniques or a whole series of court injunctions. But many campaigns were mundane, even boring, and almost neglected by the voters and media alike, in spite of their potential for high costs or for some degree of political and social change. Some proposals saw powerful coalitions of interest groups on opposite sides; others attracted only a handful of poorly organized amateurs. Only two were battles primarily between political parties.

Why would anyone want to study or read about a subject that, at least until the last decade, has been ignored by most scholars, and about which most citizens of all but a few states remain blissfully unaware? A personal odyssey, spanning fourteen years between my involvement in California's open housing referendum in 1964 and later fortuitous choice of a California vacation in late spring of 1978, just in time to see the end of the battle over Proposition 13 (the property tax cap), accounts for this study on the level that is of least direct interest to the reader. The reader should be warned, however, that

I—like many others who write on ballot questions—have been an activist as well as an analyst, with attendant strong feelings. But there are strong scholarly reasons as well. I believe such a focus to be timely and important in at least three ways: for our understanding of several important aspects of the political process itself; on policy grounds; and finally, as a contribution to the discussion about the place of direct (as opposed to representative) democracy in contemporary democratic theory.

First, analyzing campaigns and voting patterns on the initiative and referendum can tell us a great deal about the political process as it operates in the absence of the usually dominant party and candidate activities and cues. Ballot issue campaigns provide (potentially) the purest form of issue voting that exists. Do voters respond by serious information gathering and selfless decision-making, as the reformers hoped, or do they find new shortcuts in reaching their decisions? Where do they get their information? What institutions (if any) substitute for the parties and candidates in organizing and financing their campaigns? How well do media and grass-roots campaigns work in informing the voters?

In short, campaign expenditures and strategies, group decisions about alliances and/or the use of political consultants, the mobilization of volunteers, the use of the media, and the like, are important topics on which too little systematic information has been collected—aside from the well-worked area of presidential, and to a lesser extent congressional, campaigns. My primary focus will be on this subject.

The attempt to answer these questions may also shed light on the range and applicability of some major models of democracy (majoritarian, pluralist, postpluralist) or some of the cyclical arguments over the appropriate role of parties, in the sense that ballot issue campaigns are the most extreme of deviant cases: not only are parties irrelevant to this set of debates over issues (though not illegal, as they are for local nonpartisan government), but so, on the whole, are candidates. Discovering and explaining what fills that vacuum is in itself important. And this study may also cast light on the roles usually played by the missing actors, through their very absence.

Second, although this has not been my main purpose, I hope to reach some conclusions about political activation and recruitment in an issue-oriented and mainly nonpartisan milieu. This analysis may also be relevant to the debate over national primaries or a proposed national initiative, and/or other national mechanisms of direct democracy. I am particularly interested in the political recruitment and communication process of the leaders and followers who first become active as a result of ballot issues.

I have observed, in participating in several grass-roots campaigns on initiatives, a number of activists who have seldom (if ever) participated in traditional interest group activities or in campaigns for partisan office. Many of them stay to fight another day. If this is a very widespread phenomenon, it implies that while the Progressive dream of activating vast numbers of apathetic voters may not have come to fruition, that dream may nevertheless have been partially fulfilled by the provision of an alternative channel for political expression, through (for example) political movements and public interest groups.

Finally, there are also clear policy implications in studying ballot questions. The initiative and referendum process has been one way of broadening the public agenda, and thus of bringing new ideas to the attention of the wider polity. Minimum wage laws, child labor laws, old age pensions, and merit systems for public employees were only a few of the first laws enacted through the process in the early days; the bottle bill and a comprehensive land planning agency are two other recent examples.

An analogous (and valid) argument has been made for the platforms of third parties as a source of fresh ideas that frequently enter the mainstream at a later point (Stedman and Stedman, 1950). The difference in the present argument, however, is that the initiative has been a means of early *enactment* of some of these ideas, often after failing to receive majority support in a state legislature, and thus can furnish concrete evidence of how new and sometimes unorthodox policies can work. Some of these innovations have indeed proved unconstitutional, trivial, or occasionally oppressive (as have some products of legislatures); but from a policy perspective the initiative in particular has helped some states to fulfill one promise of federalism: 50 (or 22) built-in laboratories in which to sort out and test proposals before they are considered or approved on a wider scale. While a discussion of the issues per se has not been my central purpose, I shall consider, in passing, the degree to which some ballot questions have opened up important new areas on the political agenda.

The remainder of this chapter is devoted to four preliminary tasks. First, I shall attempt a very brief history of the origins and adoption of the initiative and referenda mechanisms, in the context of the Progressive reform movement, and a set of definitions of specific devices (direct and indirect initiatives, statutory referenda, constitutional referenda). Second, I will present a summary of my own survey of the ballot questions considered by all states with provisions for the statutory initiative and referendum from 1976 to 1980. Third, I will explain and justify the present research strategy: the choice of states, criteria for selection of major issues, choice of time frame, and the sources of data on campaigns and voting. Finally, I will preview the format and contents of the remaining chapters in this study.

Direct Democracy and the Progressive Reform Movement

Plebiscitary democracy, in one form or another, is at least as old as the Greek city state, although this classical form of participation was limited to free citizens. Referenda, as legitimating devices, appeared in relatively modern times in Switzerland and in France in the fifteenth and sixteenth centuries. Most relevant for the American student of democracy, however, was the consideration, by New England town meetings in the Revolutionary era, of several state constitutions drawn up to replace the colonial charters (Ranney, 1978: 5-21, 68-85).

Although every state but Delaware has used the constitutional referendum (that is, voter approval of amendments to the state constitution) almost from the very beginning, other types of direct legislation were adopted more gradually. It wasn't until the growth of the reform sentiment of the Progressives that some of the states of the Midwest and the Northwest seriously considered and adopted the initiative and statutory referendum. A trend that began with adoption of these devices in South Dakota, Utah, and Oregon between 1898 to 1902 gradually spread to nineteen more states by the end of World War I. All initiative states but Maine, Massachusetts, and Arkansas were, up to that point, still in the West and Midwest. The last four states to adopt both of these mechanisms, however, included Alaska (1959) and Florida (1972) (Ranney, 1978: 69-73).

The Progressive movement had much in common with its immediate predecessor, Populism. (The Populist Party, in fact, was an early advocate of direct democracy.) While the social and political base for the new reform advocates was more urban and middle class, and thus both more inclusive and less mistrustful of Jews, immigrants, or indeed of urban residents in general, the central intellectual thrust of both movements was quite similar. As Eric Goldman (1952: 75) puts it:

> . . . to the extent that the two movements concerned themselves with liberty, they shared an emphasis on freeing the avenues of opportunity. . . . Government was to be democratized in order to make it amenable to reform. Reform meant primarily the ending of governmental interventions that benefited large-scale capital and a rapid increase in the interventions that favored men of little or no capital.

Thus the focus, at the national level (and on the whole, the reformers relied more on federal than state action), was on antitrust action, minimum wage laws, a federal income tax, and the fostering of unionism. But unlike the populists, there was no Progressive push for nationalization of industries or a thorough overhaul of the currency, lending, and banking structure. The goal was the *restoration* of economic opportunity for the small entrepreneur, the laborer, and the farmer by using the powers of government to break up, or at least restrain, large institutions that threatened to choke off economic access. In a sense the Progressives were romantics who wanted a return of the era of smallness. The enemy was large organizations, whether public or private.

At the state level one of the main targets was the power of the railroads, particularly in the West and Northwest. Another was a whole set of symbiotic relations between, on the one hand, the dominant "interests" (mining, lumber, meatpacking, utilities) and, on the other, the state legislators who seemed to be in thrall to those with economic power. This led naturally to the other dominant theme of the movement: their preoccupation with procedural reform. While at the national level this took form in the commission as an answer to many evils, for the states and cities the solution was a host of proposals for direct democracy. These included the direct primary and nonpartisanship (both designed to cut the power of parties and bosses), the recall device, the direct election of judges, and the initiative and referendum.

One key assumption behind these procedural devices was, according to Richard Hofstadter (1960: 259), the possibility that the individual citizen's "contribution to the public weal grew not out of his pursuit in politics of his own needs but . . . out of his disinterested reflection upon the needs of the community." The problem was to devise the machinery through which this public-spirited citizen could effectively wield power. Hofstadter (1960: 261) goes on to point out that whole ethos of individual responsibility, a variant of the Yankee-Protestant ethic, was ill-adapted "to the realities of the highly organized society of the late nineteenth and twentieth century." This is a point, of course, on which I shall be concentrating in later chapters.

More specifically, the reformers hoped that this economically disinterested or neutral citizen impulse could be used to force substantive change on state legislatures that had avoided controversial topics because of their close ties to vested interests. The mere threat of a referendum (a reconsideration of a measure already passed) might prevent passage of inegalitarian legislation. The threat of an initiative petition might force the legislature's hand as well. If this failed, of course the citizens could bring their original proposals directly to the voter. (And other devices, such as the recall and direct election of judges, would in the long run prevent continued obstruction or overruling of the handful of reforms that made their way into law.)

By 1918, then, 22 states had adopted the initiative for constitutional amendments, with four more to follow in the next 54 years. Thirty-nine states have adopted the referendum for statutes (the 39 include all 26 that have the initiative), while 22 allow the statutory initiative. Fourteen, in addition, allow a constitutional initiative, or proposal by petition of a constitutional amendment. And, as mentioned, all but one state provide for voter approval of amendments passed by the legislature (Council of State Governments, 1983-84).

A more detailed definition of these mechanisms may be helpful. I shall specify, in addition, their use (or absence) in the four states of the present study.

(1) The regular *constitutional amendment*, submitted to the voters by the legislature, usually requires an exceptional legislative majority and in some states must be initially approved by two suc-

cessive sessions of that body. Thus it usually has widespread support before reaching the ballot. All four states in this study employ the mechanism, as do all states but Delaware.

(2) The *constitutional amendment by initiative,* in contrast, reaches the ballot by initiative petition, after its advocates obtain a specified number of voter signatures and is used by only 14 states. Michigan, California, and Oregon use the mechanism; Massachusetts does not.

(3) The *statutory initiative,* used by 22 states, allows proposed changes in laws to reach the ballot by initiative petition. In Massachusetts and Michigan (as in five other states) such proposals must first receive legislative approval to reach the ballot, or in lieu of that approval, additional signatures must be collected. This is called the *indirect initiative* and was also employed by California until 1966. At this writing 14 states, including California and Oregon, employ the *direct initiative* instead, whereby petition signatures of a specified number of voters are required for ballot status. The more cumbersome indirect initiative process has been justified as screening out frivolous proposals; it was repealed in California, however, partly because of its infrequent use.

(4) The *statutory referendum* allows voters to pass judgment on laws already approved by the legislature. Thirty-nine states provide for the mechanism; in some cases this is by petition, in others by vote on the legislature itself, and in still others both means are allowed. All four of our states provide for the petition method of statutory referendum; Michigan and Oregon also have the legislative version. (There is probably no significant practical difference for states allowing only the petition form, since dissident legislators as well as citizens can and do use that technique. The petition version, however, is a simpler or more attainable remedy for ordinary citizens.)

The number of signatures required for petitions to qualify varies from state to state, usually consisting of about 5-8% of the number of votes cast in the last gubernatorial election. A few states require some minimal spread of these signatures across counties; most also have a signature verification process that is stiff enough to have fostered the collection of as many as 50-100% in excess of the minimum to be sure of meeting the standards. The legal arrangements for each of the four states studied here will be specified below.

Use of Ballot Questions and Bond Issue
Submissions in the 1976-80 Period

In mid-1978 and again in 1980, I contacted all 39 states that provide for the statutory initiative and referendum, requesting copies of the ballot question for the 1976-80 period. After eventually receiving answers from all 39, I found that during the period in question, voters in 27 of these states were asked to decide on constitutional amendments; in 16 states they were presented with statutory initiatives and/or referenda; and in nine (including California) they were asked to approve bond issues. Aside from Wyoming, no reason was given for the lack of ballot questions (even mandatory submissions of constitutional amendments) in 12 initiative-and-referendum states. (A letter from the office of the Wyoming Secretary of State explained that while a few initiative petitions had been circulated, none had qualified for a period of some years. I assume a similar situation in the other 11 states.)

In the following discussion I shall omit the four states on which I will be concentrating for the remainder of this study—Massachusetts, Michigan, Oregon, and California—thus presenting data on 23 states in regard to statutory proposals, 12 on amendments, and eight on bond issues. My purpose is to provide a background "census" of issues that were considered in the late 1970s by the voters in states that encouraged direct legislation.

Table 1.1 presents information on the 12 states that in fact utilized the statutory initiative and/or referenda. Since Virginia and New Jersey voters were asked to consider only *one* issue (gambling), voter opportunities existed on most questions in only 10 other states. Procedural questions of all types arose, as they always do, with great frequency in eight of the states. Next in frequency were environmental questions (in eight states), with bottle bills and proposals for nuclear power regulation the most common. After that, taxes (seven states) and regulatory issues (three states) made up most of the remaining 1976-80 statutory questions.

A glance at Table 9.1 in my conclusion will demonstrate that this set of issues in 12 states is not markedly different from those considered in Massachusetts, Michigan, Oregon, and California, except for the omission of law and order problems from this initial list. The main reason is not, however, a lack of activity in this area but

TABLE 1.1:   Statutory Initiatives and Referenda, 1976-80, for 12
             States*

	Number of states
Procedural measures:	(8)
Legislative arrangements, executive commissions	4
Financial disclosure	2
Recall of officials	2
Other	2
Environmental issues:	(8)
Nuclear safety and waste	5
Bottle bills, litter control	7
Land and water use	4
Utility rates	1
Taxes:	(7)
Property tax limits or exemptions	6
Budget limits	2
Other	4
Other financial issues	2
Parimutual betting, lottery, gambling	5
School issues	2
Regulatory issues (drinking, obscenity)	3
Miscellaneous	3

* Alaska, Arizona, Arkansas, Colorado, Maine, Montana, New Jersey, Ohio, South
Dakota, Utah, Virginia, Washington. (Does not include Massachusetts, Michigan, Oregon, or California.)

the fact that in most states, crime control proposals require constitutional amendments. (On some other issues, including taxes and
proposals on nuclear regulation, there is considerable variation in
whether states use statutes or constitutional amendments to change
existing arrangements.)

Thus it can be seen in Table 1.2, which presents the list of constitutional amendments considered in the larger population of 23
states, that seven states considered amendments dealing with criminal issues. A total of 15, including three of the seven in the crime
control category, considered proposals on the court and jury structure as well.

As in the preceding table, Table 1.2 shows a very large number
of procedural proposals, dealing not only with the powers, salaries,
and administrative arrangements among officials but with election

TABLE 1.2:   Constitutional Amendments Submitted to Voters in 23 States, 1976-80*

	Number of states
Procedural measures:	(23)
Legislative, executive, bureaucracy	21
Salaries, benefits	8
Courts, juries	15
Local officials	7
Election procedures	10
Constitutional revision	7
Tax and revenue issues:	23
Environmental issues:	(8)
Nuclear regulation	2
Land use	6
Mineral rights/issues	2
Prisoners, crime control, gun control	7
School issues	3
Lottery, gambling, bingo	4
Regulatory issues:	(14)
Utilities	4
Commerce, transportation	7
Drinking age	1
Right to work laws	3
ERA	2
Miscellaneous	4

* Alaska, Arizona, Arkansas, Colorado, Florida, Georgia, Idaho, Illinois, Kansas, Kentucky, Maine, Montana, New Hampshire, New Jersey, New Mexico, New York, Ohio, Rhode Island, South Carolina, South Dakota, Utah, Virginia, Washington. (Does not include Massachusetts, Michigan, Oregon, and California.)

rules and arrangements for a constitutional revision commission as well. All 23 states in fact considered amendments in the procedural category.

Tax proposals were by far the most popular subject for amendments (as they also were in our four states) after procedural topics were sorted out. Again, voters in every one of these 23 states considered at least one proposal. An amazing number of these proposed amendments dealt with highly specific subjects, such as tax exemptions for swine (Georgia), urban renewal (Florida, Virginia), disabled veterans (Virginia), and solar energy (Georgia, Nebraska).

The narrow scope of these proposals is of course due to the extreme specificity of the state constitutions being amended, few of which are noted for either brevity or a high level of abstraction.

As was also the case with statutory initiatives, environmental proposals and regulatory issues are also very common topics for constitutional amendments. Land use amendments were proposed in six states, and a host of regulatory proposals for almost every conceivable economic sector appeared in 11 states. Note also that the ubiquitous "right to work" proposals, a popular cause in some quarters for at least three decades, appeared on the ballots of three states, while the more contemporary ERA amendment was considered in two, in addition to the Massachusetts campaign.

There are no real surprises in either table, in part because grouping issues into manageable categories sometimes robs most lists of any individual flavor. I might therefore note in passing that among the environmental issues in Table 1.1 was the poignant reminder of the enormous change in prestige of George McGovern (in only four short years from 1972 to 1976) in the form of a South Dakota initiative to authorize the hunting of mourning doves. There was also a hotly debated proposal over the location of Alaska's new capital; a fair number of controversies over casinos, jai alai enterprises, state lotteries, horseracing, and bingo in churches that set good citizens against each other. And the citizens of Georgia not only were asked to cope with taxes on swine but on widows, PTAs, mobile homes, and private airports as well.

The final table in this chapter, on bond issues presented to voters, is potentially even less informative if caution is not used in aggregating the data. This is because officials in one or two states (often Alaska) in almost every substantive category have proposed a bond issue of sufficient magnitude to dwarf all the others on the same topic. For this reason, the name of the state and amount requested is specified separately in the table when one or two issues dominate a category.

Proposals for bond issues, constitutionally mandated in only a few states, are not strictly speaking referenda with details of policy to be judged by the voters. Yet some observers trace the "taxpayers' revolt" back to an increase in the number of school bond issues defeated at the local level. Most of us too would agree with the textbook adage that budgets are platforms or policies in action. And in one of the four states studied intensively here—California—battles over the parklands and Lake Tahoe bond proposals, although low-keyed, were very similar in support and opposition patterns to other environmental controversies. Thus it is appropriate to conclude this brief census of issues by summarizing the proposals for bonds put before the voters in eight states (not including California).

The most obvious fact to be gleaned from Table 1.3 is that Alaska, as a relatively large, undeveloped, and new state, is playing "catch up" with the others, especially in regard to capital facilities. Fully $1.4 million, or almost one-third of the eight state totals proposed, was Alaska's. Clearly "catch up" in very specific areas was going on for other states as well: New York's economic recovery program and highway system, Washington's water policies, and New Jersey's prison and park systems. Thus there is little point in drawing conclusions about relative distribution of resources in a year or even in a decade. The next decade may see other states replacing old facilities or developing new resources in a previously neglected area.

In addition, knowledge about the relative share of state and local funds, and about the long-term borrowing of other states, would be essential for any meaningful inferences. It should be noted, however, that the voters in these eight states—most of which are also among those using the statutory initiative and/or referendum as well—were expected to make 76 separate decisions involving $4.5 billion over a span of five years. This averages almost 10 decisions and $567 million for each state.

Having completed a very brief survey of the constitutional amendments, ballot questions, and bond issues considered in several states, I am now ready to discuss the research strategies which enable a manageable analysis.

Research Strategy: Choice of States, Issues, and Information Sources

THE FOUR STATES

While it was feasible to collect information on ballot proposals in all 39 states employing the statutory referendum, and in the somewhat smaller set that uses an initiative as well, clearly the focus of a more detailed analysis of campaigns and outcomes had to be narrowed. I began, quite naturally, with Massachusetts and California

TABLE 1.3:   Bond Issues Considered on Ballots of Eight States, 1976-
80*

Subject	Number of separate proposals	Amount (in millions)	Largest proposals (in millions)	
State facilities and buildings	8	$1,024	$969	Alaska
Economic action program	1	750	750	New York
Highways, trans-portation	15	750	500	New York
			149	Alaska
Flood control, water sewage, pollution	13	857	575	Washington
			92	Alaska
Prisons	9	279	180	New Jersey
Parks, recreation fish, wildlife	8	277	200	New Jersey
			68	Alaska
Schools, education	12	258	120	Alaska
Housing	3	132		
All Other	7	109		
TOTAL	76	$4,536	(millions)	

* Alaska, Florida, and New Jersey voted in even years; Maine, New York, Rhode Island,
Virginia, and Washington voted in odd years.

because I have worked on ballot campaigns while living in both
states and was familiar and intrigued by what I had observed and
experienced. In addition, both states were historic political innova-
tors in their regions, and both had mixed industrial-urban, agricultural, and mountainous areas which promised a considerable range
of subject matter for ballot consideration. Finally, the choice of
Massachusetts also allowed, initially, a contrast of the indirect with
the direct initiative process—a contrast, as it turned out, that made
little difference except in the number of ballot questions considered.

The next set of choices was based on the desirability for both
regional and partisan-ideological diversity. Michigan was selected
not only as typical, in some ways, of the upper-Midwestern band of
former Progressive strongholds that includes Wisconsin, Minnesota, and the Dakotas, but because it is a strong party and union

state, with a strong industrial base in the Detroit area. Like the other
three states in our study, however, Michigan also includes a large,
more conservative, nonurban hinterland.

Finally, for maximum contrast I added Oregon to the list, as a
somewhat more Republican state (on state level elections), and one
with weaker parties, a weak union movement, and a less developed
economy than any of the other three. Oregon is also a pacesetter on
ballot issues, particularly on land use and environmental politics,
taking tremendous pride in its contrast to California's embrace of
rapid economic development. And finally, because of more stringent limits on campaign activities during the petition qualification
state, I expected and indeed found a contrasting campaign style.

While it might have been desirable to add yet a fifth state either
from the South (where only Florida, Arkansas, and Oklahoma
employ the initiative) or from the three lower Midwestern states that
use the mechanism (Ohio, Nebraska, Missouri), a desire to keep
both the research task and the final published work manageable
precluded this option. Since no states in the Middle Atlantic or
southern New England areas employ the initiative (although voters
consider constitutional amendments that originate in the legislature), I have selected a fairly representative and yet diverse group
of states that use the initiative and statutory referendum. Certainly
almost every conceivable kind of issue came forth in the seven years
covered, including some that were frivolous as well as momentous,
deeply divisive as well as routine, and in some cases devious and of
dubious constitutionality.

THE CHOICE OF ISSUES

Over 150 questions reached the ballot in these four states in the
period initially chosen for study (1976-80), and the addition of the
1982 elections pushed that figure over 200. Thus some analytical
grounds had to be devised for narrowing the set of issues for more
intensive analysis. Unfortunately, simply choosing those on which
the greatest spending, publicity, or controversy occurred was not
an appropriate strategy given my central focus on the impact of
campaign strategies, spending, and publicity on both the campaign
process and outcomes. While a random process might have been
feasible, and would have helped narrow the field to a more manageable set than the issues ultimately chosen, I would have risked

eliminating either some deviant cases that later proved analytically fruitful or some cases that allowed three- and four-state comparisons of campaigns on the same issue.

Thus my choice of the 72 ballot questions on which to concentrate was made in several stages. I began by selecting what seemed to be important, high-impact proposals or ones with less far-ranging effects that appeared to be controversial by a careful reading of the ballot pamphlets in three states and the wording of the question itself on the Michigan ballot. (There is no voters' information pamphlet in Michigan.) I then added several additional questions, still relying on ballot pamphlets, that seemed either to be counterparts to proposals made in other states (for example, tax caps or alternatives or law-and-order proposals) or to include issues in the same substantive areas as the more controversial proposals (for example, the parklands bond issue in California and the advisory question on a deep water port in Massachusetts).

Some of the choices made at this stage were deliberate efforts to include proposals that I suspected would attract little or no spending or attention in order to compare media coverage, poll data (when available), and outcomes on a range of high- and low-saturation controversies. In a few cases, issues around which I expected a heated controversy (for example, the newsman's shield proposal in California) stayed on the back burner, at least in regional newspapers. In other instances (the drinking age controversies in Michigan) I initially underestimated both the public and media response.

The next step was the addition of a few more controversies after examining both the voting totals and the first few weeks of newspaper coverage during the final campaign period (the eight weeks preceding the election). In this way, for example, I added both the self-service gas and land use proposals in Oregon and the comprehensive water plan in California (all 1982 issues). I did, unfortunately, make a few errors by omission, particularly in California, where so many issues reach the ballot that it is hard to spot the controversial ones on the first pass through newspaper microfilms.

On the short list of major issues I regret omitting are: chiropractor licensing and greyhound racing in California, "denturists," animal traps, and the first effort to repeal the land use act in Oregon, and an early proposal on utilities in Michigan. After discovering the amount of attention given to these issues, generally late in the campaign, I decided (rightly or wrongly) that the potential insights to be gained did not justify the time and effort involved in retracing my steps through microfilmed newspapers or financial and voting reports from the states, which in some cases are reproduced only as requested on individual issues. Thus this study includes almost but not all of the controversial and important issues for the 1976-82 period. It also includes a great many issues that were virtually ignored by press and public. I do not believe, however, that the selection process in any sense biased my conclusions.

THE TIMEFRAME

It is perhaps desirable to make some brief comments about the span of this study. My initial choice (made in the summer of 1978) was the 1976-80 period. I reasoned that a return to the 1976 elections would be analytically fruitful if only because of the incredible range of earlier issues with which I was already familiar: nuclear power, gun control, a proposal by the United Farm Workers, the ERA, to name only a few. Naïvely anticipating a compact study that would only consume two or three years of work, I also decided to include 1980, simply to be sure that there were a goodly number of issues.

The subsequent decision to add 1982 was made reluctantly, given the wealth of information on the first set of 50 campaigns. The overriding consideration, however, was the dual existence of a great many "replays" (e.g., the bottle bill, gun control, property taxes) and the addition of a new level of question on the ballot in all four states, namely the nuclear freeze. By hindsight, the rich information on the 22 additional issues chosen amply justified the decision.

Why then have I not also surveyed the 1984 data, finally available as my writing neared completion? First, because in no sense has my major purpose been a hot-off-the-presses descriptive account of campaigns and their results. I believe my analytical goal—to explain the dynamics of these campaigns and their outcomes by taking an intensive look at key variables like spending, media coverage, advertising, endorsements, strategies, and voter attitudes and involvement—has been well served by the 72 campaigns in the moderate time period covered. My somewhat distant observation of the 1984 campaigns in three states (there were no 1984 ballot questions in Massachusetts) also indicates that no startling new campaign techniques or reversal of tendencies among either strategists or voters were evident. Thus there is little reason to burden the reader with an additional chapter simply to write a trendy book.

Finally, it will be noted that I did not include an off-year election in California (on school busing) or any of the controversial city-level referenda campaigns on issues like nuclear free zones, taxes, racial issues, and the like. Again, tempting as some of these campaigns were, the same line of reasoning was followed: enough is enough (perhaps even too much).

SOURCES OF INFORMATION
ABOUT CAMPAIGNS AND OUTCOMES

The most important sources for this study were the official documents and reports issued by state agencies: the voting returns (by county), the voters' information pamphlets (in all states but Michigan), and the reports on campaign contributions and spending made available by the offices of the secretary of state, or in the case of California by the Fair Political Practices Commission. Other crucial sources included microfilm editions of major regional newspapers, including poll data, editorials, advertisements, and the like, my own (nonrandom) interviews in two states, and discussions with family members, colleagues, and fellow activists, and finally the handful of scholarly studies of campaigns in the four states during the relevant period. (These included a few in-depth analyses of tax and environmental issues and a substantial literature on campaign finances and reform.) David Magleby's excellent (1984) study, primarily on California voting patterns with some information on Massachusetts and Oregon as well, might have been helpful, but it appeared too late in my own research efforts. Some of Magleby's concepts are, however, incorporated in the analytical chapters that follow.

Some interesting, and at times frustrating, differences in the availability of public reports came to light almost immediately. All four states released full information on the vote in a moderately timely fashion; the availability of the Massachusetts data by cities and town was especially useful, since the small number of counties (14) would have rendered county correlations almost useless. (As it turned out, my extensive work on relating voting returns to census variables was of extremely limited use. As with other scholars, I found demographics of little explanatory value for ballot question voting.)

Voters' information pamphlets varied in the three states that provide them. Both California and Massachusetts give relatively brief
summaries and explanations, as well as arguments pro and con. The
Massachusetts arguments take the form of minority and majority
reports from the legislature, since the Massachusetts initiative is
indirect. In California and in Oregon, major opponents and advocates are asked to submit brief pro and con statements, and the California pamphlet also includes an official estimate of costs which
sometimes becomes a source of later campaign debate. In Oregon,
until 1982, the pamphlet also carried paid one-half page advertisements, available at $300 each, used by whatever individuals and
organizations wanted to present their views. This practice, which
amounted to a partial state subsidy, was discontinued in 1982 for
budgetary reasons.

Financial reports on both contributions and expenditures were
made, in helpful detail, by California and Oregon officials throughout the period. Official Michigan reports did not exist prior to the passage of relevant legislation in 1978, forcing me to rely on newspaper
estimates of expenditures for the earlier elections. In Massachusetts, almost predictably, state officials collected financial information but did not compute totals from the weekly reports, nor did
they print information for distribution. By the time I requested the
data, I was informed that the 1976 and 1978 reports had been discarded because of "scarce office space." Thus in this state as well
as in Michigan, I have used newspaper data for earlier elections.
This is presumably quite accurate since it is based on official material that once was (in theory) available to the public.

I have used the five major regional newspapers (one for cach state
and one each in southern and northern California) in a variety of
ways, in full realization that if time and resources had been available, it would have been preferable to study several papers in each
state (varying in circulation, area covered, and ideological stance)
plus videotapes of major TV ads and other coverage. I used microfilms of the *Boston Globe*, the *Detroit Free Press*, the (Portland) *Oregonian*, the *Los Angeles Times*, and the San Francisco *Chronicle*,
covering the two months before all elections in each state. In California this involved April-May newspapers as well as September-
October, since ballot questions are considered in primary as well
as general elections. My experience in clipping the *Boston Globe*
during the six months before an election, and scanning microfilms

of the *Los Angeles Times* for an equivalent period, satisfied me that very little information is actually available before about October 15, except for an occasional feature on a petition drive.

The newspapers were used for information on campaign activities, extraneous events that might affect voters (including simultaneous candidate campaigns), positions taken by officials, relevant groups and party organizations, and (when available), the shifts in public opinion polls over time. All editorials endorsing or opposing measures, as well as columns and features, all paid advertisements and accounts of TV and radio advertising (as well as court injunctions, threats to invoke the FCC Fairness Doctrine, and the like), and ongoing reports in states where I had little other information about spending were particularly valuable. Sometimes factual information was incomplete or puzzling for a nonresident; if it was important, I usually tried to clarify the point through alternate sources, and as a last resort through family and collegial contacts.

All of these major regional newspapers reflected, to some degree, a liberal bias on most issues, at least in comparison with many citizen interviews and published polls. It was also clear, from my own first-hand observation of one California campaign in spring 1978 and participation in all four autumn campaigns in Massachusetts, that there were gaps in the newspaper coverage. One problem was the sparse coverage of events or voter sentiment outside of the major metropolitan areas of the newspaper's circulation (Michigan's Upper Peninsula, for example). Another was the lack of follow-up on some events, such as an account of the outcome of a legal controversy over advertising.

The most frustrating gap, from my perspective (aside from being unable to watch TV ads in other states), was the lack of any first-hand knowledge about public awareness or responses to the many colorful events in the campaigns. How many voters in San Francisco actually came into contact with the thousands of farmers and farm workers who poured into the cities just before the vote on the Chavez proposal? How deeply were they moved (if at all)? How many bumper stickers or decals were prominently in view, as they were in Massachusetts, in campaigns on the bottle bill elsewhere? I can only guess at the answers to questions like these or infer them from the final vote, except on those happy occasions when the newspaper interviewed large numbers of voters at length. (The *Boston Globe* and the San Francisco *Chronicle* made this effort more frequently than did the others.)

I am reasonably satisfied, however, that despite the liberal editorial stance of these newspapers, there was little if any systematic bias in coverage of events (whether speeches, spending, strategic errors, or degree of grass-roots activity.) I base this both on the ample amount of coverage provided, at least on the major controversies, to the side opposing the newspaper's editorial stance, as well as my own assessment of coverage in Massachusetts, where I had access to alternate media sources. In any case, the newspapers were used as general informants rather than for a systematic content analysis. Had the impact of the press per se been my major research question (or had more research resources been available), I might have cast a wider net to study statewide media coverage.

Preliminary Comments about the Scholarly Literature on Ballot Questions

When I first began, in 1978, to search for background material for this work, I found very few comprehensive studies on referenda. Butler and Ranney's (1978) volume of essays had just appeared; other than that, there were some excellent but primarily one-state survey and appraisals by Crouch (1950), LaPalombara (1950), Bone and Benedict (1973), and others, an extensive literature on campaign finances that mostly ignored ballot questions, and scattered work on individual campaigns, such as Wolfinger and Greenstein's (1968) analysis of California's 1964 campaign on open housing.

In stark contrast, in the years between 1979 and 1984, I have been pleased to note a modest resurgence of interest in referenda, perhaps associated in part with the national attention accorded the tax revolt, or simply because—as is often the case—several scholars simultaneously noticed a gap in scholarly knowledge. Whatever the reason, a number of studies have appeared on voter motivations and rationality, campaign finances, the use of the FCC Fairness Doctrine, and political reform and on a number of substantive issues that cross state boundaries. Since I shall make numerous (and lengthy) references to the post-1978 literature in the course of discussing my own data, I only pause at this point to mention a few studies that have been especially valuable to me.

Two works that yielded a variety of helpful hypotheses for my analysis were those of Daniel Lowenstein (1982), on campaign finances in California, and John Shockley (1980), on finances, advertising, and grass-roots campaigning in Colorado. Even more important, since we lack systematic survey data of our own, was the extensive research of Sears and Citrin (1982) on the tax revolt and two studies by the Henslers (1979) and by Kuklinski and associates (1982) on public attitudes toward nuclear power. While there is no real substitute for primary survey data, this work by other scholars, in combination with scattered newspaper interviews, went a long way in filling a gap on two of the more important issues covered here.

A Preview and Outline of this Study

I shall begin, in Chapters 2 and 3, with a descriptive overview of the history, political structure, and campaigns and outcomes of the four states. This background material sets the stage for the analytical chapters that follow. It also presents the major controversies in their political *context*, in the belief that, for example, the fate of some questions depended in part on the number of issues and candidates competing for scarce campaign resources and voter attention during any given election.

Chapter 4 is the first of four chapters dealing with the major elements of the 1976-80 campaigns, in this case expenditures. Here I establish the critical importance of campaign spending, even for measures where that spending is low, looking in detail at expenditures, public opinion poll data, endorsements, and the final vote. Considerable attention is also given to those cases where the low-spending side was victorious.

Chapters 5 and 6 consider two contrasting types of campaign: those that rely heavily on media advertising and those that utilize extensive grass-roots efforts. In both cases questions are raised about the effectiveness of differing strategies from the dual perspectives of voter activation and education, and the prospects of election victory.

In Chapter 7 I turn to the knotty question of voter rationality. My conclusions are quite positive in regard to some traditional myths about voter confusion and negativism in relation to problems like exceptionally long ballots or confusing and technical language. I am less sanguine, however, about the incidence of instrumental voting among any but the most knowledgeable voters. Contrasting campaigns and voter responses on the tax and nuclear power issues are examined in several states.

Chapter 8 gives an overview of the 1982 campaigns and outcomes in all four states, returning again to the related themes of spending, media and grass-roots campaigns, and voter rationality. Utilizing 22 issues, some of which are replays from the earlier period, I find both a marked increase in the level of spending, on style as well as position issues, and a noticeable increase in the professionalism of grass-roots campaigns.

In Chapter 9 I summarize and assess my findings from the perspective of both the Progressive reform and pluralist models of democracy. I find that the 1976-82 campaigns and voter responses on the ballot issues fall short, in some significant ways, of both pluralist and Progressive expectations, although I am somewhat more optimistic about the agenda-expanding and political recruitment impact of these efforts at direct democracy. I conclude by critiquing some major proposals for campaign reform.

2

AN HISTORICAL AND POLITICAL
PROFILE OF FOUR STATES

This chapter presents a summary of the history, politics, and relevant legal arrangements in the four states included in this study: Massachusetts, Michigan, Oregon, and California. I will begin with a brief profile of each state (its history, governmental structure, and the major problems of the 1976-82 period), concluding with a four-state comparison of the laws governing initiatives, referenda, and campaign finances. This contextual information is given in some detail because of its importance for understanding the contrasting campaign strategies and outcomes analyzed in later chapters. Differences in both demographics and political traditions, for example, help to explain Oregon's ban on paid signature collection for initiative petitions as opposed to Californians' extensive reliance on professional campaign consultants. Similarly, different answers to tensions between environmental concerns and the dictates of economic health must be understood against the backdrop of both cultural norms and the economic resource base of each of the four states.

Massachusetts: A Profile[1]

Massachusetts may be described as a paradoxical blend of old and new traditions: Old Yankees and new immigrants, troubled old shoe, paper, and textile mills cohabiting with a modern and flourishing electronics industry; a proud heritage of political and social reform predating the Civil War coupled with the scourge of intolerance stretching from the Salem witch trials to racial confrontations over school busing in the 1970s. Contemporary politics is dominated by a Democratic majority split into conservative and mul-

31

Land Area: 8,257 square miles				
	1976	1978	1980	1982
Estimated population	5,809,000	5,781,000	5,771,000	5,737,000
State revenues	$4,104,904,000	$5,669,948,000	$6,824,000,000	$7,676,000,000
State expenditures	$4,939,813,000	$5,520,145,000	$6,377,000,000	$7,986,000,000
Labor force (nonagricultural)	2,341,900	2,516,500	2,893,000	2,603,200
Insured unemployed	5.5%	6.9%	6.6%	7.6%
Per capita income	$6,114	$7,258	N.A.	$11,128

tiple liberal factions. For most of the 1976-82 period, a governor noted for his focus on administrative efficiency, economic development, and liberal social policies has presided over a political system sporadically under investigation for corruption among state contractors, transit officials, legislators, and even members of the judiciary.

Although economic issues dominated most political debates, unemployment remained the lowest in any of the four states studied, markedly under the national average as well. The energy crisis touched off debate in the legislature over offshore oil exploration, the development of nuclear power, and the control of nuclear waste, sometimes reaching the ballot as well. Apart from tax and environmental issues, however, the ballot questions that generated the most conflict were part of the larger liberal-conservative debate over "style" issues: capital punishment, gun control, the ERA, the nuclear freeze.

HISTORICAL TRENDS

A leader in the American Revolution and one of the original colonies, Massachusetts boasts the oldest written constitution of any continuing democratic body in the world and is the only state still using the original document, first adopted in 1790. In stark contrast to early religious oppression, the Massachusetts Declaration of Rights served as a partial model for the federal Bill of Rights.

Initially the population was divided between a sophisticated and wealthy mercantile class, located in the Boston area and strongly pro-Federalist, and an agrarian-Democratic hinterland of small farmers supporting Jeffersonian principles. Following the War of 1812, however, the rise of the new textile industry and the first major wave of immigrants from Ireland ushered in an era of economic and social diversity. It was this period too that witnessed not only a "flowering" in the intellectual field (Emerson, Thoreau, Longfellow) but one of crusaders in regard to education (Horace Mann), slavery (William Lloyd Garrison), women's suffrage (Susan B. Anthony), and a host of other issues.

As the abolitionist movement gained support, Massachusetts voters shifted their support to the new Republican Party; simultaneously, they increasingly found their livelihood in small manufacturing as shipping and agriculture declined. Finally, the twentieth century saw further economic diversification as textiles, shoes, and paper began to move South, to be replaced mainly by electronics and high technology—a natural trend in a state that is also a leader in higher education.

As can be seen from the figures at the beginning of this chapter, Massachusetts population did not grow in the 1976-82 period, while at the same time state expenditures rose from $4.9 million to $7.98 million for each of the seven years. Per capita personal income continued to rise, however, and was only slightly lower than that of California throughout the period. While unemployment has remained relatively low by national standards, double digit figures have plagued some metropolitan areas in the southern part of the state, notably Fall River and New Bedford.

The period between 1840 and World War I saw a continuing influx not only of Irish immigrants but of Italians, French Canadians, Portuguese, and others. More recently, Massachusetts cities have also experienced an increase in Hispanic and Asian populations. (The 1970 population of Boston, site of a court-ordered school busing program, was over 15% Black as well.) Thus the initial English stock has been supplemented with a major foreign born population which is both politically and culturally diverse: in the late 1970s about one-half were Catholic and 4% were Jewish, leaving the descendents of the Puritans (today primarily Congregationalist, Unitarian, and Episcopalian) in the minority. This shift has had major implications for the political style of the state, superimposing, among other things, some of the values and techniques of the immigrant-based political machine on the town-meeting, consensual ethos of the old Yankee population.

The rise of organized labor should also be noted. The labor movement was weak in Massachusetts, as elsewhere, before the Civil War, although child labor legislation was enacted at the state level as early as 1842. Labor unrest surfaced, however, in some of the smaller mill cities like Lawrence and Lowell at about this time. In 1869 the first state labor board in the country was established to investigate factory conditions in Massachusetts: one result was the enactment of a ten-hour workday for women. In 1912 a minimum wage law was passed, partly as a result of a long and bitter strike in Lawrence. Seven years later Governor Coolidge broke a major police strike in Boston by calling in federal troops. By the time of the New Deal and the Wagner Act, however, Massachusetts had developed a strong labor movement, which began to play a major role in the Democratic party. Today the teachers unions, in addition to more traditional industrial unions, carry considerable clout in elections.

GOVERNMENTAL STRUCTURE AND POLITICS

The Massachusetts Constitution provides for a governor and lieutenant governor of the same party serving four-year terms and for a legislature consisting of a 40-member Senate and 240-member House, all serving two-year terms. Several aspects of the legislative process are unique: Massachusetts is the only mainland state to provide for the unlimited right of citizens to petition the legislature itself. Privately introduced bills are guaranteed a hearing (however brief) by a joint legislative committee, and all bills are reported to the floor after hearings. Such a practice does not guarantee more than perfunctory treatment; it does, however, contribute to a log jam at the end of sessions, which together with the considerable arbitrary powers of the Speaker of the House contributed to a highly publicized demand for legislative rules reform in 1982-83. (Modest streamlining was enacted by the legislature itself, but an initiative petition calling for sweeping changes was disallowed by the Attorney General's office and thus failed to reach the ballot in 1984.)

In the 1960s and 1970s the Democratic Party dominated the state legislature, as well as the delegation to the United States Congress. The Governor's office, however, has shifted between the two parties. Two Democrats with markedly contrasting views have held the office since 1976: Michael Dukakis, 1975-78 and 1983 to the present, and Edward King, 1979-1982. Dukakis represents the liberal wing of the party, while King spoke for the more conservative business-oriented wing of the party and made no secret of his admiration for Ronald Reagan.

Massachusetts counties are judicial units (maintaining courts and jails) with no independent taxation power. Local governing authority rests in the hands of the 312 nonpartisan towns and cities. The town meeting, along with a modern hybrid, the "representative town meeting" consisting of several hundred elected members, is still the dominant form of local government. State revenues are raised by a combination of the personal income tax, a corporate tax, and a limited sales tax which was raised from 3% to 5% in 1975. Local governments still rely most heavily on a combination of the property tax and state grants-in-aid for state-mandated programs, notably in the field of education.

MAJOR ISSUES AND EVENTS IN MASSACHUSETTS, 1976-82

One is immediately struck by the *variety* of political and social issues that have emerged prominently in Massachusetts in the past decade. (Comparable diversity is found in California but not in Michigan and Oregon.) In addition, the state has been relatively free from the natural disasters that plagued both California and Oregon during the period. Finally, Massachusetts is unique in the amount of attention given to corruption in high places, at least among the four states studied here.

The year 1976 saw considerable debate over the state budget, especially with reference to what was then seen as a high level of unemployment (5.5% of the insured workforce, 8.8% adjusted for seasonal unemployment). The AFL-CIO called for a strike of state workers which lasted for four days. Concern continued over two issues that were to surface on the ballot in later years, busing for desegregation and restoration of the death penalty. There were a host of controversial ballot issues, including gun control, the ERA, a bottle bill, and the graduated income tax. Voters gave the state's electoral votes to Jimmy Carter.

In 1977 public attention turned to court reform and to judicial remedies for past wrongs. Following the recommendation of a select commission headed by Archibald Cox, the legislature approved a consolidation of the complex court structure. A suit by the Wanpanoag Indians for 16,000 acres of Cape Cod was sent into adjudication, and Governor Dukakis issued a proclamation reversing the 50-year-old finding of guilt in the Sacco-Vanzetti case.

Nineteen seventy-eight was a year of election upsets: incumbent Governor Dukakis was defeated in the Democratic primaries by conservative Edward King, who went on to win the general election. Senator Edward Brooke, the state's Republican black Senator, was defeated by Paul Tsongas, after a year's revelations of Brooke's problems that included a divorce and accusations of tax irregularities. The only major state ballot issue proposed differential taxation of residential and industrial property. This measure, approved by the voters, arose from public concern over a 1975 court decision requiring uniform assessment at 100% of full value.

In 1979 three appointees of newly elected Governor King were forced to resign because of alleged improprieties, and in 1980 reports of widespread corruption in the award of state contracts led to the establishment of a special blue-ribbon commission to investigate the subject. Racial problems, never entirely absent since a 1974 court-imposed desegregation plan for Boston schools, surfaced again in the fatal shooting of a black high school athlete. Opposition to busing—and ugly demonstrations—continued.

In 1980 Massachusetts voters chose a Republican president for the first time since the Eisenhower years, on the same ballot that saw passage of "Prop. 2 $1/_2$"—a property tax cap similar to California's earlier Proposition 13. Thus economic concerns were highly salient to voters. Two emotional style issues also surfaced in the autumn. One arose over the circulation of a pastoral letter by the archbishop of Boston a week before the congressional primary urging Catholics to vote against candidates who supported government-funded abortions. The two targets of the letter (James Shannon and Barney Frank) were subsequent victors in both the primaries and the general election; the furor over the letter, however, did little to foster good will between Protestants, lay Catholics, and the church hierarchy.

The second major issue concerned a 1979 law establishing capital punishment in Massachusetts. In October the State Supreme Judicial Court found it unconstitutional on grounds that it was "impermissibly cruel." This decision laid the groundwork for the 1982 ballot proposal to amend the constitution.

Economic problems in the wake of Prop. 2 $1/_2$ were dominant in 1981. State employees went without pay for two weeks when the state legislature failed to approve a state budget by the end of the fiscal year. The MBTA (the transit authority in eastern Massachusetts) raised fares from 50¢ to 75¢ in a move that saw riders desert an already undependable and allegedly inefficient and corrupt system.

The 1982 election dominated the news in that year. Former Governor Dukakis made a strong comeback, winning both the primary and general elections. Since Massachusetts lost one congressional seat through the post-1980 census redistricting, two popular incumbents, Barney Frank (D) and Margaret Heckler (R), were forced to battle, amid charges of favoritism in drawing the new boundaries.

Frank was elected in what was interpreted as a referendum on Reagan's policies, while Senator Kennedy was reelected for his fourth term despite continuing controversy over his personal life.

Finally, Massachusetts voters were asked to pass judgment on a number of controversial ballot proposals, including the death penalty, the bottle bill, the nuclear freeze, the control of nuclear power and radioactive waste, and an almost neglected issue which in any other year would have received major attention—aid to private and parochial schools.

Michigan: A Profile

Historically and culturally, Michigan has three major regions: the vacation area and mining territory of the Upper Peninsula, the rich farmland originally settled by pioneers from New England and New York, and the urban manufacturing areas characterized by ethnic and racial diversity, labor strength, and sporadic unemployment.

Tourism is Michigan's second major industry, with well over $3 billion spent annually, not only in the forest and small lake region of the Upper Peninsula, but along the 3200 mile freshwater shoreline of three Great Lakes. To the South, one-third of the state's land area is devoted to farming, with a variety of grain and vegetable crops, the third largest apple production in the country, and livestock products important to the economy. Yet it is the third Michigan—Detroit, Lansing, Grand Rapids, and other major industrial areas—that occasionally makes national news with racial unrest, protracted strikes, and grave problems of unemployment. Fully one-quarter of the state's workers are involved in the manufacture of autos and auto parts, accounting for about 40% of the nation's auto production.

Although economic problems dominated the news for at least four of the years covered by this study, Michigan's historical role as an educational leader and as an integral part of the early Progressive reform movement still manifests itself in present-day political style and activities. Educational and environmental issues, as well as economics and crime control, were key topics for legislative/ballot activity throughout the 1976-82 period. Another political factor of note is the state's strong, competitive two-party system. This stands in stark contrast to the fragmented, individualistic Califor-

Land Area: 58,216 square miles

	1976	1978	1980	1982
Estimated population	9,157,000	9,141,000	9,233,000	9,258,000
State revenues	$6,938,098,000	$9,689,212,000	$11,449,000,000	$15,035,000,000
State expenditures	$7,668,334,000	$9,070,835,000	$10,507,000,000	$13,295,000,000
Labor force (nonagricultural)	3,135,300	3,552,300	3,426,800	3,190,600
Insured unemployed	5.6%	7.0%	14.0%	14.9%
Per capita income	$6,173	$7,619	$9,403	$10,790

nia style, on the one hand, and the one-party dominance in Massachusetts, at the other extreme.

HISTORICAL TRENDS

Michigan was first explored in the early seventeenth century by French fur traders. The area came under British control in 1763, at the end of the French and Indian War, and became a part of the United States in 1783. After an early period of slow growth, rapid settlement came with the opening of the Erie Canal. Agriculture and lumbering were the dominant activities at first. In the 1840s copper and iron mines were established on the Upper Peninsula, and Michigan remained a leading producer until almost the end of the nineteenth century. By the turn of the century, new ore sources in the West and in neighboring Minnesota eclipsed Michigan's production, but by then the state economy had begun to diversify beyond farming, forestry, and mining products.

Michigan, after statehood in 1837, supported the Democratic Party until 1854, when strong antislavery sentiment (as in Massachusetts) prevailed. After the Civil War the strongly probusiness Republicans dominated state politics and national elections in Michigan, until the time of the New Deal. Agriculture and timber remained dominant in the 1870-1900 period, although a strong business class was developing in the southern transportation centers as well. It was during this period that the population doubled, largely because of migration from Canada, England, and Germany, and during the 1890s, from Poland and other parts of Eastern Europe.

Michigan suffered less farm unrest than neighboring states, partly because of a relatively diversified economic base. Thus while the electorate backed the Greenbacks in 1892, strong support for the more radical Populists failed to materialize. At the turn of the century, a vigorous reform movement was begun under Governor Hazen Pingree; the next two decades saw, if not an outright embrace of Progressivism, the introduction of the major mechanisms (initiative, referendum, recall, the direct primary). A new state constitution, enacted in 1908, provided for home rule for Michigan cities.

The state had already served as an educational pioneer. In 1921 a Department of Conservation with broad powers on water pollution, fish and game management, and reforestation was established. Now, with the beginnings of organized labor, Michigan also became one of the first states to enact workmen's compensation laws.

Small local labor organizations had predated Michigan statehood. Both the Knights of Labor (1878) and the AFL (1889) organized on a statewide basis even before the reform era. But the development of the new auto industry, while accelerating urbanization and attracting a new work force, created problems for labor organizers. The elite craft union structure was not geared to organizing the range and number of unskilled, nonapprenticed workers that joined the fledgling auto industry. It was not until the coming of the United Auto Workers, and employment of an extensive sit-down strike in Flint in 1936-37, that the union movement was taken seriously. By 1941, when Ford became the last company to recognize a union shop, about 30% of the state's labor force was organized. By 1975, 38.4% of the work force in Michigan was unionized. This is the highest percentage in the nation.

The Depression brought tremendous economic hardship to the state's population. Recovery finally came with the peak production activity of World War II, which also attracted new migrants from the South. One result was an explosive race riot in Detroit in June 1943. Part of the friction was of course due to intense competition for jobs in an economy that had become increasingly dependent on one industry. Another was a clash of cultures, of first- and second-generation Southern Europeans, Italian, and Canadian immigrants with newly arrived rural southerners.

By the mid-1970s Michigan had developed a strong two-party system, in fact moving into the Democratic column in most national elections since 1936, but continuing to elect several progressive Republican governors. The population was diverse, with blacks comprising 11% of the total and the number of Hispanics increasing as well.

Dominant religious affiliations include Catholics, Lutherans, and Methodists, with a fairly strong Prohibitionist sentiment remaining from earlier times. The most divisive issues, however, are economic—not surprising, since unemployment levels have remained at alarming levels since 1980. The problems are of course amplified by a leveling off in population, and thus in potential revenue sources, at a time when, as in Massachusetts, state expenditures continue to accelerate.

GOVERNMENT AND POLITICS

Under Michigan's present constitution (adopted in 1963) a jointly elected governor and lieutenant governor serve four-year terms. The legislature consists of a 38-member Senate (with four-year terms) and 110 members of the House, serving for two years. There is a centralized administration, a nongraduated income tax for revenues, and strong guarantees of civil rights. One interesting feature of the Constitution is a provision that in 1978, and every 16 years thereafter, the question of constitutional revision must be submitted to the voters. This became a highly partisan issue in 1978.

The state's major income sources are a 4% sales tax, special taxes on cigarettes, liquor, gasoline, and motor vehicles, and more recently the income tax. Local governments and schools depend heavily, as elsewhere, on the property tax.

In 1982 Michigan voters elected the first Democratic governor in twenty years. Republican governors, however, have included the likes of Romney and Milliken, representing the liberal wing of the party; and the decades of the 1960s and 1970s have seen the enactment of progressive legislation like open housing (1968) as well as the environmental legislation found elsewhere. In 1979 the Republican governor twice vetoed legislation to cut off welfare payments for abortions. Thus while Michigan politics is usually pictured as highly partisan, a strong moralistic/evangelical strain cuts across these party lines; environmental interests sometimes confront *both* business and labor; and racial friction does not always follow party lines.

MAJOR EVENTS AND ISSUES IN MICHIGAN, 1976-82

Gerald Ford carried his home state in the 1976 election. Michigan voters also approved a variety of crime control measures (for example, limitations on parole), approved the highly publicized bottle bill by a 2-1 margin despite large expenditures by opponents, and rejected a proposal for a graduated income tax.

The economy was not yet a major issue in the state as a whole since unemployment was low, car manufacturing was on the rise, and a UAW strike had been settled after a 28-day walkout. Crime control had become a major issue in Detroit, where 1000 policemen were among the city employees affected by a midyear budget crisis. After a rampage at a rock concert in August, a citywide evening curfew was declared for those who were 17 or younger. Simultaneously, state police were ordered to intensify patrols on the freeways because of crimes against stranded motorists. Finally, a forest fire in late July destroyed over 72,000 acres of Upper Peninsula timberland. This is the only case of a natural disaster dominating Michigan headlines during the 1976-82 period. But man-made disasters involving chemicals were soon to emerge.

In 1977 the major issue was the chemical contamination of farm products by the accidental addition of PBB to cattle feed in 1973. (This topic received national coverage as well in the print media and on programs like "Sixty Minutes.") The governor, who had originally claimed that problems were minimal, now reversed himself to impose stringent restrictions on PBB sales.

Another man-made disaster receiving considerable publicity was the increase in highway accidents involving double-tanker fuel trucks. The legislature resisted public demands that double-tankers be banned from the highways on the grounds that such a ban would increase already-high fuel costs to Michigan consumers. The governor then ordered state police to enforce stricter highway safety standards on truckers.

Nineteen seventy-eight saw Governor Milliken reelected by a substantial margin while Democratic Senate contender Carl Levin unseated the Republican incumbent, Robert Griffin. Voters rejected two stringent financial proposals on the ballot but approved a constitutional amendment limiting government spending to 9.5% of the state's total personal income. The electorate also raised the legal drinking age to 21, despite substantial out-of-state funding and the efforts of college students for the opposition.

The PBB controversy continued to rage, as the circuit court ruled, in the first suit against the state and the Michigan Chemical Company, that low levels of PBB were harmless. Finally, the economy appeared to be in good health, with a high level of sales and production reported by the auto manufacturers. Chrysler announced a new preferred stock issue for public sale.

By 1979, even though unemployment rose only 0.2% at midyear in comparison with 1978 figures, an economic crisis—which was to dominate the news for at least the next four years—was clearly in the making. Chrysler projected a $1 billion loss by year's end and requested federal assistance to remain solvent. Wayne County failed to meet the public payroll in October, after being denied permission to borrow against future revenues. The governor blamed the county's decentralized government structure and appointed a special task force to study the problem.

In 1980 the auto industry declared losses of $3.7 billion at the end of the third quarter, and Chrysler stood near bankruptcy. Official unemployment figures stood at 14% of the insured portion of the work force, but the newspapers reported that far more people were receiving aid of some sort from the federal or state government. The state budget was cut back to the 1979 level ($10.5 billion) in spite of revenues of $11.4 billion, with a sharp reduction in the level of aid to schools and local communities. Over 900 state employees were laid off, and Detroit reduced its police force by 15%.

A tremendous groundswell for tax cuts, partly as a result of "Proposition 13 fever" carried over from California, brought forth three separate ballot proposals. Michigan voters not only rejected all three but voted against all seven ballot questions for the year, including a proposal to lower the drinking age. One result of the campaigns on taxes, however, was a promise by legislators to make property tax relief a top priority for the coming years. (Comprehensive relief was not forthcoming in either 1981 or 1982 despite these promises.)

Nineteen eighty-two saw a continuing high level of unemployment (11.8%), modest profits for the auto industry but relatively low production figures, and an abortive proposal by the governor to launch a comprehensive economic development program including a 20% property tax reduction. One month after announcing the plan, the governor withdrew the tax proposal on grounds that it would only increase the deficit.

Voters responded to the continuing recession in 1982 by supporting Democratic candidates, reelecting U.S. Senator Donald Riegle, and choosing James Blanchard, who ran on the slogan of "jobs, jobs, jobs," as the first Democratic governor in twenty years. Two ballot proposals to limit automatic increases in utility rates were also approved.

Economic news continued to be grim: official unemployment rose to post-World War II highs of 14.9%, or 16.1% adjusted. Moody's Investors' service credit rating put Michigan at the bottom of the list of states. The auto industry, partially as a result of Chrysler's comeback, announced modest profits, but sales remained slow by the end of the year.

Thus in a period spanning only seven years, there is a clear shift in the public agenda of one state from high diversity (economic, environmental, racial, crime control, and morality issues) to an almost exclusive focus on one crucial area, economics. This trend is only an exaggeration of national tendencies, and not too different from Oregon as well. It does serve to illustrate, however, the way in which an economic base can critically influence both the larger political arena and the scope of debate over ballot questions.

Oregon: A Profile

Because the Oregon economy depends heavily on natural resources (notably timber and water), sound environmental policies have been a major concern for most of the twentieth century. Oregon's history as more than a land of scattered farms and trading posts spans less than a century; the period of pioneer isolation was thus brief, with settlers from the diverse traditions of New England, New York, Canada, and the Midwest. The most distinctive heritage is probably that of the Progressive reform era, dating from about 1902, with the introduction of the initiative process, to 1912, with the establishment of women's suffrage. This tradition has continued to the present, when Oregon has again led in reforms. It was, for example, the first state to pass the graduated income tax, a bottle bill, and a ban on aerosol products using fluorocarbon propellants.

Yet for all the progressive emphasis, Oregon retains elements of a strong conservative, relatively parochial, religious heritage. As a result, fluoridation of local water supplies is unusual, state-funded abortion is controversial, and a proposal for gun control would probably be rejected out of hand, given both the hunting tradition and the individualistic strain.

In addition, the Oregon economy has yet to diversify to a degree adequate for stable employment during a national downturn. Thus in the period studied here, Oregon—like Michigan—was forced to cut many widely supported social programs. This has happened in spite of the strong labor movement, the reform tradition, and the sense of social responsibility characteristic of Oregon politics.

HISTORICAL TRENDS

Although brief visits of the Spanish explorers to the Oregon coast apparently occurred in the seventeenth century, the first overland exploration awaited the Lewis and Clark Expedition of 1802-4. There was early fur trading in the area, and a few Methodist mis-

	1976	1978	1980	1982
Land Area: 96,981 square miles				
Estimated population	2,288,000	2,402,000	2,570,000	2,633,000
State revenues	$1,941,187,000	$2,638,018,000	$3,499,000,000	$4,423,000,000
State expenditures	$1,783,168,000	$2,272,393,000	$2,906,000,000	$3,817,000,000
Labor force (nonagricultural)	861,800	986,400	1,032,600	964,600
Insured unemployed	4.8%	5.5%	8.3%	10.1%
Per capita income	$5,769	$7,007	$8,938	$10,008

sionaries settled in 1834. About 900 settlers—the largest single influx to that time—arrived in 1843, the same year in which a provisional territorial government was established. By the time statehood was attained in 1859, the beginnings of a sparsely settled agricultural society were in place.

Three significant external events hastened Oregon's early development. The first was the California Gold Rush in 1849, which provided a major and enlarged market for farm produce. The second was the later mining rush to Montana and Idaho, further expanding Oregon's produce markets. Finally, the completion of the Northern Pacific Railway in 1883 gave the state a major overland link, increasing both the population influx and the market for farm and lumber products. Thus when first-growth timberland in the Great Lakes region was exhausted (about 1900), the lumber industry moved to the Pacific Northwest.

Oregon, like California, is divided by two major north-south mountain ranges—the Coastal Range and, further east, the Cascades. Between these two ranges extends the fertile Willamette Valley, where the largest cities (Portland and Eugene), as well as much of its agricultural land, are located. Farm holdings in this area are relatively small, producing fruit and vegetables; on the coast cheese and other dairy products are produced. To the east of the Cascades, in an area covering about two-thirds of the state, the land is arid, experiences a wide range of temperatures, and is mainly used as grazing land or for wheat. This part of the state is very sparsely settled, with large farms or ranches the norm.

Over 30 million acres (almost half the total area) of Oregon land is forested (two-thirds in national or state reserves). While the state's oldest economic activity is agricultural, Oregon has been the nation's largest producer of lumber since 1939.

There was no significant labor movement in Oregon until the expansion of the lumber industry at the turn of the century. The IWW struggled in Oregon, from 1905 to 1917, for better pay and working conditions, only to meet the opposition of a counter-organized Lumbermen's Protective Association. After the LPA's refusal to negotiate, 85% of the West Coast mills were closed by strikes, which then received little public support. The IWW failed as a union, but in the long run their goals were achieved through state action. In 1913, for example, Oregon passed a minimum wage law and set maximum working hours for women. That year also saw

passage of workmen's compensation. In 1965 the law was extended
to cover farm workers, a decade before similar action in California. As of 1970, 31% of Oregon's nonagricultural work force was
unionized.

Oregon's population is more homogeneous than the other states
in this study. As of the mid-1970s, about 97% of the population was
white, with 13,500 Indians living mainly on reservations, and a small
Asian and black population largely in the cities. Most Oregonians
are native-born, with the principal place of origin Canada or Western Europe.

This is not to say that no tension has existed. There was a brief
period after World War I when the Ku Klux Klan attempted (unsuc-
cessfully) to gain control of the state government through electoral politics. Pockets of nativists sentiment undoubtedly remain,
although there was no overt sign of this in the referenda campaigns
studied.[2] Portland, in contrast to Boston, Detroit, and Los Angeles,
experienced no race riots in the 1960s or earlier. This of course is to
be expected in a state where the nonwhite population is all but missing, where there are only 350 industrial establishments employing
more than 100 people, and where population density, even in Portland, remains low.

GOVERNMENT AND POLITICS

Oregon's constitution, adopted in 1857, drew on the Michigan
and Indiana constitutions. It was not amended until 1902, when Progressive mechanisms were added. It provides for a governor (with
no lieutenant governor) who is limited to two consecutive terms
and a legislative assembly of 30 senators (four-year terms) and 60
representatives (two-year terms), convened only in odd-numbered
years. Most cities operate under home rule, with the larger cities
having city managers.

Politics was dominated by Democrats until the Civil War, then
swung between Republican and Democratic leadership. Populists
were important between 1890 and 1900, sometimes holding the balance of power. The Progressive Party, led in Oregon by William
U'Ren, was important from 1900 until the end of World War I, and
it was during that era that major reforms were enacted. U'Ren and
his followers convinced the public that the state legislature had
been captured by special interests—notably the railroads—and that

direct democracy would return power to the people at large. About 150 constitutional amendments were adopted between 1902 and 1976. (Oregon has used the initiative and referendum process more frequently than any other state.)

Republicans were ascendant until 1932. By 1929, however, both the agriculture and the lumber industry were suffering from the beginnings of economic stress, and state leaders also came to see the importance of public power. Thus from 1932 to 1944 the state supported the New Deal and began to reap the benefits not only of the newly constructed Bonneville Dam but of massive reforestation, irrigation, and flood control projects.

Since World War II there has been a gradual resurgence of Republicanism, with the governorship and U.S. Senators split between the two parties. Into the sixties there was continuing hydroelectrical development and entry of some new industry in the chemical, electronics, and metal-processing fields. But the dominant environmental concerns have made the business climate somewhat uncertain, and future development will probably proceed slowly, if at all. Oregonians, like Coloradans of late, have been wary about economic growth on the nearby California model.

MAJOR EVENTS AND ISSUES IN OREGON, 1976-82

Oregon experienced two natural disasters which were relevant to the economy, and thus to the political decisions of this period. One was an intense three-year drought from 1977 to 1979, seen as the worst since the 1930s. The second was a series of eruptions from Washington's Mt. St. Helens, 30 miles from the border, in October 1980. This not only injured and killed people and destroyed farmland—it displaced election news in the media for several days during the 1980 campaign. Environmental issues, and beginning in 1979, the condition of Oregon's economy dominated the news throughout the period.

The 1976 election witnessed the highest voter registration and turnout in the state's history. This was not so much a reflection of interest in the presidential contest (which Ford won by 2000 votes) as it was in some of the 12 ballot measures. A proposal for a moratorium on nuclear power development was defeated after an enormously costly campaign. Incumbent Congressmen (all Democrats) were returned to office, and Norma Paulus was chosen as Secretary of State—the first woman to achieve statewide office in Oregon.

In 1977 the legislature wrestled with several environmental issues. One concerned controlled field-burning, which spokesmen for the important perennial grass-seed industry argued was essential for pest control. After extensive debate, the legislature agreed to continue the program for limited areas. A second new law, pushed by environmentalists, prohibited the sale of aerosol cans using fluorocarbon propellants.

On the local level the opening of the Trojan nuclear plant near Mt. Ranier set off intense demonstrations, and several local school boards announced large budget cuts after voter rejection of an increased school tax rate. Both the Trojan plant and the plight of local schools were to remain controversial over the next several years.

The 1978 election saw a moderate Republican tide. Republican Victor Atiyeh defeated incumbent Governor Robert Straub, while incumbent Mark Hatfield, also a Republican, was reelected to the Senate. Oregon voters, nevertheless, rejected both the Proposition 13-style property tax proposal and a more moderate alternative. State legislative leaders announced that the tax issue was of the highest priority for 1979.

Several teachers' strikes resulted from a failure to agree on contracts. And finally, protests continued at the Trojan nuclear plant, despite suspension of its operating license for structural reasons and a shutdown for much of the year.

By 1979, after continuing debate on the Trojan reactor, hearings on safety compliance were announced. Another environmental issue was the question of Forest Service use of the herbicide 2,4-D, while a third explosive issue arose with the discovery of leaking nerve gas containers near an Army depot in eastern Oregon. And finally, the debate over field-burning continued without resolution.

But by now troubling economic news began to rival environmental issues. When the drought continued and a plague of forest fires caused heavy losses in the farm and lumber industries, both unemployment and slowed construction rates became cause for alarm. Unsold housing inventories were up 200% nationwide, in part because of high interest rates and a shortage of mortgage capital.

In June 1980 Governor Atiyeh announced an anticipated revenue shortfall of $204 million. At the heart of the problem was overdependence on the lumber industry. Since state revenues came almost entirely from personal and corporate income taxes and Oregon's unemployment rate was beginning to rival Michigan's, there was no easy way to avoid a drop in revenues. Exacerbating the problem were two external shifts as well: a new technique for processing plywood from southern pine had halved the market for Oregon plywood, and the Japanese began importing logs in place of finished lumber from the Northwest.

Atiyeh thus proposed stringent budget cuts, beginning with closing parts of the university system, including the medical school. While the threatened closings never materialized, the budgets of all state schools were cut to the bone, with a freeze on both new hiring and the replacement of retirees. Personnel at other state agencies were cut as well.

The 1980 elections were conducted against this backdrop. Oregon gave its vote to Reagan and to incumbent Republican Senator Packwood but left control of the state legislature to the Democrats. A second effort to cut property taxes was defeated, while a much-revised proposition curtailing nuclear power and nuclear wastes was approved.

Nineteen eighty-one saw almost nothing but continuing bad news. Lumber and plywood mills closed across the state, and several aluminum producers who had been attracted to the Columbia Valley by the cheap power of an earlier era began cutting production. Unemployment now stood at 8.8%, with an additional 74,000 workers having exhausted their benefits. All sections of the state budget were cut.

In 1982 the governor was forced to call three emergency sessions of the legislature to cope with the continuing budget crisis. After brief debate on a sales tax, the Assembly chose two other tactics—a deeper cut in higher education, and an appropriation against the surplus in the State Accident Insurance Fund. In the meantime, voters reelected Governor Atiyeh but sent a Democratic delegation to Congress. A ballot measure to limit property taxes was narrowly defeated, while a nuclear freeze resolution was approved by the voters.

California: A Profile

California—a land of firsts and superlatives. An exotic history, multicultural and trendy, yet a political heritage like Oregon writ

Land Area: 158,693 square miles

	1976	1978	1980	1982
Estimated population	21,520,000	22,083,000	22,925,000	23,669,000
State revenues	$22,124,617,000	$26,108,228,000	$31,058,000,000	$39,552,000,000
State expenditures	$20,533,635,000	$22,439,586,000	$28,319,000,000	$38,846,000,000
Labor force (nonagricultural)	8,515,500	9,015,100	9,803,800	9,901,500
Insured unemployed	7.6%	8.1%	6.6%	10.2%
Per capita income	$7,151	$7,911	$10,047	$11,923

larger. A people plagued recently with unemployment, bitter arguments over taxes, and some racial unrest. A state that has provided leadership, both in the concrete sense of presidents and candidates, and by bringing new issues onto the public agenda.

California is our most populous state and one with a rich and diverse resource base, aside from a perennial water shortage. It is first nationally in both industrial and agricultural income, rich in mineral resources, possessed of the most extreme topography in the country. Almost half of the state's forest land (100 million acres) is in the public domain. There are also five major national parks, a national seashore, and 175 state parks. Yet in the 1970s over half of the population lived in metropolitan areas, mainly along the coast.

A north-south rivalry continues in part because of water problems (most of the water is in the north; much of the need is in the south) and in part because political and economic power was historically lodged in the north but is now shared. San Francisco Bay Area voters are, on the whole, the most liberal in the state and often watch with dismay as their causes are vetoed by the south, which outnumbers them. At the same time, inhabitants of the Central and Imperial Valleys may resemble their midwestern or southwestern forebears more than they do the residents of coastal cities. Those who live to the north and east of the Sierra Nevada mountain range are still another species both politically and culturally (Wolfinger and Greenstein, 1969).

HISTORICAL TRENDS

California (and indeed the West Coast in general) was one of the last places to be settled by Europeans. Although both Cabrillo and Drake explored parts of the coast in the sixteenth century, the first serious settlement began in 1769 with the establishment of the missions. A period of Mexican rule from 1821 to 1848 saw mission lands and much of the hinterland divided by royal grants into large ranches, establishing a Spanish aristocracy, traces of which can still be found today. During this period a small number of settlers began to trickle in from the east as well.

American forces occupied California in 1846 as part of the Mexican-American War; two years later the territory was included in land ceded to the United States. Ironically, gold had been discovered at Sutter's Ford nine days before the treaty was signed, unbeknownst to the negotiators. In the Gold Rush following the news, California's population rose from 15,000 (1848) to 100,000 (1849), surpassing the 60,000 needed for statehood. A constitution modeled largely on Iowa's was ratified in 1849, and statehood was granted the next year.

Thus the earliest settlers, aside from the large numbers of Indians originally there, were Spanish; less than a century later they were vastly outnumbered by American adventurers, predominantly of European and English stock. The next large migrations came just after the Civil War, when Chinese laborers were imported to complete the transcontinental railroads, followed a few decades later by the Japanese.

Between 1850 and 1879 three major economic activities were dominant: some of the new settlers became farmers and ranchers, many more were seeking gold, and still others were completing the Southern Pacific Railroad connection. Vigilante justice prevailed in the mining camps and near the railroads, there was a growing anti-Asian sentiment, and railroad owners gradually learned to manipulate the state legislature. With the continuing influx of new citizens, including more middle-class farmers, the time was ripe for a full-scale reform movement.

Thus in 1879 Californians adopted a new constitution (still in effect, though much amended), largely in response to railroad power. It curtailed the legislature's authority, established controls on both public utilities and private corporations, and vastly restricted further Chinese migration. A few decades later even more drastic steps were taken, under reform governor Hiram Johnson. These included the direct primary (1909) and the initiative, referendum, and recall (1911).

A shortage of water has always been a problem, with the first major efforts at diversion and control as early as 1913, when the Owens Valley Aquaduct was built. Federal efforts in the Central Valley were stalled in the 1930s because most California farming, characterized by exceptionally large holdings, was ineligible for Bureau of Reclamation subsidies. Eventually the state developed its own project to assist large owners and to help meet water needs of urban southern Californians as well. In 1960 voters approved a project on the Feather River to bring northern water to the south. In 1982 yet another element in the state's water plan became a controversial ballot issue.

The Depression was severe for California farmers, along with the newcomers who sought new work or new land, because much of California's produce (fruit, exotic vegetables, nuts) was considered a luxury for family consumption. Problems of the elderly, of newcomers, of farmers facing foreclosure combined to give birth to a unique movement called EPIC (End Poverty in California), led by Upton Sinclair. His subsequent campaign for governor so frightened voters that a Republican victory was inevitable.

World War II brought an industrial boom, and in its wake a population boom as well, as the shipping and aircraft industries expanded. Thus manufacturing came to replace agriculture as the major source of jobs. By the 1970s trade and light electronics had become dominant. Oil was discovered in Los Angeles in 1892, and since that time offshore resources have been developed in significant amounts as well, spawning no small amount of political and jurisdictional conflict. California ranks third in the country in current extraction of mineral and mining resources.

The labor movement was born in California at about the same time that statehood was achieved. In 1850 the San Francisco Typographical Society became the first union organized west of the Rockies. The next year saw organization on the docks, and soon the beginnings in other crafts. The movement was slow, however, in Los Angeles, partly because of labor violence involving the outspoken antiunion offices of the *Los Angeles Times*.

Farm workers were difficult to organize because so many were migrants, were geographically dispersed, and were intimidated by powerful and well-organized growers. It wasn't until Cesar Chavez organized a grapeworkers strike and mobilized a nationwide boycott that union contracts were accepted, in the 1960s, by large growers. By the 1970s growers managed to encourage rivalry (and more favorable contracts) with the Teamsters. After the legislature passed an agricultural labor relations law in 1975, guaranteeing secret elections and providing for hearings of grievances, the United Farm Workers won most of the union elections. Inadequate funding for the ALRB and refusal of many growers to grant access to organizers, however, gave impetus to one of the first initiative petitions to reach California voters in the 1976-82 period—one that lost despite vigorous campaigning and significant spending by supporters.

In the late 1970s California was blessed with an unparalleled resource base, a well-educated population, and an economy that was not dependent on any one sector. Yet the rumblings of economic discontent were heard in 1978 even before unemployment reached double-digit figures in 1982. And racism, which had reared its head over Asians in the past, became visible again in the arguments over school busing and to some degree over illegal immigrants. Thus even sun-blessed California was not immune to the darker currents in politics that have swirled in other states.

GOVERNMENTAL STRUCTURE AND POLITICS

Californians elect both a governor and lieutenant governor for four-year terms. These officials are not always of the same party, the most recent example being Democrat Jerry Brown and Republican Michael Curb. All but two governors between 1898 and 1975 were Republicans.

The legislature consists of 40 state senators and 80 state representatives. Meeting annually, it is among the most professional in the country in terms of staff, research, and availability of printed records. Party unity has been weak, even under the relatively strong leadership of Jesse Unruh.

California counties are important administrative units, since they have jurisdiction over a fair amount of unincorporated (but by no means vacant) land situated between cities. The larger cities operate under home rule charters, mostly utilizing the manager-council structure. There are also a large number of special districts (i.e., water, sewage, irrigation, and the like) as well as school districts which in many cases cut across city lines. Most local units in California have been preoccupied with meeting the challenge of the massive population and economic growth of recent decades.

MAJOR EVENTS AND ISSUES IN CALIFORNIA, 1976-82

The weather and natural disasters were of major concern in California as they were in Oregon: a two-year drought that put farm crops in jeopardy was followed in 1978 by the largest annual rainfall in the twentieth century, resulting in severe flooding problems and mudslides in the Los Angeles suburbs. A severe earthquake in 1978, major forest fires 1978-79, and the invasion of the Mediterranean fruit fly in the summer of 1981 also caused havoc and, in the latter case, considerable political grief for the governor.

Bizarre criminal events also dominated the headlines for brief periods: the aftermath of the Patti Hearst kidnapping, the kidnapping of school children and their busdriver (1976), the so-called freeway murders (1981), and just before the period under consideration, two efforts in 1975 to assassinate President Ford, in Sacramento and San Francisco.

In 1976 President Ford narrowly won California's election by a 49.7-48.0% margin over Carter, and incumbent Democratic Senator John Tunney, who had faced primary opposition from activist Tom Hayden, was defeated by S.I. Hayakawa. Voters were asked to consider 30 ballot questions (15 each in June and November), including an agricultural relations act and a proposed restriction on nuclear power. Both were defeated.

Nineteen seventy-seven was, by contrast, a quiet year. The legislature approved restoration of the death penalty, overriding Governor Brown's veto. It also prohibited bank mortgage "redlining," i.e., refusal to grant mortgages in poor locations. Brown's appointment of Rose Elizabeth Bird as Chief Justice stirred considerable controversy, which resurfaced repeatedly in later years.

Proposition 13—a drastic and controversial property tax cap—dominated the news for most of 1978, as what seemed to be the entire citizenry debated its probable effects and then, after its June passage, worried about the results. November saw Jerry Brown easily reelected, a small Republican gain in the California delegation to the Congress, and several major ballot proposals, including a ban on hiring homosexuals in the public schools and a Clean Air Act establishing nonsmoking sections in public places. Both were defeated in campaigns that set new records for spending.

In 1979 the anticipated state budget cuts did not occur, and in fact state aid to local schools increased. Further state action included tax credits for employers hiring welfare recipients and a $1 billion appropriation for public transit. All of this was possible because of an accumulated state surplus of $5 billion and angered many Proposition 13 supporters.

Governor Brown launched his campaign for the presidency amid a series of setbacks in California: an attempt to appoint Jane Fonda to the State Arts Commission was rejected by the Senate, several skirmishes were lost to the University Regents, and work on the $1.4 billion Diablo Canyon nuclear power plant continued despite Brown's opposition and sporadic demonstrations by environmentalists. Brown withdrew from the presidential race in April of 1980.

Californians split their voting decisions between the two parties, supporting Reagan over Carter, but returning Democrat Alan Cranston to the Senate.

The Clean Air Act was again defeated, as was a proposed cap on state income taxes authored by Howard Jarvis, one of the authors of Proposition 13. And, in a long-awaited decision, the state supreme court upheld the constitutionality of the death penalty by a 4-3 vote.

Three major state environmental issues also reemerged in three different jurisdictions. In spite of considerable opposition, the U.S. Congress exempted the Stanislaus River from the National Wild and Scenic Rivers Act, enabling the New Melones Dam to be completed. A U.S. District Court overturned the state nuclear safety laws passed in 1976, declaring federal jurisdiction over the production of nuclear energy. And the state legislature authorized a $5.1 billion expansion of the peripheral canal project, approximately doubling the amount of water to be transferred from the northern to the southern part of the state.

Nineteen eighty-one was a year of fiscal troubles, controversy over the medfly, and extreme party rancor over reapportionment. In early October the governor issued an executive order imposing some $460 million in budget cuts—the long-delayed impact of Proposition 13. (This was also the year in which unemployment rose to 7.4%; it was to climb in 1982 to 10.2%.) The "medfly" problem surfaced in the summer when the U.S. Department of Agriculture announced a quarantine on California produce as a result of an infestation of the Mediterranean fruitfly. Brown had been advised by state experts to undertake aerial spraying with Malathion but had refused to do so on environmental grounds. A belated decision to spray did not save the governor from a tremendous drop in popular support.

The major battle, however, came over the Democratic legislature's reapportionment plan for the two new seats in Congress. The Republicans, claiming deliberate gerrymander of district lines, placed the issue before the voters on the June 1982 ballot. (The voters rejected the plan.)

Controversy continued over the Diablo Canyon reactor, with over 1000 arrests of demonstrators. The NRC in Washington revoked a preliminary operating license, pending an investigation of safety of the design.

In 1982 consistently bad economic news competed for voters' attention with controversial elections. Unemployment was the worst in 42 years, placing California well above the national average. There was a sharp increase in both unpaid property taxes and mortgage foreclosures, with a drop in tax revenues as well. The legislature drafted more restrictive rules on welfare and medical care for the poor.

Record spending occurred in the elections, with over $40 million in the primary contests and $60 million in the general election. Former Governor Brown lost to San Diego Mayor Pete Wilson in his bid for the U.S. Senate, but 28 Democrats out of a California delegation of 45 were sent to Congress, including three women, three blacks, and three Chicanos.

Voters rejected two redistricting plans in June and November. They also rejected the expensive peripheral canal project. In November, while giving bare majority support to the nuclear freeze resolution, they rejected both the bottle bill and a stiff gun control bill, in campaigns that once again attracted huge out-of-state spending.

Thus it is clear that the public mood in California (like Oregon) had shifted in complex and not invariably happy ways over a period of only seven years. Public attitudes on spending stiffened with visible economic distress. Major environmental arguments, notably over nuclear power and water resources, seemed almost impossible to resolve. Law-and-order issues occupied what room remained in the spotlight. And arguments over how to divide the "spoils" of population growth (two new Congressional seats) aroused partisan ire, as they do elsewhere every decade. In some cases politicians were made scapegoats for problems not entirely in their domain. All of these trends illustrate the fact that California, as the nation's largest and perhaps most flamboyant state, magnifies tendencies that can be observed elsewhere.

Laws Governing Initiatives, Referenda, and Campaign Finances

Michigan and Oregon laws about the proposal of ballot questions by popular petitions are quite similar, with the exception of initiative *statutes*. In Michigan constitutional amendments proposed by initiative require the signatures of 10% of the number of voters in the last gubernatorial election, as do referenda on laws previously enacted by the legislature. Statutory initiatives, however, are indirect—requiring legislative review in addition to signatures of 8% of the voters—before going onto the ballot. In Oregon, while initiative amendments require 8% of the voters' signatures, statutory changes proposed by initiative and referenda only require 6% and 4% respectively, of the number voting in the last election for governor. Oregon initiatives are direct—that is, they do not require legislative approval. Both states require simple majority approval for these proposals to take effect.

California requirements, quite stringent under the original 1911 legislation, were eased in 1966 and 1974. Constitutional amendments by initiative require signatures of 8% of the number of voters in the last election, while statutory initiatives and referenda require 5%. But the referenda method is actually used very infrequently in California because signatures must be filed within 90 days of the date of legislative adjournment, a very short period in a state with low-density cities and an area of 158,653 square miles (26 times the area of Massachusetts). Thus Californians who want to repeal a law are more likely to use the initiative route instead, simply proposing a law that forbids a given legislative action. (This happened, for example, on open housing, in 1964.)

Massachusetts, unlike the other three states, uses the *indirect initiative* for both statutes and constitutional amendments. (California also provided for a seldom-used indirect initiative until the mechanism was repealed in 1966.). An initiative statute requires signatures of only 3% of the number of voters participating in the last election, with a limit of 25% from any one of the state's 14 counties. This proposal (after certification by the attorney general, who may reject it on substantive grounds) must then be submitted to the state legislature. It becomes law if passed by the legislature and signed by the governor (or repassed by a two-thirds majority over a veto); if defeated, however, it may still go on the ballot if an additional half percent of the voters' signatures are collected. (Many Massachusetts initiatives, including the 1980 property tax cap, reached the ballot after initial rejection by the legislature.) Final voter approval requires not only a majority of "yes" votes but approval by at least 30% of all those participating in the general election.

An initiative to amend the Massachusetts Constitution also requires 3% of the gubernatorial voters' signatures, with no more than 25% from a single county. In this case, however, the proposal must be approved by a quarter of the members of two successively elected legislatures, meeting each time in joint session. If the legislature fails to act favorably, the proposal is dead. Finally, a referendum proposal requires 2% of the voters' signatures, after which it is placed on the ballot for approval or rejection, in accordance with the usual requirement: a majority of yes votes plus approval by at least 30% participating in the election. As will be clear in the next chapter, the more stringent requirements of the indirect initiative (despite the low number of signatures) has meant that Massachusetts voters have been presented with fewer initiatives than those in other states. To some degree this is true of Michigan as well.

All four states have laws requiring financial disclosure on ballot questions, although Michigan's rules were not enacted until 1978, and Massachusetts officials neither compile a cumulative report nor retain information on past elections for any significant period of time.[3] Michigan and Massachusetts require two reports (one shortly before the election, the second 30 days and 60 days after the election, respectively), while Oregon asks for three (one 30-31 days before, one 7-12 days before, and the final accounting 30 days after the election). California, in contrast, requires an initial report for the signature collection period, then periodic reports in the six weeks preceding the election, and a final accounting no later than 65 days after the election.

The California requirements, established by the sweeping Political Reform Act of 1974, exemplify the determined efforts in several states to plug loopholes that have allowed monied interests to dominate the referendum process. The act established a Fair Political Practices Commission, which is empowered to audit financial statements, investigate violation, issue cease-and-desist orders, levy fines, and institute law suits. It attempts to prevent the establishment of fronts that conceal the activities of utilities, corporations, and other organizations (under benign names like "Citizens for X") by requiring full disclosure of the names of campaign committee officers in addition to financial data. The act also addressed itself to the absolute amount of spending in an effort to reverse the trend toward multimillion dollar campaigns in California. This was attempted by imposing a spending limit of 8¢ per person of voting age (totalling $1.15 million in 1976) and a prohibition against more than a $500,000 difference between the two sides on a given question.

The California Supreme Court, following the reasoning of *Buckley v. Valeo* (424 U.S.1, 1976), struck down the limits on campaign spending while leaving the remainder of the act in force. The court stated that these limits interfered with constitutionally guaranteed freedom of expression. This decision, along with the 1978 *Bellotti* case in Massachusetts, where the state supreme court overturned a prohibition on corporate spending (also on free speech grounds), illustrates the very narrow area left to the state in limiting or prohibiting campaign activities by the affected interests. All four states place limits on anonymous contributions and on involuntary contributions by government employees; Michigan and Oregon also limit the conditions under which corporations and unions may solicit contributions. The justification is obvious: an effort to prevent expensive, self-interested advertising campaigns from entirely dominating battles over ballot questions, leaving little chance for success to a popular but underfunded grass-roots cause. As I shall demonstrate in Chapter 4, the fears are real. Yet there is a genuine dilemma here, in that an overly-stringent regulation of campaign finances may also hinder free speech and petition.

Finally, three of these states (all but Michigan) attempt to inform the voter by distributing voters' pamphlets before the elections. The Massachusetts pamphlet contains a relatively clear summary of each proposal, the text of the law or constitutional provision to be changed, and a brief argument by each side. The California pamphlet provides, in addition, rebuttals to the initial pro and con arguments and an official statement of the anticipated financial impact of proposals. Finally, the Oregon pamphlet—through the period of this study—allowed concerned individuals and groups to publish advertisements (at $300 per advertisement) opposing or supporting proposals.[4] Even at this subsidized rate, only about six to eight advertisements per measure were printed, except on the more controversial causes, where as many as 20-25 might appear. In at least one case (the fluoridation issue) it was only through an advertisement that the extremely limited scope of the proposal (because of a mistake in wording) was publicized.

California's 1974 reform act also mandated both an avoidance of obscure or technical language and a change in type and format to make the information on ballot questions more easily understood. This may have been partially in response to a 1973 Loyola University study that found the reading level of state, county, and local propositions beyond the comprehension of an estimated two-thirds of Los Angeles voters (Brestoff, 1975). While the new California format is indeed more attractive than either the old pamphlet or those in Oregon and Massachusetts, my assessment of comprehensibility is pessimistic. While the language and explanations are relatively straightforward, many of the issues (especially taxes, nuclear power, and criminal law) are so intrinsically technical that I wonder whether cosmetic efforts alone can do much to help all but the most determined voters. It should also be mentioned that while Michigan voters (like those in the vast majority of states) have no ballot pamphlet, explanations of the proposals on the ballot itself are clearly written. And the state also finances publication of the full text of questions in major regional newspapers. I shall return to the whole question of voter comprehension and the information-provision of ballot pamphlets in Chapter 7.

Conclusion

Beneath the major differences in size, location, resource base, and unique histories, there are obvious commonalities in both the political heritage and the recent political experiences of these four states. All four share in a common progressive tradition, although in Massachusetts this was not formally associated with the Progressive Party. Thus three (all but California) were pioneers on labor legislation, three (all but Oregon) in educational reform, and all stood with the North on slavery. All four states opted for Republican presidents until the New Deal. And finally, each state includes strong conservative/parochial elements, just beneath the progressive overlay, that occasionally emerge as racism or as rejection of some of the trappings of modern (urban) life. Examples include battles over self-service gas and fluoridation in Oregon, homosexuals and the peripheral canal issue in California, desegregation issues in both California and Massachusetts, and most of all, insistence on bureaucratic cutbacks and lower welfare expenditures, via tax caps, by substantial numbers in each state. Frequently these anti-modernization surges took the form of controversies brought to the ballot.

All four states clearly felt the contradictory national tides on environmental issues as well. Two of the governors (Brown and Milliken) were politically embarrassed by balancing and shifting on these priorities; two of them (Brown and Straub) also became embroiled in nuclear power controversies, initially at the level of mass demonstrations and ultimately through sweeping ballot proposals that looked like bans on future development. All four states—but especially Michigan and Oregon—faced unacceptable economic choices in a rising tide of failing industries and high unemployment, partly as a result of broader national trends.

Yet there were also several unique cultural traditions molding both the public agenda and ultimately the major electoral decisions in each state. Oregon, in particular, usually tilted toward the environmental side in a clash between economic and conservationist priorities, even though her voters can least afford to do so given a weaker (and less diverse) resource base than that of the other three states. Michigan's politics seem the most low-keyed (or least flamboyant) of the four; and as the next chapter will demonstrate, voter participation is somewhat lower. Massachusetts voters are probably more cynical about government spending or even the accurate translation of the popular will into public policy. (As the only state of the four, in this period, with continuing scandals about political corruption, the cynicism may be justified.) And California, with enormous size and geographical diversity, is more prone to overt regional conflict, bizarre issues, and expensive campaigns on referenda.

While the analytic chapters that follow will draw, from time to time, on these unique cultural-historical factors to explain differences in campaign strategies and outcomes, it is nonetheless important to remember the commonalities as well. All four states are among the leaders in the passage of innovative legislation, whether by the ballot or the legislature. The people in all four states have high rates of voting participation in contrast with the national average. And, except for Massachusetts, voters in these states have *used* (almost to excess) their right to pass direct legislation over a period of many years. Even in Massachusetts, concerned groups have been highly successful recently in working their way through the maze of the indirect initiative process, despite frequent roadblocks requiring extra efforts.

The next chapter will describe the 15 campaigns involving ballot questions in these four states: three general elections in four states, with three additional June primary elections in which propositions were also considered by California voters.

Notes

1. Information for all four states was obtained from major newspapers during the election campaigns and from relevant news in the national media, particularly from *Newsweek, The Progressive,* PBS programs, and "Sixty Minutes." Visits and correspondence with colleagues and friends in three states clarified some points. The statistics at the beginning of each section were obtained from *The Americana Annual* (1976, 1978, 1980, 1982.)

2. Fundamentalist and Evangelical churches flourish in Oregon, and some were active in the 1976 campaigns against abortion and fluoridation. None of the public campaign arguments or advertisements stressed the overtly religious themes characteristic of the 1978 antihomosexual campaign in California.

3. I was unable to obtain official reports on Massachusetts campaign finances for the 1976 and 1978 elections because, according to the official responding to my request in early 1981, all but the 1980 reports had been destroyed on grounds of "limited storage space." Thus I rely in later chapters on figures published in the *Boston Globe* for those two elections. It should be noted that officials in other states, who also received my request in early 1981, were universally helpful in providing information.

4. Oregon no longer carries subsidized advertising in the ballot pamphlet. This change is part of the stringent economic cutbacks discussed in this chapter.

3

AN OVERVIEW OF
FIFTEEN ELECTIONS, 1976-80:
POLITICAL CONTEXT AND ISSUES

In Chapters 4 through 7 the impact of campaign spending, advertising, endorsements, and grass-roots organizing will be assessed for 50 major ballot questions in the 1976 to 1980 period. There will be an opportunity to compare and explain campaigns and outcomes on, for example, 16 tax proposals, three efforts to limit nuclear power development, two bottle bills, and a variety of crime control measures. This procedure has the effect, however, of lifting individual battles out of a very rich campaign context. Because I believe the political backdrop can be important for both campaign strategies and for voting decisions on specific issues, I begin this chapter with a broad description, year by year, of the 15 campaigns studied here.[1]

I want ultimately to answer questions like the following: Do ballot questions fare better in presidential or off years? In primary or general elections? Do voters behave differently in campaigns focused on a single issue or on several major controversies? Do activist groups experience a shortage of funds and campaign workers in multiple issue years or in years when hotly contested candidate races are competing for limited resources? Why do some groups cooperate closely on multiple issue campaigns while others virtually ignore potential allies? How does this affect their choices?

I thus start with an account of the overall campaigns, both to lay the groundwork for answering these questions and to give the reader some feel for both the major issues and some of the campaign tactics. I will then discuss two sets of contextual factors: the simultaneous candidate races (presidential vs. off year; primaries vs. general elections) and both the number of and relation between ballot issues considered in the same campaign, as well as the presence or absence of coalition activities on those issues. The conclusion offers some preliminary remarks on campaign strategies and resources—elements which will then be dissected in detail in the remainder of the book.

The 1976 Campaigns

The 1976 presidential election is unlikely to be labeled by future historians as memorable, decisive, or realigning. Neither Carter nor Ford was a striking orator, no major new scandals emerged from the closet, and neither political party broke new ground on either the issues or campaign strategies. Thus it is not surprising that newspaper coverage and campaign activity were relatively low-keyed in three of the states studied here. The exception was Michigan, home of the Republican incumbent Gerald Ford, where coverage was high in both the presidential and senatorial races. Oregon held no election for the Senate, while in Massachusetts Senator Kennedy, the incumbent, won in a landslide against nominal opposition. The California contest, in which Republican S. I. Hayakawa defeated Democrat John Tunney for the Senate, was more colorful (and expensive), but even this campaign failed to arouse the sort of public excitement characteristic of many senatorial or gubernatorial races.

In all four states, however, ballot issues virtually monopolized the news and in some cases provoked bitter controversies. One or two issues were clearly dominant in each state except for Massachusetts. The dominant propositions were Michigan's bottle bill (on which interest groups, newspapers, and citizens concentrated, almost ignoring a property tax proposal), Oregon's (November) and California's (June) nuclear power controversies, and in the California general election, a proposal to legalize betting on greyhound racing coupled with one to strengthen the new Agricultural Labor Relations Board. All but the Michigan bottle bill were defeated in campaigns that set records for negative spending on campaign advertising.

The Massachusetts campaigns, in contrast, presented special problems for both voters and grass-roots organizers because five of the nine propositions (an unusually high number for the state) were liberal proposals, supported by many of the same public interest groups, endorsed by the same officials, and competing for the same limited campaign resources. These issues were the Equal Rights Amendment, gun control, a bottle bill, the graduated income tax, and a proposed flat electric rate to replace the quantity discount that benefited large consumers. Only the ERA was approved by voters. I shall discuss the Massachusetts campaigns more fully at the end of this chapter as an example of a multiple issue election where coalition activity was absent. Many of the other 1976 campaigns will be considered, as well, in Chapters 4 to 6, when I assess the relative effectiveness of grass-roots and media strategies.

Turnout in 1976 in all four states was reasonably high despite a lackluster presidential campaign. Participation ranged from a high of 82% of registered voters in Massachusetts and California to the lower levels of 74% and 71.5% in Oregon and Michigan. It can also be seen, from Table 3.1, that participation in individual states remained high across the board on the most controversial propositions as well as in the presidential and major statewide elections, with blanks from less than 10% of those voting. In both California elections, in fact, the number of blanks (or drop-off) on the most controversial proposition (the nuclear power issue in June, the ALRB amendment in November) was lower than in the U.S. senatorial race.

Another point of note in Table 3.1 is the *range* of voter participation on ballot questions. In Massachusetts, for example, the percentage of blanks increased from a level of 6-8% on the most contested issues to a high of 11% on the advisory question on a deep sea port and oil refinery. The latter was ignored by many voters primarily because of its nonbinding status. The drop-off is more striking in California and Oregon, where only 4-6% of the voters ignored the multimillion dollar campaign issues on, for example, nuclear power, but 18-20% blanked routing constitutional amendments submitted by the state legislature.

In summary, all five 1976 elections saw high turnout (71.5% or better) despite a low level of interest in the presidential campaign in all states but Michigan. In four of the five elections, a single proposition dominated the news; in the fifth, Massachusetts voters grappled with five major issues. Nevertheless, in all but one of these campaigns (the California primary), the clear drawing card for participants was an opportunity to vote on the presidency: only 2-3% of

TABLE 3.1: Summary of 1976 Turnout and Participation in Candidate and Ballot Question Elections

State	Registered voters	Voting in election	Percentage blanks		
			President	Senator/ Governor	Top 3 questions and last (by % voting)
Massachusetts	3,145,551	2,954,262 (82.5%)	2%	4% (Sen.)	Bottle bill 6%
					Gun control 7%
					ERA 8%
					Oil refinery 11%
Michigan	5,202,379	3,719,694 (71.5%)	2%	6% (Sen.)	Bottle bill 9%
					Tax cap 12%
					Quality of rep- resentatives 12%
					Gradual income tax 13%
Oregon	1,420,146	1,048,561 (73.8%)	2%	(no elect.)	Nuclear Power 4%
					Fluoridation 7%
					Gas tax 7%
					Amendment validation 18%
California (June)	8,710,756	6,323,651 (72.6%)	7%	15% (Sen.)	Nuclear Power 5%
					Bingo 11%
					School bonds 12%
					Historical proposition 19%
California (November)	9,980,488	8,137,202 (81.5%)	3%	8% (Sen.)	ALRB 5%
					Greyhound 6%
					Coastal bond 13%
					Unsecured property tax 20%

voters blanked this contest, in contrast to about 4-8% in statewide races and a range of 4-20% on ballot issues. The California primary, in contrast, saw a higher level of participation on one ballot question (95% on the antinuclear power initiative) than on the presidential race (93%).

Finally, the 1976 elections included expensive, negative media campaigns in all four states: five major battles on ballot questions attracted expenditures exceeding $1 million, with the California ALRB in fact involving more than that amount on each side. While extravagant campaigns are an old story in California, this level of spending was new to the other three states. Yet several of these ballot issues also generated skilled grass-roots operations as well, including one that won in the face of heavy spending (the Michigan bottle bill), one that came close with 49.6% of the vote (the Massachusetts bottle bill), and a third that won handily in the absence of heavy spending but with considerable latent opposition (the Massachusetts ERA).

The 1978 Campaigns

Despite the fact that 1978 was an "off year," voter interest ran high on selected issues or candidates in all four states, news coverage was intense (especially in Massachusetts and California), and voter turnout ranged from 57% in Michigan to 70% in the California general election. The main attractions varied considerably, from general elections in two states where popular incumbents were overturned (Governor Straub in Oregon, Senator Brooke in Massachusetts) to two where highly emotional style issues (smoking and homosexuality in California, the drinking age in Michigan) dominated the political debates. And the California primary drew a record turnout on Proposition 13—the property tax cap that was to dominate the initiative scene in many states in the elections that followed— while voters displayed relatively little interest in a gubernatorial contest involving Jerry Brown and a large field of challengers.

In Massachusetts interest in statewide candidates was far more intense than it was on the seven ballot questions, none of which was an initiative. Incumbent Republican Senator Edward Brooke, the only black in the United States Senate, was dogged throughout his campaign by questions on both his divorce and his income taxes and was ultimately defeated by a relative newcomer, Representative Paul Tsongas. Interest was also moderately high in the race for governor, between Edward King, a conservative Democrat whose September defeat of the liberal incumbent (Dukakis) had taken many by surprise, and Francis Hatch, a liberal Republican, who lost in a close finish. The only major ballot question concerned property tax classification—a last-ditch effort to satisfy those who were already threatening to bring a California-style tax cap to the voters. This complex proposal to tax residential, commercial, and industrial properties at different rates was approved by a substantial majority of voters (66-34%) after a multimillion dollar campaign more noteworthy for arguments over both the contradictory claims and the expenditures of both sides than for any degree of enlightenment. (Media coverage was thorough on Question 1, but a very large number of voters remained both confused and undecided even the weekend before the election.)

In contrast, voters in each of the other three states divided their attention among several acrimonious ballot question controversies. The Michigan electorate was almost equally preoccupied with three different kinds of issues: a proposal to raise the drinking age from 19 to 21, three different tax reduction measures including one tied to vouchers for education, and two proposed changes in the criminal code concerning bail and mandatory sentencing. None of these campaigns drew a high level of spending, although totals on the three tax issues exceeded $1.3 million. Four of the six major proposals were approved, including both crime control proposals, the most moderate tax measure, and the higher drinking age. The latter was the only issue attracting large grass-roots efforts, in this case by university students opposing the change.

Oregon's campaigns on ballot questions, despite competition for voters' attention by a close campaign in which the incumbent Democratic governor (Straub) was ousted by Republican Atiyeh, as well as an uneven Senatorial contest, attracted an extraordinary amount of voter attention on three style issues. This level of interest is surprising given relatively little press coverage and only modest spending by either side. While two of these issues (abortion and the death penalty) almost certainly evoked what David Magleby (1984: 129) calls "standing" opinions (opinions formed long before the election and difficult to change), a third, on the licensing of "denturists," was not one with which large numbers of people were familiar. Both the denturist and abortion issues received more votes than the race for senator, and the former came within 5200 votes (less than one-tenth of a percent) of the vote for governor. Voters approved both the death penalty and denturists, while defeating the proposal to ban state funding for abortions.

Finally, there is a sharp contrast between the two California elections. First, the June primary was completely dominated by Proposition 13, the property tax cap, and the more modest legislative alternative, Proposition 8. Blanks on Proposition 13 were left by only 3.5% of 6.8 million voters (a high primary turnout of 69% of registered voters), in contrast to 15% blanks in the gubernatorial primary, which involved 19 candidates. An even more unusual element in this campaign was the virtual necessity for almost every statewide candidate (even those low on the ballot) to make public statements on the tax issue. In addition, both incumbent senators entered the fray, with Cranston opposing and Hayakawa supporting Proposition 13 "with some misgivings." (As discussed in later chapters, candidates and incumbents are normally well-advised to remain silent on controversial ballot issues, since they stand to lose a great deal if they misjudge voter sentiment. Jerry Brown, in fact, later moderated his strong opposition to the tax cap, even implying that he had favored the idea from the start.)

Readers of either the *Los Angeles Times* or the San Francisco *Chronicle* might never have guessed, through most of the campaign, that there were 11 other questions on the ballot, including one school bond issue that also (by a margin of 15,000) drew more votes than the governorship. Coverage of the debate on taxes was so pervasive that news items and advertisements appeared on the sports pages (because of the impact on funding for school athletic programs) and even occasionally in the society section of these newspapers.

The November election was a return to a more normal pattern for California: only 3% of the 7.1 million voters blanked the final gubernatorial contest, won easily by Jerry Brown, with a slight drop in voter attention to three hotly argued style issues: a legislative proposal on the death penalty and initiatives on nonsmokers' rights and on homosexual teachers. The fact that the race involving candidates drew fewer blanks (3% in contrast to 4% on smoking, 5% on homosexual teachers, and 12% on the death penalty) should not, however, lead us to ignore one characteristic common to both the June and November elections: the intense anger of campaign activists and of many voters. What had begun in June as anger at government (and specifically at welfare spending) somehow spilled over into the seemingly unrelated issues of individual (smoking) rights, personal morality, and the rising crime rate. The debates and advertisements were ugly and intense, as well as expensive. While a $6.4 million expenditure against the smoking proposal was not surprising, given the economic stakes for tobacco companies, the $2.3 million cost of arguing the homosexual issue, almost evenly divided among opponents and supporters, sets a record for spending on a style issue. In the end, Californians rejected both the antismoking proposal and the ban on homosexual teachers but accepted the death penalty.

One of the most obvious points in Table 3.2 is the drop in voter participation in 1978 in contrast to the previous presidential election: the range is now from 57% in Michigan to 70% in California, with a drop of about 11-16% in each case, except in the 1978 California primary where the turnout of 68.9% was only 3.7% lower than the earlier presidential primary. A second point of note is the similar pattern of participation on ballot questions in all but the Michigan election: about 3-8% blanks occur on the most popular issues, with a drop to 17-25% on the less controversial items. In Michigan, however, fully 90% of those casting votes made choices on even the least of the 11 questions they faced, on a railroad development authority.

There is no simple explanation for this difference between Michigan and other voters. It does not seem to reflect the intensity or extravagance of the campaigns in the four states, since Michigan was the one state with no campaign exceeding $1 million, and even the tax issues failed to generate the level of vitriol characteristic of both the 1978 campaign in California and the later counterpart in Massachusetts. Nor does the 1978 pattern continue into 1980 in Michigan.

The 1980 Campaigns

The 1980 presidential campaign generated far more national interest than that of 1976, with the added excitement of a third candidate, John Anderson, whom many feared would split the normal Democratic vote; a charismatic newcomer to national politics as Republican standard bearer; and a seemingly endless crisis over American hostages in Iran that many blamed on the incumbent. Not surprisingly, turnout in Oregon and Massachusetts returned to the high level characteristic of presidential years, ranging from 77% to 81%. (This, however, was actually a few points lower than the 1976 level in Massachusetts and Michigan.) In contrast, however, Michigan turnout was lower, at 69.5%, and California experienced its lowest turnout in two decades in both the primaries and general elections of presidential years, despite the presence on the

TABLE 3.2:   Summary of 1978 Turnout and Participation in Candidate
             and Ballot Question Elections

State	Registered voters	Voting in election	Percentage blanks		
			Senator	Governor	Top 3 questions and last (by % voting)
Massachusetts	2,962,904	2,044,076 (68.9%)	(none)	4%	Tax classification 5% Voters' pamphlets 17% Government budget 18% Census procedure 11%
Michigan	5,230,345	2,984,829 (57.1%)	5%	4%	Drinking age 6% Vouchers (ed.) 6% Parole denial 7% RR Development Authority 10%
Oregon	1,482,339	937,423 (63.2%)	5%	3%	Denturists 3% Abortion 5% Death penalty 5% U.S. balanced budget 17%
California (June)	9,934,841	6,843,001 (68.9%)	(none)	15%	Property tax cap 4% Tax alternative 8% School bonds 14% Administrative agency 25%
California (November)	10,129,986	7,132,210 (70.4%)	(none)	3%	Smoking 4% Homosexual teachers 5% Death penalty 12% Public utility commission 21%

ballot of both a former governor as presidential candidate and several hotly debated propositions.

All five campaigns were characterized by high spending, heavy
newspaper coverage, and at least one bitterly divisive proposition.
Three of these issues were those of style: reruns on the drinking age

in Michigan and smoking in California, and an Oregon proposal forbidding the use of leghold traps. Several others involved both old and new economic issues: three tax caps, rent control, and limitations on nuclear power. Outcomes were quite mixed on the reruns: Michigan and California voters stood firm on their previous decisions to restrict drinking to 21 or older and to reject restrictions on smoking, while Oregon voters approved a modified restriction on nuclear power plants, reversing the earlier 1976 decision. Massachusetts approved but Michigan rejected a Proposition 13-style property tax cap, while Howard Jarvis, co-author of the 1978 tax cap, saw his follow-up proposal on income taxes defeated by California voters.

The Massachusetts campaign provided the starkest possible contrast to that state's 1976 election. First, to the surprise of many observers, the electorate reversed its previous support of President Carter and its longstanding loyalty to Democratic candidates by opting for Ronald Reagan in a close three-way outcome (Reagan 41.9%, Carter 41.7%, Anderson 15.2%). More to the point from the present perspective, in place of the earlier multiple focus on several important ballot issues, voter attention was concentrated on just two campaigns: the presidential race and the battle over "Prop. 2 $1/_2$," the property tax cap. Although there were five other ballot questions, only Question 3, a last ditch alternative to the tax cap authored by the state Teachers' Association, attracted much public attention. (There were no races for senator or governor in 1980.) The dominant tone in public debates and private discussions on both the tax issue and the presidency was one of anger over the economy and the seeming indifference or ineptitude of public officials in relieving the financial distress of the middle class. Thus the tax limitation was approved by a substantial margin (58.6-41.4%) despite warnings by state and local officials that cutbacks in essential services would follow. Voters further vented their anger by overwhelmingly rejecting Question 4, a proposed pay raise for legislators, by 88.2-11.7%.

The Michigan campaign, as in Massachusetts, was concentrated on the ballot issues and the presidency since there were no other major contests for office. Michigan again supported the Republican candidate, with 49% for Reagan, 42.5% for Carter, and 7% for Anderson. Here, however, the resemblance ends. In more than one way the 1980 election was a rerun of Michigan's 1978 experience. Taxes were again the dominant issue, with three separate proposals, including a property tax cap, under consideration. (All three were rejected by majorities ranging from 56% to 79%.) In addition, a proposal to restore the drinking age to 21 was rejected by 62-38%. The remaining three issues (all of which were placed on the ballot by the legislature) were largely neglected both in the campaigns and ultimately by voters.

It is worth noting that this is the only election of the 15 in which every ballot measure was defeated by the electorate. These election outcomes cannot, however, simply be interpreted as voter negativism or (as in Massachusetts) as anger at the government. First, a quick-cure tax cap (a partial outlet for voter anger) was defeated in Michigan. Second, Michigan voters, in rejecting the lower drinking age, were actually reaffirming their own 1978 decision on a very different kind of issue. The more interesting question concerns the contrasting outcomes in Michigan and Massachusetts (both states with strong Democratic parties, strong unions, and at least the beginnings of economic distress in 1980) on the tax cap. This contrast, together with Oregon and California outcomes, will be considered at length in Chapter 7.

The Oregon campaign was unique among the 15 studied in that a major natural disaster, the eruption of Mt. St. Helens, blacked out election coverage for a three-day period in mid-October. The events at Mt. St. Helens (actually in Washington but with major loss of life and property in Oregon) was of course covered extensively in California and the other two states as well, but it failed to dominate the media and public attention in other campaigns. I might note here that local natural disasters in California (mudslides and forest fires), extensive strikes in Michigan, and the nationally important 1980 Iranian hostage crisis also occasionally preempted news coverage in the regional newspapers and television broadcasts in various November campaigns—but never for the extended period experienced in Oregon. Nor did the 1980 Carter-Reagan debates, although they seem to have attracted far more coverage (especially in Oregon) than had been the case for debates in 1976. Despite the three-day news hiatus, however, Oregon turnout was about 3.5% higher (77%) than it had been in 1976.

There was one close three-way race in Oregon, ultimately won by incumbent Senator Robert Packwood with 52% of the vote; but this campaign received less media attention than several controversial ballot measures. In fact, once again there were more votes cast on the three most controversial measures than on the senatorial contest, with blanks ranging from 5-6% on three measures (the leghold traps issue, a gas tax increase, and nuclear power regulation) to 6% (about 38,000 fewer participants than on nuclear power) on the senatorial race. These figures compared to 2% blanks (27,000 voters) on the presidency.

As in Michigan, three of the eight measures considered in Oregon were reprises of earlier battles: a pair of tax reduction proposals (one a tax cap, the other a compromise plan) and a scaled-down proposal to regulate nuclear power plants. The tax proposals, in high spending campaigns by Oregon standards (a total of $418,500), were decisively defeated by 63-37% and 72-28% majorities largely because of vocal opposition from both moderate business interests and a host of local and state officials. The Oregon electorate reversed itself, however, on nuclear power, by a relatively close vote of 53.2-46.8%. There were several new elements in this campaign, including a narrowing of the 1976 proposal, somewhat less activity and spending by an overconfident opposition, and finally— perhaps most important of all—the relatively fresh memory of the March 1979 accident at Three Mile Island. Both the ban on leghold traps and the proposed increase in the gas tax were defeated by overwhelming majorities.

Two days before the June 1980 primary in California, the *Los Angeles Times* predicted a high voter turnout because of intense interest in three ballot measures. Voter turnout in fact dropped from the level of earlier primaries to a low 63.3% of the 6.77 million registered voters. The *Times* was correct, however, in expecting relatively low interest in both the senatorial campaign (which included incumbent Alan Cranston and former Los Angeles Mayor Sam Yorty) and the presidential primary. More votes were cast on 10 of the 11 propositions than on senatorial candidates, and six also received more votes than presidential choices.

The three measures on which most action took place were all initiatives: a surcharge on oil profits, a limitation on local rent control, and an income tax cap proposed by Howard Jarvis. All three were defeated, two by substantial margins of 60% or more, and the third (the oil tax) by 56-44%. It was clearly the propositions that brought many voters to the polls, since 94-96% voted on these three (with an additional three on veterans bonds, disaster relief, and a newsman's shield law receiving votes from about 89% of the electorate), in contrast to 88% voting their presidential preferences and 83% participating in the senatorial primary. There are three other points of note about this election: an unusual amount of *coalition activity* among opponents of two proposals (rent control and the income tax cap), the injection of strident *arguments over personalities* associated with the issues, and a level of *threatened litigation* and invocation of the FCC Fairness Doctrine that is unusual even for California. This campaign will be discussed further at the end of this chapter.

The general election apparently did little to restore voter interest. Although 77% of the 11.4 million registered voters went to the polls, with a 52.7% majority for Reagan, turnout was below the 82-88% showing in the presidential years from 1964 to 1976. Only one of the 11 propositions attracted much attention, and this (the only initiative on the ballot) was a modified version of the Clean Air (nonsmokers) proposal defeated two years earlier. The only other contests of major interest were those of Senator Alan Cranston, who won by 56.5% in a low-keyed campaign, and decisions on two bond issues on state acquisition of parklands, also reruns of earlier efforts. While few voters blanked their ballots on the president, senator, or Clean Air Act, blanks on the remaining propositions ranged from 12 to 18%.

While national concern about both the Iranian hostage crisis and the poor state of the economy surely affected Californians as well as other Americans, I do not believe it can in any way account for the ennui in this campaign or in the June primary a few months earlier. There were, for example, eight days in October when no news items, letters, editorials, or advertisements on *any* issues appeared in the *Los Angeles Times*; the absence of coverage was even more striking in the *Chronicle*. There simply seem to have been no issues, apart from occasional outcries and complaints to the FCC over the $1.1 million opposition campaign of tobacco companies on the Clean Air Act, that caught the fleeting attention of more than a small number of voters. Although Oregon's repeat performance on nuclear power and Michigan's reconsideration of both the drinking age and tax issues were far from earthshaking in intensity, they clearly excited more interest than any California campaign. And Massachusetts battles over both the presidency and the tax cap dwarfed all other political news in that state, even among those whose interest in politics was shallow and sporadic.

Table 3.3 presents, in summary form, the information on 1980 participation discussed above. Note that while both turnout rates and percentage of blanks in the November presidential vote are quite similar in the four states (as is the level of participation in the Oregon and California senatorial races), there is a marked contrast between states in blanking patterns on the ballot questions. Both Massachusetts and California illustrate the characteristic pattern of elections where one issue was dominant: blanks rise from 5% on the Massachusetts tax cap to 11-19% on other issues, and in California from 6% to a 12-18% range. In contrast, Oregon voters especially show their concern over several issues, with 94-95% participation; and even the issue least voted-on, a state bond issue for prisons, saw 89% participation.

Campaign Contexts and Participation on Ballot Questions

PRESIDENTIAL VS. OFF-YEAR ELECTIONS

Past election returns have shown a regular pattern of higher turnout in presidential years than in the intervening off-year elections. General elections, in addition, usually attract more voters than do primaries. This difference varies, of course, with the perceived closeness of races for state office and the presidency, the issues raised, the record of incumbents, and the like. Nevertheless, there is little question that presidential campaigns activate some voters who show less interest in races for the Congress, for state office, or for local elections in other years. The preceding tables in this chapter thus have shown, as expected, a drop in turnout of 10-13% between 1976 and 1978 and a subsequent increase of 7-14% from 1978 to 1980 in the four states. In addition, it also was shown that while the number of blanks in the presidential contests remained constant at 2-3% of those voting (in two presidential elections in all four states), the blanks in statewide races ranged from 3-8% and on ballot questions from 3-25% of participating voters. (All of this information is given in Tables 3.1-3.3.) The real question, then, is whether there are systematic differences (other than in turnout) in presidential and off-year elections that somehow spill over into campaigns and voting on ballot questions.

There is some disagreement in the scholarly literature on this point: Angus Campbell's (1966) findings from studies of the Eisen-

TABLE 3.3:   Summary of 1980 Turnout and Participation in Candidate and Ballot Question Elections

			Percentage blanks		
State	Registered voters	Voting in election	President	Senator/ Governor	Top 3 questions and last (by % voting)
Massachusetts	3,156,672	2,566,807 (81.3%)	2%	(none)	Proposed tax cap 5% Tax alternative 11% Legislative salary 11% Emerging law 19%
Michigan	5,725,713	3,978,647 (69.5%)	2%	(none)	Property tax 8% Drinking age 8% School tax 12% Lieutenant governor Power 16%
Oregon	1,569,222	1,209,691 (77.1%)	2%	6%	Leghold traps 5% Gas tax 5% Nuclear power 6% Prison bonds 11%
California (June)	10,694,660	6,774,184 (63.3%)	12%	17%	Income tax cap 4% Energy surtax 6% Rent control 6% Reapportionment 19%
California (November)	11,361,623	8,775,459 (77.2%)	2%	5%	Smoking 6% Parklands 12% Lake Tahoe bonds 12% Tax valuation 18%

hower years stressed the importance of both education and age for differential turnout in presidential and off years; Wolfinger and associates (1981) found only age to be important (young voters drop out disproportionately in off years) in examining 1972-74 data. They also found a somewhat higher percentage of conservatives in mid-term elections. Magleby (1984: 78-83) confirms these findings and goes on to demonstrate that drop-off on proposition voting in

California, Massachusetts, and Washington does not change in presidential years. This is in accord with my own findings in the four states, reported above: about the same percentage of voters participate in both presidential and off-year elections on the more important propositions. I have found, in addition, no systematic conservative shift or shifts in outcomes on issues of special interest to younger voters (e.g., the drinking age) when comparing presidential and off years. Measures receiving a good deal of "liberal" support (for example, nuclear power, bottle bills, and the graduated income tax) fared about equally well in both kinds of years. Oregon voters, for example, initially rejected a nuclear power proposal in 1976 then approved a modified version in 1980—both presidential years. Tax caps were approved and rejected in both election contexts as well. In short, the type of election year does not by itself provide an explanation for differing outcomes on ballot issues.

One other possibility, however, calls for brief examination: Are there fewer *campaigns* on ballot questions in presidential years (quite apart from outcomes), since some of the limited resources needed for petition drives and later precinct work have been preempted by the presidential contest? We do not find this to be the case. In Massachusetts, for example, where the indirect initiative process in itself discourages a large number of initiatives, there were no initiatives on the ballot in 1978 (the off year), in contrast to four in 1976 and three in 1980. The total numbers for all four states were, however, 17 in 1978 (the off year), in comparison to 14 each in 1976 and 1980—a slightly but not significantly higher showing.

There may, however, be other important contextual differences that matter greatly for campaign strategies and voting behavior. One of these, I would argue, is the question of single versus multiple issue campaigns and, as a secondary point, the degree of overlap, cooperation, or autonomy of campaign actors and activities. In one sense this is simply another way of approaching the all-important question of availability of resources.

Single vs. Multiple-Issue Campaigns and Coalition Formation

The 15 elections studied here are almost evenly divided between those where the bulk of media attention, spending, or grassroots efforts went to one issue (or in one case two) and those in which three to five issues competed for attention and resources. The seven single-issue campaigns involved tax caps or tax classification (California, 1978 primary; Massachusetts, 1978 and 1980), nuclear power (California, 1976 primary), a bottle bill (Michigan, 1976), and nonsmokers rights (California, 1980), with the double issue campaign in California (1976) focusing on Chavez's ALRB proposal and on greyhound racing. Note that such campaigns occurred in three states, in all three election years, and in both primary and general elections. Multiple-issue campaigns included a few where several major proposals came from ideological cousins (although not always from formal allies), notably the 1976 campaign in Massachusetts (five liberal proposals) and the 1980 primary campaign in California (two conservative proposals and one from liberals, with all three attracting both overlapping support and opposition). By far the most common pattern, however, was one in which three or more issue clusters were involved—for example, the drinking age, crime control, and taxes in the 1978 Michigan election or denturists, abortion, and the death penalty in Oregon, also in 1978. In campaigns involving multiple-issue clusters there was usually very little overlap from one issue to another in organizational support or opposition. Table 3.4 presents a summary description of the 15 campaigns and also estimates the level of media and public interest in the election on both candidates and ballot questions.

It should be emphasized that I am *not* attempting to treat level of interest as a dependent variable; the fourfold table is simply a convenient means of presentation. Similarly, level of interest in candidate campaigns is presented only for information: there is no implication that high level of interest in candidates, for example, caused the moderate to low level of interest in issues marked "*" at the bottom of the table. In the Michigan and Oregon cases, the fact that several issues were reruns (property tax, drinking age, abortion, death penalty) probably dampened voter interest; the extraordinary complexity of the Massachusetts tax classification issue is undoubtedly relevant as well.

The remaining task is to compare and contrast some of the single- and multiple-issue elections in rather general terms, since many of the campaigns on individual issues (tax caps, bottle bills, nuclear power, parklands, and several style issues) will be discussed at length in later analytical chapters.

TABLE 3.4:   Single and Multiple-Issue Campaigns, 1976-80

Single Issue Campaigns	Multiple-Issue Campaigns
High-interest on ballot questions[a]	
*Mich. 1976 (bottle bill)	Mass. 1976 (ERA, gun control, bottle bill, electric rate, income tax)
Cal. 1976P (nuclear power)	Ore. 1976 (nuclear power, gas tax, fluoridation)
Cal. 1976G (ALRB, greyhounds)	Mich. 1978 (taxes, drinking age, crime control)
Cal. 1978P (property tax cap)	*Cal. 1978G (homosexual teachers, death penalty, smoking)
*Mass. 1980 (property tax cap)	*Ore. 1980 (leghold traps, gas tax, nuclear power)
	Cal. 1980P (income tax cap, rent control, oil surtax)
Moderate or low interest on questions	
*Mass. 1978 (tax classification)	*Ore. 1978 (dentures, abortion, death penalty)
Cal. 1980G (smoking)	

[a] Level of interest judged by media coverage, opinion polls, and final number of blanks on most controversial issues.
* Indicates high level of interest in one or more candidate election.

In some single-issue elections there simply were no other major issues that successfully reached the ballot. This is true in the Massachusetts (1978, 1980) and California primary (1978) elections that focused on tax issues. In other elections potentially controversial measures somehow never took off in the face of high spending media campaigns for or against the dominant proposal. For example, a tax cap in Michigan (which predated California's Proposition 13) was totally lost in the spending, grass-roots activity, and public relations efforts on the bottle bill; a potentially controversial proposal to legalize bingo received less attention than the (at that time) unprecedented nuclear power moratorium proposed to Californians in June 1976. The most interesting point that can be made about single-issue campaigns, at this stage of the analysis, is the potential advantage they present to those who rely on grass-roots strategies, namely in the near-monopoly in recruiting campaign workers not involved in candidate operations. This advantage was one of the major differences between the (successful) bottle bill campaign in

Michigan and its (defeated) counterpart in Massachusetts in 1976, where workers were spread in the latter state among five different campaigns that appealed to the same liberal constituency.

The 1976 Massachusetts campaigns are worth comparing to the June 1980 campaigns in California because of the contrasting strategies employed by liberal activists. Although several Massachusetts organizations endorsed two or more proposals, there was no move to form coalitions or to publicize more than one issue in the same group rallies, fundraisers, or advertisements. (This individualistic behavior is typical of most of the multiple-issue campaigns studied here.) In California, in contrast, joint campaigns and coalitions formed on both sides of two major issues, and occasionally joint advertisements appeared on all three.

Five controversial liberal proposals, four of which evoked heavy opposition spending, were submitted to Massachusetts voters on the 1976 ballot. Three of these, the bottle bill, a gun control law, and a proposed flat electric rate, were proposed by initiative. The other two, the ERA amendment and a graduated income tax, took the form of constitutional amendments submitted by the legislature. Only the ERA was approved by voters (by a 60-40% majority), although the bottle bill came close, with a 50.4-49.6% defeat. Spending was high by Massachusetts standards, with one campaign (the bottle bill) exceeding $2.6 million, a second (the flat electric rate) at $550,000, and two others (gun control and the graduated tax) over $100,000. In three of these four campaigns, supporters were outspent by margins ranging from 11-1 to 40-1. Thus the only way that supporters could hope to win was through strenuous grass-roots efforts and by staging events that would attract free media coverage.

The grass-roots efforts of both the bottle bill workers and the victorious, low spending movement on behalf of the ERA are discussed in detail in later chapters. Both issues brought forth an ambitious canvassing effort, accompanied by imaginative public events. In the case of the other three proposals, however, opposition workers appear to have not only outspent but outorganized supporters. One puzzling question is why this happened, given the honor roll of prominent individuals and organizations that backed these issues. The gun control proposal, for example, was endorsed (with some reservations) by the governor, his Republican predecessor, the Boston Police Commissioner, Common Cause, and the League of

Women Voters. The latter two groups and the governor joined with conservation groups to support the bottle bill, and with Mass Fair Share (a blue-collar group), the ADA, organized labor, and the Council of Churches in working for the graduated tax, which also had the approval of the legislature. It was only the proposal for the flat electric rate (an innovative measure that forbad the quantity discount given to large consumers, thus, it was argued, both lowering residential rates and encouraging conservation) that saw one of these groups, Mass Fair Share, standing almost alone against some of its allies on other measures, namely the governor and the AFL-CIO.

Many observers attributed the liberal defeat on all but the ERA to the division of limited campaign funds and workers among too many causes, in contrast to well-funded opposition groups who were fighting one cause each: the gun and sportsmen's clubs, the Citizens for Limited Taxation, the beverage, liquor, and retailers interests, and the Associated Industries of Massachusetts. This was undoubtedly true; and given both the overwhelming negative spending advantage and the sharply negative vote (69-75% against the proposals) on all but the bottle bill, it is hard to see how the liberals *could* have won these uphill races. Yet one wonders why there was no pooling of efforts by the groups that supported more than one cause—e.g., joint press conferences by Common Cause, the League, and the governor on behalf of two or three measures; joint fundraising parties; a division of labor on leafletting.

The failure of Fair Share to combine its efforts on behalf of the flat electric rate and the graduated tax, for the obvious reason that its allies on one measure were opponents on the other, provides a clue to the answer. Proponents of each cause feared that multicause rallies, fundraising, or leafletting might alienate part of an already slim constituency; thus each cause was handled in separate events, and even single-cause activities were only loosely coordinated by the various endorsing groups.

All of this seems quite reasonable from a strategic standpoint, particularly from the perspective of long-range organizational survival. Many interest group analysts would support the idea that espousal of many, seemingly unrelated causes may antagonize more members than are gained by adding new issues. It does not, however, explain the contrast between the 1976 Massachusetts liberals and both sides in the June 1980 campaigns in California, who indeed formed coalitions and conducted joint events on major ballot issues.

California voters faced 11 ballot proposals in the 1980 primary, in addition to preliminary contests for the presidency and on the Senate seat held by Alan Cranston. As discussed above, general participation dropped from the 68.9% level of the 1978 primary to 63.3% of registered voters, despite the presence on the ballot of three controversial propositions. But in this election more votes were cast on *ten* propositions than for the senatorial candidates, and in six cases the vote also exceeded that for the presidency.

Two of the three initiatives were sponsored by Howard Jarvis and a coalition of conservative business, real estate and development interests. One, Proposition 9, would have capped state income taxes, while the other, Proposition 10, sought to impose limits on local authorities to impose rent control. Opposition groups included the California Federation of Teachers, the AFL-CIO, NOW, the Grey Panthers, and the American Association of Retired People. In addition, the opposition included a figure easily as colorful as Jarvis in the person of Tom Hayden, whose Campaign for Economic Democracy in fact was the major radical force on the Santa Monica City Council, one of the local authorities whose laws were the target of Proposition 10.

Part of the controversy centered on Jarvis's abrasive style, part on the unprecedented level of spending ($6.8 million on rent control, $5.4 million on the income tax cap, with supporters outspending the opposition 37-1 and 2-1 respectively), and part, in the case of rent control, on what was widely denounced as one of the most fraudulent advertising campaigns in several decades of California politics. (Proponents implied in both the petition drive and in early ads that the proposition supported rent control, when in fact it would overturn existing ordinances on the local level.) Both propositions were defeated by decisive majorities (60.8-39.2% and 64.5-35.5%), as was the third controversial measure, an oil surtax proposal supported by liberals.

The campaigns began in a style that is common in California when high economic stakes are involved. Both sides sponsored debates and forums, issued press releases, and purchased large amounts of radio and television time. The unusual feature of the campaigns on Propositions 9 and 10 was the moderate amount of long-term coordination, especially by opponents of the measures. Opponents, for example, conducted a joint voter registration drive in the San Fernando Valley in late April. Senior citizens and minority people then held joint workshops on strategy as well as fundraisers featuring Hollywood stars. Joint rallies and press conferences spotlighting Governor Brown, Mayor Bradley, Tom Hayden, and representatives of the United Farm Workers were common toward the end of the campaign.

The opposition campaign, despite the atmosphere of cooperation, the extensive training given to workers, and the visible presence of celebrities, was nevertheless far from flawless: two separate fundraising "galas" had to be canceled, for example, leaving a meager treasury of only $178,000 in the rent control fight, against supporters' $6.6 million. Tom Hayden, too, drew some unfavorable coverage and probably lost some votes for his earlier anti-Vietnam activities and his marriage to fellow-activist Jane Fonda. Thus, without the stylistic flaws and strategic errors of the Jarvis forces (for example, overspending on the petition drive for Proposition 9, leaving relatively little for later advertising), plus the fraud issue on Proposition 10, voters might not have been moved from initial confusion and vague approval to the ultimate opposition of election day. But this cooperative canvassing and the barrage of broad-spectrum media events (many of which received free coverage) certainly helped the opponents' cause and ultimate victory.

Why this strategy, in contrast to the "go it alone" and single-issue approach of the Massachusetts liberals? Why, for example, weren't the more moderate teachers' unions, representatives of the aged, and prominent officials careful to dissociate themselves from Hayden's radical Campaign for Economic Democracy? My educated guess is that—given the Proposition 13 experience two years earlier—the moderates overestimated the appeal and skill of the conservative forces in arousing public anger and economic fears and thus gratefully accepted alliances where they could find them.

Then, too, truly massive grass-roots efforts are usually essential in California to counteract big spending—massive efforts that usually are difficult without some pooling of resources across a range of organizations and several issues. And finally, it is probably fair to characterize many California campaigns as more polarized than those in Massachusetts and elsewhere. Liberal-radical coalitions were not unprecedented in the state, as witnessed by the successful combination of civil libertarians, unions, officials, and a highly visi-

ble gay and lesbian alliance in opposing the 1978 proposal to forbid
hiring of homosexual teachers and school administrators. That coalition, incidentally, faced a cooperative right-wing-fundamental-
ist effort on behalf of both the homosexual teachers issue and an
amendment on the death penalty. What I am arguing is that the California campaign style is frequently not only expensively geared to
media blitzes—it often forces moderates to join hands with radicals
and to count victory or defeat more important than organizational
or ideological niceties, especially when the stakes are high. If conservative campaigns in other states continue to increase in cost and
to become more professional (that is, run by campaign consultants
and media experts), liberal multiple-issue coalitions may arise more
frequently outside of California as well.

Conclusion

This account of 15 elections in four states has highlighted the context in which the major campaigns on ballot questions took place.
While I have found the anticipated ebb and flow of voter turnout
during the four-year presidential cycle, I have not found that the
existence of presidential races or hotly contested campaigns for the
Senate or governorship make a great deal of difference for the simultaneous battles about propositions. Instead, ballot question campaigns seem to take on a life of their own. The existence, for example,
of multiple controversies as opposed to one or two seems to matter more for campaign resources and strategies, and ultimately for
public attentiveness, than the parallel contests conducted by major
candidates.

I have noted, in passing, the impact of high spending and intensive advertising on some campaigns, of endorsements by celebrities and public officials (and of the more characteristic attempts of
candidates to avoid position-taking), of grass-roots efforts to register
voters, to leaflet and canvass, and to create media events. Occasionally I have discussed the moods of the voters themselves: disin-
terest, confusion, occasional anger. In the next four chapters I will
zero in on all of these elements of ballot issue campaigns. I will
concentrate on 50 ballot questions, all of which were important and/
or controversial in themselves or were similar to issues that were
important in other campaign contexts in the four states.

Note

1. My major information sources for this chapter are the *Boston Globe, Detroit Free Press,* (Portland) *Oregonian, Los Angeles Times,* and (San Francisco) *Chronicle* for the two months preceding the general elections, and in California for the primary as well, in 1976, 1978, and 1980. Election returns and financial information came from official state sources, listed in full under References at the end of this study, except for the two elections in Massachusetts and Michigan, where spending data came from the newspapers.

4

CAMPAIGN EXPENDITURES

Campaign expenditures, and their role in elections, have long been of interest to political scientists as well as to reformers. This has been particularly true since the rise of the campaign PACs in the wake of congressional reforms of the 1970s and the continuing importance of costly media advertising in national campaigns. While a good deal of scholarly attention has focused on spending in presidential and congressional campaigns, comprehensive studies are only beginning to appear on money and campaigns on ballot questions.[1] This seems a reasonable place to begin the present analysis for one very strong reason: I find that campaign expenditures are the single most powerful predictor of the vote. In fact, in 40 of the 50 issues studied for the 1976-80 period, the high-spending side won.

This high-spending victory was true for low-salience style issues like fluoridation as well as highly controversial matters like property tax caps and nuclear power. It held for noncorporate as well as corporate spending. Is this simply reconfirming the obvious point that "money talks"? Quite apart from the lack of consistent evidence that "money talks" for *candidate* races,[2] I disagree for two reasons. First, we must ask *why* money matters so much. Is it simply a matter of sensible contributors supporting obviously winning causes? Or is there a genuine conversion effect in costly media campaigns? Second, given the fact that the ten deviant cases include several major issues where the outcome varies from state to state, notably nuclear power and bottle bill proposals, it is important to understand the conditions under which high spending *fails* to pre-

Author's Note: An earlier version of this chapter was presented as a paper, "Winning State Referenda: Money vs. Peoplepower," at the 1983 Annual Meeting of the American Political Science Association in Chicago.

dict the vote. Was it the content of the issue, the campaign strategies, or what?

The discussion in this chapter will begin with a presentation, in
summary form, of the 50 ballot questions, with spending and voting figures obtained from official sources. I will then attempt to sort
out those cases where money appeared to make a difference, that
is, where spending seemed to reverse an initial stance of the electorate and/or to have an important impact apart from endorsements
and activities of other political actors and the media. Finally, I will
focus on the ten deviants, with particular emphasis on cases where
outcomes varied from state to state.

Expenditures and Voting on Fifty Issues

For ease of discussion, we have divided the 50 issues on two
dimensions: first, following Berelson's usage (1954: 184), into
"position" and "style" issues, and second, in terms of probable
economic impact. Berelson defines position issues as those which
raise the question "in whose *interest* should the government be
run?" Style issues, in contrast, involve "self-expression of a rather
indirect, projective kind." This rather loose definition creates some
problems in classification, since some campaigns shift from stylistic to position arguments over time, and others may find one
side emphasizing style while the other argues position. Since the
typology is used here primarily for heuristic purposes, however,
the arbitrary classification of some mixed cases is not a major
problem.

The magnitude of economic impact is fairly easy to predict, since
an official estimate appears in the ballot pamphlet in some states
and looms large in campaign debates. (Even when contenders disagree on the exact amount, they do not disagree generally on whether
it is "high" or "low." The environmental field presented some
problems, however, in classifying issues on Berelson's dimension.
Opponents of nuclear power regulation stressed economics, while
sponsors of proposals stressed style, as did many voters, in the surveys on this issue (Hensler and Hensler, 1979). (This was also the
case for bottle bills.) Thus I classified these proposals as style
issues. In the case of the four California coastal park bond issues,
however, most of the ballot pamphlet and campaign discussion

centered on economics (costs and benefits to voters), so, with some misgivings, these were classified as low-impact position issues. Table 4.1 presents the classification, together with data on expenditures and election outcomes.

Table 4.1 shows a number of ballot questions where campaign spending exceeded $1 million. Six of these are position issues—four dealing with tax caps, one with rent control, and one with an Agricultural Labor Relations Act brought to the ballot by Chavez and the United Farm Workers. Six more are style issues with high economic impact, concerning nuclear power, smoking, and the bottle bill. Perhaps the most interesting case, though, is the California initiative to ban the hiring of homosexual teachers—a style issue with low economic impact which attracted $2.3 million in campaign spending. It is also the one instance where noncorporate spending exceeded $1 million.

It should be noted that nine of the 13 top-spending campaigns occured in California, which is the most populous state of the four studied, and also a testing ground for many new propositions. Campaigns attracting $500,000-999,000 show more geographic spread—five in Michigan, two in Massachusetts, one in Oregon, and one in California.

Next, Table 4.1 shows that over two-thirds of the ballot questions in this study fall into two categories: position issues with high stakes (15 out of the 19 deal with major tax proposals) and style issues with low stakes, where the most common type (six out of 16) involves law enforcement. All of the seven style issues where economic stakes are high are environmental questions; four of the eight we have classified as position issues with low stakes also involve the environment.

Finally, Table 4.1 shows my central finding: in 40 of the 50 issues studied, the high-spending side won at the polls. The deviant cases (marked "*" on Table 4.1) include two where spending exceeded $5 million and three where it was under $100,000. A range of issues is represented, with three instances (the Michigan bottle bill, Oregon nuclear regulation, and California parklands bond issue) where the high spending did in fact win *on the same issue* in other elections in the same state or elsewhere. I shall return to some of these "deviant" campaigns in the next section.

Before proceeding to specific campaigns, two more trends in Table 4.1 deserve separate attention. They concern the distribution

TABLE 4.1: Expenditures and Voting on 50 Major Ballot Issues in California, Massachusetts, Michigan, and Oregon, 1976-80 (* indicates cases where high-spending side lost election)

| Ballot Question | Spending (in thousands) | | | Vote |
	Pro	Con	Total	
Position Issues, High Impact (N = 19)				
*Ban on local rent control without referendum, Cal-80	$6,655.2	$ 178.3	$6,833.5	35.5-64.5%
*Income tax cap, Cal-80	3,633.6	1,777.7	5,411.3	39.2-60.8%
Property tax cap (Proposition 13), Cal-78	2,158.6	2,000.2	4,158.8[a]	64.8-35.2%
Legislative alternative to Prop. 13, Cal-78	2,000.2	2,158.6	4,158.8[a]	47.0-53.0%
Agricultural Labor Relations Act, Cal-76	1,358.4	1,898.6	3,257.0	37.8-62.2%
Tax classification (differential rates), Mass-78	900.6	554.8	1,455.4	66.4-33.6%
Property tax cap, Mich-80	140.5	581.6	722.1	44.2-55.8%
Vouchers, private school, Mich-78	239.4	351.2	590.6	25.7-74.3%
Flat electric rate, Mass-76	150.0	400.0	550.0	25.3-74.7%
Property tax limit (compromise), Mich-78	292.1	239.8	531.9	52.5-47.6%
Property tax cap, Mass-80	430.5	101.2	531.7	58.6-41.4%
Property tax cap, Ore-80	31.4	311.0	342.4	36.9-63.1%
Property tax cap, Mich-78	22.9	270.6	293.5	27.3-72.7%
Property tax cap, Ore-78	83.9	153.6	237.5[a]	48.3-51.7%
Legislative alternative to tax cap, Ore-78	153.6	83.9	237.5[a]	45.1-54.9%
Property tax limit, Mich-76	97.0	100.0	197.0	43.0-57.0%
Graduated income tax, Mass-76	7.0	115.0	122.0	26.5-73.5%
*Legislature's plan, property tax limit, Mich-80	74.5	1.6	76.1	25.7-74.3%
Graduated income tax, Mich-76	"modest"	"modest"	"modest"	27.8-72.2%

(continued)

TABLE 4.1:   Continued

Ballot Question	Spending (in thousands)			Vote
	Pro	Con	Total	
Position Issues, Low Impact (N = 8)				
*Parklands bonds, Cal-June 80	91.0	26.4	117.4	47.0-53.0%
Urban coastal bond, Cal-76	43.8	0	43.8	51.5-48.5%
*Lake Tahoe bonds, Cal-Nov 80	24.2	0	24.2	48.2-51.8%
Tax exempting solar energy, Cal-80	18.5	0	18.5	65.5-34.5%
Coastal parklands bond, Cal-Nov 80	10.1	0	10.1	51.7-48.3%
Limit local taxes, state aid to education, Mass-80	0	0	0[b]	35.7-64.3%
Shift school tax to state income tax, Mich-80	0	0	0[b]	21.2-78.8%
Constitutional convention, balanced budget, Ore-78	0	0	0	82.6-17.4%
Style Issues, High Economic Impact (N = 7)				
Clean Air Act (nonsmoking sections), Cal-78	700.6	6,411.3	7,111.9	45.6-54.4%
Nuclear power ban, Cal-76	1,257.1	4,033.6	5,290.7	32.5-67.5%
Clean Air Act, Cal-80	1,024.8	2,732.0	3,756.8	46.6-53.4%
*Bottle bill, Mich-76	117.0	1,316.0	1,433.0	63.8-36.2%
Nuclear power ban, Ore-76	238.1	985.2	1,223.3	42.0 58.0%
Bottle bill, Mass-76	56.5	2,587.5	2,644.0	49.6-50.4%
*Nuclear power regulation, Ore-80	34.8	600.0	634.8	53.2-46.8%
Style Issues, Low Economic Impact (N = 16)				
Antihomosexual teachers, Cal-78	1,033.7	1,279.9	2,313.5	41.6-58.4%
Broaden death penalty, Cal-78	657.9	12.4	670.3	71.1-28.9%
*Lower drinking age, Mich-80	523.3	28.3	551.6	38.4-61.6%

| Ballot Question | Spending (in thousands) | | | |
	Pro	Con	Total	Vote
*Raise drinking age, Mich-78	41.4	194.4	235.8	57.1-42.9%
Denial of bail, Mich-78	203.0	0	203.0	83.4-16.6%
Convene state constitutional convention, Mich-78	55.8	83.5	139.3	23.3-76.7%
Prohibit state-funded abortion, Ore-78	50.5	81.2	131.7	48.3-51.7%
Ban handguns, Mass-76	8.4	93.9	102.3	30.8-69.2%
Collective bargaining, troopers, Mich-78	72.8	0	72.8	56.0-44.0%
ERA, Mass-76	66.5	2.3	68.8	60.0-40.0%
Antifluoridation, Ore-76	3.7	13.4	17.1	43.0-57.0%
*Restore death penalty, Ore-78	0	15.0	15.0	64.3-35.7%
Mandatory sentencing, Mich-78	13.9	0	13.9	74.5-25.5%
Deep water port, Mass-76	0	0	0	65.3-34.7%
Newsmen's shield, Cal-80	0	0	0	73.3-26.7%
Ban on racial school assignments, Mass-78	0	0	0	70.1-29.9%

a. In both the California (June 1978) and Oregon (November 1978) elections, the campaign committees opposing the tax cap supported the alternative, and those supporting the cap opposed the alternative; thus financial reports were combined.
b. In Massachusetts and Michigan in 1980, committees favoring these proposals spent most of their funds on opposing the tax cap proposals.

of spending among the four types of issues and the ratio of spending by the winners and losers on specific issues. Table 4.2 presents the distribution of expenditures by category of issue.

Note a strong pattern of self-interest among campaign contributors, namely, a higher level of spending on issues where the economic stakes are high. Over half of the high-stakes position issues, and all of the high-stakes style issues, attracted spending in excess of $500,000. In contrast, only three low-stakes issues (homosexual teachers and the death penalty in California, the drinking age in Michigan) attracted this sort of money.

TABLE 4.2:   Distribution of Campaign Expenditures by Issue Type

Spending	High Stakes Style (N = 7)	High Stakes Position (N = 19)	Low Stakes Style (N = 16)	Low Stakes Position (N = 8)
$1,000,000 or more	86%	32%	6%	—
500,000 - 999,999	14%	26%	12%	—
100,000 - 499,999	—	—	31%	12%
0 - 99,999	—	—	50%	88%
	100%	100%	99%[a]	100%

a. Does not total 100% because of rounding

At the other end of the spectrum there were eight high-stakes issues where spending was under $500,000. Six of these concerned property tax reduction in Michigan and Oregon, where the average spending level was markedly lower as a whole than in California in particular, but also than in Massachusetts.[3] The other two were not given much chance of passage (or discussion) by the press.

Before assuming that high spending on high-stakes issues simply implies rational economic self-interest on the part of corporate contributors, it is necessary to examine who spent what on which side. Table 4.3 presents the data.

Twenty-six of the campaigns involved corporate spending, although just over one-third saw a divided industry with some banks, the Chamber, and individual firms supporting one side, while the state association of manufacturers and realtors supported the other. Almost every mixed case involved the property tax, with corporate support split between a cap and the legislative alternative. In some cases where corporate support was united, contributions were quite diverse, including banks, utilities, large manufacturers, electronic firms, and organizations like the Chamber. This was the case, for example, in the three proposals involving nuclear power. In other cases, such as the two clean air initiatives or the proposed limitation on local rent control in California, only the industry most involved was active—major tobacco companies or banks and real estate interests in these cases. In some cases (notably on the bottle bill, clean air, and nuclear proposals) the fact that a great deal of corporate money came from out of state became a campaign issue, although in no case did that argument seem to change the election outcome.

TABLE 4.3:   Main Source of Funding, By Voting Outcome

| | *Funding Source for High-spending Side* | | |
	Corporate	*Corporate mixed—some corporate spending on both sides*	*Non-Noncorporate*
Top 20 issues ($500,000+)			
Won	8 (73%)	4 (80%)	3 (75%)
Lost	3	1	1
	11	5	4
Remaining Issues[a] ($203.00-$499,000)			
Won	4 (67%)	4 (100%)	10 (77%)
Lost	2	0	3
	6	4	13
Percentage of all issues			
Won	71%	89%	76%

a. The seven issues on which no spending was reported are not included.

The financial advantage of winners over losers in the top 20 issues ranged from a high of 53-1 (broadening the death penalty in California) to near parity in three cases (two tax cap initiatives and the proposed ban on homosexual teachers in California). In seven instances the winners outspent the losers by 8-1 or more. All but two of these cases (the drinking age, limits on rent control) involved corporate spending.

Finally, it can be seen that the frequency of deviant cases, that is, those where the high spenders lost, is not related either to the phenomena of *corporate* spending or the magnitude of the spending. Over 70% of the cases supported by high spenders won in each of the three categories (corporate, mixed, noncorporate). In fact, referring back to Table 4.1, we can see that four deviant cases involved total expenditures of less than $100,000 per election; in addition, two of these were style and two were position issues. In short, neither very high spending nor an extraordinary spending ratio (rent control, nuclear power, Oregon—1980) guarantees victory; corporations do not always fare better than private parties; and deviant cases are found in all four types of issues. To sum up, then, thus far I have shown that the high-spending side won in 80% of the issues studied here, but the amount of that money, the source, or the kind of issue does not seem to determine victory or defeat.

Does Spending Follow Opinion or Mold It?

Let me now address the question of whether spending patterns simply follow trends that would have existed without such spending either among opinion leaders (the press, prominent political actors) or the general population. I will do this in two different ways, first, in this section by comparing spending and endorsement patterns, and by looking at the poll data that are available *over time* on several issues. In the next section I will compare deviant and winning cases on the bottle bill, nuclear regulation, coastal bond issues, and the drinking age in an effort to untangle the effect of money versus other variables.

Public opinion poll data, usually commissioned by the newspapers (and, in addition, in California by the Field Poll), were reported on 32 issues, including all 20 where spending exceeded $500,000. Newspaper editorials (endorsements) were written on all issues, and public stands taken on 20 issues by major political figures, such as the governor and/or major candidates for office. Thus we are able to assess the relation between general public views, expenditures, editorials, and prestigious endorsements on at least 32 major issues. The reader should remember, however, that 18 are not covered in the discussion that follows.

Table 4.4 shows five categories of issues in terms of the relationship between poll results, expenditures, and outcomes. First, there are five issues where public opinion remained constant throughout with few undecided voters even at the beginning, where campaign expenditures coincided with the public preferences, and where the final outcome was decisive (a split of 60-40% or more). These are cases where (by hindsight) spending seems to have been superfluous given the margin of victory. It should be noted that four of the five are low-impact style issues.

A second category of issues (four cases) is similar, in that polls showed a consistent set of public attitudes which ultimately prevailed in the election, and where campaign spending was predominantly on the winning side. In all four cases, however, there was voter confusion over the meaning of these proposals and indecision

TABLE 4.4:   Poll Data, Expenditures, and Endorsements for 32 Issues[a]

Issue	Poll	Editorials	Major Political Endorsements	Vote
Category 1: Expenditures, polls, and outcomes consistent and one-sided (N = 5)				
Cal. death penalty*	Consistently pro	Con	Mixed	71.1-28.9%
Mass. gun control	Consistently con	Pro	Mixed	30.8-69.2%
Mass. ERA	Consistently pro	Pro	Pro	60.4-39.6%
Mich. denial of bail	Consistently pro	Pro	—	83.4-16.6%
Mich. vouchers for private schools	Consistently con	Con	—	25.7-74.3%
Category 2: Expenditures, polls, and outcome consistent; public uncertainty early (N = 4)				
Cal. nuclear ban*	Con	Con	—	32.5-67.5%
Mass. tax classifi-cation*	Pro	Pro	Pro	66.4-33.6%
Ore. nuclear ban (1976)*	Con	Con	—	42.0-58.0%
Mass. property tax cap*	Pro	Con	Mixed	58.6-41.4%
Category 3: Measures where public opinion changed to outcome consistent with spending (N = 15)				
Cal. property tax cap (Prop 13)*	Early con; erosion over time	Con	Mixed	64.8-35.2%
Cal. tax alternative*	Pro; erosion	Pro	Mixed	47.0-53.0%
Mich. property tax cap* (1978)	Early pro; late polls disagree	Con	Mixed	27.3-72.7%
Mich. tax alternative* (1978)	Early con	Con	Mixed	52.5-47.5%
Ore. property tax cap (1978)	Slightly pro, erosion	Con	Mixed	48.3-51.7%
Ore. tax alternative	Slightly pro	Pro	Mixed	45.1-54.9%
Mich. property tax cap* (1980)	Slightly pro	Con	Mixed	44.2-55.8%
Mich. property tax limit (1976)	Early pro; erosion	Con	Con	43.0-57.0%
Mass. graduated income tax	Early pro; erosion	Pro	—	26.5-73.5%
Cal. farm labor relations*	Early pro; late con or undecided	Con	Pro	37.8-62.2%
Cal. clean air-78*	Early pro; late con	Con	—	45.6-54.4%
Cal. clean air-80*	Early pro; late con	Con	—	46.6-53.4%

(continued)

TABLE 4.4: Continued

Issue	Poll	Editorials	Major Political Endorsements	Vote
Cal. ban on homosexual teachers*	Early pro, late con	Con	Con	41.6-58.4%
Mass. bottle bill	Steady erosion (June, 73%; October 56% pro)	Pro	Pro	49.6-50.4%
Mass. flat electric rate	Began pro; steady erosion	Con	Con	25.3-74.7%

Category 4: Measures where opinion changes in direction of spending but not enough to change outcome (N = 2)

Issue	Poll	Editorials	Major Political Endorsements	Vote
Ore. property tax cap-80	Early con, late slightly pro; large number undecided	Con	—	36.9-63.1%
Mich. raise drinking age	Early very pro; close pro later	Con	—	57.1-42.9%

Category 5: Deviant cases: money and outcome differ (N = 6)

Issue	Poll	Editorials	Major Political Endorsements	Vote
Mich. bottle bill*	Consistently pro	Pro	—	63.8-36.2%
Mich. lower drinking age*	Pro Oct. 25; no other polls taken	Pro	Pro	38.4-61.6%
Cal. income tax cap*	Early mod. pro; erosion later	Con	Con	39.2-60.8%
Cal. limit on local rent control*	Early pro; erosion later	Con	Con	35.5-64.5%
Mich. coalition tax plan (1980)	Early pro; late con	Pro	Pro	25.7-74.3%
Ore. death penalty	Consistently pro	Con	—	64.3-35.7%

a. No polls taken on 18 issues not included in table.
* Expenditures exceeded $500,000 on these measures.

on the part of many, even toward the end of the campaign. In two cases the final vote was close as well. These were indeed complex proposals on taxes or nuclear power regulation, where campaign spending may not have been essential for victory, but where it probably contributed to the final decision. Note that all four occasioned expenditures over $500,000, of which by far the largest part went into advertising.

The third and fourth categories, which include a total of 17 cases, consist of outcomes where money seems to have been important. In category 3, where two-thirds of the 15 campaigns saw spending in excess of $500,000, the initial stance of voters was steadily eroded and finally reversed on election day. A vote closer than 60-40 was cast on all but four of these issues. It is no accident that at least one property tax issue (along with compromise alternatives) in all four states appears in this category, as do some other very complex proposals, the flat electric rate, and Chavez's agricultural labor proposal. In each case the economic stakes were very high, the public mood was angry but unfocused at the outset, and considerable voter education was needed. Campaign advertising seems to have been very effective in turning the voters around on these issues.

The two issues in category 4, the Oregon 1980 tax cap and the Michigan initiative to raise the drinking age, saw both a lower level of spending and a less effective shift. In both cases the high-spending side won, but in both opinion shifted during the campaign *away* from the side which finally won. Thus we would argue that particularly in the case of the 57-43% split in Michigan, these are cases where the outcome might have been different without that spending.

Finally, category 5 consists of six deviant cases where polls were taken. In the case of the Michigan bottle bill the large expenditures of opponents probably had little impact: even the early polls showed strong support, and a well-run grass-roots campaign helped to guarantee the eventual 64-36% outcome. The Michigan effort to lower the drinking age shows a similar pattern, as does that of the Oregon death penalty; and it should be noted that all three are style issues where attitudes may have developed, at least for a number of voters, long before the election.

In the other three cases expensive and heated campaigns seemed to accomplish the opposite of intended effects; an initial favorable public reaction (albeit with a high proportion of confused and undecided voters) changed to strong margins of rejection by campaign's end despite public relations and advertising efforts by supporters. I shall consider these deviants at greater length shortly.

The editorial stance of the major newspapers and the stance of major statewide office-holders or candidates is also shown in Table 4.4. In 21 of the cases shown, the press and dominant spenders were on the same side. (The figure is 29 out of 43 cases in our larger sample where spending occurred; in one additional case, the *Los Angeles Times* and San Francisco *Chronicle* took opposite views.) In 20 cases at least one major political actor took a public stand.

(This happened most frequently in California and Massachusetts.) The newspapers and politicians agreed in 11 cases, disagreed in one (the California farm labor proposal), and in eight cases the politicians themselves were split. It is interesting that seven of these cases were the property tax cap and its alternative. (The press opposed all but the Oregon alternative.) The eighth case was the death penalty in California, opposed by Governor Brown and supported by candidate Younger. *In only one case* out of 50 was there a party split with both parties vocal: this was the proposed constitutional convention in Michigan, which incumbent Democrats believed to be to their advantage.[4]

In the 12 cases where political actors agreed, seven were on the side of the high spenders while five were on the low-spending side. I believe this finding may be time-bound, since many of these public stands were taken by Governors Dukakis (Mass.) and Brown (Cal.), both outspoken and activist liberals who were succeeded by less vocal conservatives.

In any event, the data indicate that while there is considerable overlap between high spending and press endorsements (about $2/3$ of the 20 cases) and some between political actors and spending ($7/12$), there are no grounds for arguing that the money simply goes to issues which have elite support (or vice versa). In fact, two more points need to be made: first, the *voters* do not automatically follow elite endorsements, and second, the elites are themselves more divided than the above figures would imply.

On the first point, the voting outcome was in agreement with the major regional paper 32/49 times. In the case of political actors, the voting outcome agreed with these actors 8/12 times. On the second point, as will become clear in the next section, there were many instances where different sets of business interests were on opposite sides of an issue. This was particularly true of tax issues.

Note that major political incumbents or candidates took public stands on only 20 of the 32 most controversial propositions; in addition, many of these endorsements were made reluctantly, near the end of the campaign. Except in cases where their position was well-known before the campaign, they had a great deal to lose by backing what might become the losing side. Governor Brown, in particular, found himself waffling at the end of the Proposition 13 campaign, even appearing after adoption to take partial credit for a measure he initially opposed. Furthermore, reporters seldom pressed candidates about their views on any but the most controversial proposals; thus we know little about their stands on the remaining 18 propositions covered in this study.

To summarize the findings thus far, I have found that (1) the high-spending side won on all but ten ballot issues in campaigns that involved expenditures ranging from a few thousand to several million dollars; (2) with one notable exception (homosexual teachers), campaigns exceeding a million dollars were ones involving high economic stakes; (3) in 17 out of 32 cases, voter opinion (from poll data) was reversed in the direction of campaign spending, and on all but two of these issues, that reversal was enough to change the outcome; (4) and finally, spending and elite endorsements were not always in accord, and in fact disagreement frequently existed between the press and political actors or among actors themselves.

While I shall reserve, for later chapters, a detailed across-the-board discussion of campaign strategies and interest-group acties, more light can be cast on these findings by a brief comparison of deviant and winning campaigns on a few issues. This is my next task.

The Deviants: Lessons for Underdog Strategists?

There were ten deviant cases where the high-spending side lost the election. Eight of these were in California and Michigan, with two in Oregon; otherwise they show both a range in total spending (from $15,000 to $6.8 million) and in type of issue evenly divided between style and position issues and in terms of the economic stakes involved. Table 4.5 summarizes these issues, including the expenditure, voting, and endorsement data discussed above and an assessment of the level of campaign activity apart from advertising.

Let me briefly dispose of the last three issues on the table. In my judgment, the Michigan drinking age and Oregon death penalty issues were very much like some others we have discussed (such as fluoridation in Oregon, the death penalty in California) where no amount of campaign expenditures or activity would be likely to change the outcome. Even press endorsement of the losing side had little impact. These were low-impact style issues on which a large number of voters had strong predispositions not readily swayed by a campaign. This may be akin to party preferences in the pre-1964 era.[5]

TABLE 4.5: Deviant Cases, Showing Expenditures, Level of Activity, Endorsements, and Voting Outcomes

Issue	Issue Type[a]	Expenditure	Press	Actors	Political Campaign Activity	Outcome
Mich.80—Tax reduction	PH	$ 75,000	pro	pro	Mod. hi-pro	25.7-74.3%
Cal.80—Income tax cap	PH	$5,411,000	con	con	High	39.2-60.8
Cal.80—Rent control	PH	$6,833,000	con	con	High	35.5-64.5
Cal.80—Lake Tahoe Park	PL	24,000	pro	—	None	48.2-51.8
Cal.80—Coastal parks	PL	117,000	pro	pro	None	47.0-53.0
Ore.80—Nuclear power	SH	635,000	con	—	Mod.hi	53.2-46.8
Mich.76—Bottle bill	SH	$1,433,000	pro	—	High-both	63.8-36.2
Ore.78—Restore death penalty	SL	15,000	con	—	Mod.con	64.3-34.7
Mich.78—Raise drinking age	SL	236,000	con	—	Mod.con	57.1-42.9
Mich.80—Lower drinking age	SL	552,000	pro	pro	Mod.pro	38.4-61.6

a. PH = position, high stakes; PL = position, low stakes; SH = style, high stakes; SL = style, low stakes

The stories of the Oregon nuclear power initiative and the two California bond issues, however, differ in that voters actually *reversed* their views in the span of a few years. In California there had been a history of low-keyed campaigns which usually resulted in voters approving funds to acquire and improve new coastal parklands. In 1976, for example, voters approved a $280 million urban coastal bond issue in a very low-spending campaign. But in June 1980 the omnibus proposal for a $495 million parklands issue was rejected by 53-47%, despite endorsements by Governor Brown, Mayor Bradley, and prominent legislators. Voter opposition was probably aroused by the *broad range of the proposal* itself, which included funds for water conservation grants, the expansion of state fisheries, and the acquisition of lake as well as coastal property.

In November supporters split the defeated parklands proposal into two separate questions: Prop. 1 providing $285 million for coastal parklands, and Prop. 2 proposing $85 million for lands in the Lake Tahoe basin. Once again the campaign was almost invisible, although an impressive array of environmental and labor groups, the League of Women Voters, and several mayors endorsed Prop. 1. Ultimately voters approved Prop. 1 (51.7-48.3%) while rejecting Prop. 2. I interpret this as a clear voters' preference for a less sweeping (and less costly) proposal. (The geographically limited Tahoe proposal of course had less widespread support.)

The same point (that narrowing the scope of measures can increase voter support) can be made in regard to the three nuclear power proposals. Two nuclear initiatives were defeated in 1976, in California and Oregon. Both involved very high opposition spending ($4.2 million vs. $1.26 million in California; $935,000 to $238,000 in Oregon), as well as skilled advertising campaigns that brought the combined weight of the scientific and economic authorities against the proposals in both states. But another major reason for the decisive defeats (67.5-32.3% in California, 58-42% in Oregon) was probably the sweeping nature of those early initiatives. California's Prop. 15 was successfully labeled a "ban" by opponents because it not only prohibited future construction of nuclear power plants unless stringent safety and liability standards were met, but would have reduced existing plants' operating levels. The earlier Oregon proposal was almost as restrictive in that it required both an extensive public hearing process and a two-thirds vote of the legislature for future construction.

What made the difference in the 1980 Oregon campaign? One likely difference was the nationwide impact of the nuclear accident at Three Mile Island in March 1979. Both the 1976 and 1980 campaigns featured arguments on safety; those arguments were probably more convincing in 1980. The second change, however, was the narrow scope of the new proposal. The 1980 version proposed local referenda for new sites and prohibited the reprocessing of nuclear fuels but no longer required the two-thirds legislative majority for initial authorization.

The 1980 campaign was relatively low-keyed and inexpensive: opponents spent $600,049 to supporters' $34,811. Coverage was also relatively light, with, for example, only six short articles and two editorials in *The Oregonian* between October 1 and election day. (There were 18 articles as well as three editorials in 1976.) Finally, the eruption of Mt. St. Helens from October 17 to 19, 1980, virtually preempted other news in Oregon for several days before the election, the one instance (in 15 elections) where a major event of any kind seems to have had this effect on the coverage of ballot questions by the press.

While there were at least four differences in this case between the deviant victory and the earlier defeats, one crucial factor was the modification of a proposal originally seen as too extreme or comprehensive. This was the feature shared with the California parklands deviant. I would also guess that there was some spill-over from the educational efforts of the 1976 campaign, although the high number of uncertain voters in campaigns that are reruns (e.g., the California clean air proposals) warns against such an assumption. But I would *not* argue that an increase in grass-roots skills and activities made the difference on this issue; indeed, campaign activity dropped from several thousand precinct workers in 1976 to a modest core in 1980, as did the magnitude of spending by advocates.

Grass-roots organization, with the funding needed to support and coordinate a large number of volunteers, does seem to have made a difference in two other expensive campaigns. These were the 1980 California fight over restrictions on local rent control, where opponents spent $178,000 to $6.6 million by supporters, and the 1976 bottle bill campaign in Michigan, where supporters spent $117,000 to $1.3 million by opponents.

Note that in both of these cases, the victorious side was hope-lessly outclassed by opponents' resources (30-1 in California, 12-1 in Michigan). Yet supporters reached that "minimum critical mass" needed to support a staff and to finance some media advertise-ments. The California opposition was probably also helped by the state-versus-local control argument, thus gaining some support from those who would normally oppose rent control per se.[6]

I shall concentrate here, however, on the Michigan bottle bill campaign, since the deviant case in Michigan can be contrasted with a losing campaign in Massachusetts in the same year. Here is a profile of the two elections:

Spending	Polls	Press	Campaign Activity	Vote
Mass. $56,476- 2.6 million	Strongly pro throughout	pro	Pro: Governor, LWV, Com- mon Cause, Audubon So- ciety Con: Retail Assoc., AFL- CIO, bottlers	49.6-50.4%

| Mich. $117,000-1.3 million | Early pro, some erosion over campaign | pro | Pro: Amer. Farm Bur., State Police, conservation groups, pediatricians Con: similar to Mass., without unions | 63.8-36.2% |

Two points are obvious in the comparison: first, that while both sets of supporters were vastly outspent, the Massachusetts groups never raised enough to mount more than a shoestring operation; second, that the Michigan base of support was markedly broader than that in Massachusetts.[7] Part of the difference lay in the campaign context as well. In Michigan the bottle bill all but preempted news coverage of even the presidential campaign, not to mention the other three ballot proposals, only one of which (a tax limit) occasioned much spending or public interest. In Massachusetts, in contrast, there were eight proposals before the voters, *five* of which (the bottle bill, ERA, handgun ban, a flat electric rate, and the graduated income tax) contended for the resources of roughly the same liberal constituency. Spending by supporters of ERA and the flat electric rate exceeded pro-bottle bill spending by over 2-1 and 4-1 respectively, and many organizations like Common Cause, Mass Fair Share, and the League were forced to spread their limited human resources over several issues.

The Michigan campaign used three different arguments: the aesthetic/conservationist on litter, the economic costs of throwaways, and the issue of safety (cut glass hazards for children, livestock, and tires). It was this last argument that helped bring the active support of the Farm Bureau, the State Troopers Association, and the Michigan Chapter of the American Academy of Pediatricians, which is normally inactive on ballot questions. In contrast, Massachusetts supporters completely overlooked the safety argument and in fact became embroiled in an endless debate with spokesmen for bottlers and retailers on whether passage would mean a net gain or loss of jobs in the state. The Michigan campaign was colorful, featuring several "cleanathons" in which supporters collected and publicized photographs of discarded bottles and compared amounts collected with similar sites in Oregon (where legislation had been in effect for some years). The Massachusetts campaign, while thoroughly covered, was drab and unemotional both in comparison with its Michigan counterpart and in contrast to fights on other issues in Massachusetts.

It would be simplistic to argue that the level of supporters' spending was all that mattered in the two bottle bill campaigns. What is argued is that a strong grass-roots effort can only succeed against a high-spending media effort if it has the logistic support to mobilize volunteers, stage media events, and coordinate regional activities in the case of a decentralized campaign. This usually requires far more than the $56,000 available in Massachusetts. Even with more funding however, the Massachusetts effort would still have suffered from the competition for volunteers and coverage that came from the multiplicity of liberal causes on the ballot.

I shall continue the discussion of both grass-roots and media-intensive campaigning in Chapters 5 and 6. In the meantime, however, it is worth noting that strong grass-roots activity is one of the four variables I have found important for underdog (i.e., low-spending) victories. The others are the relative scope of proposals, the degree to which proposals support or oppose existing cultural values (especially on style issues like the death penalty or drinking age), and the overall electoral context, i.e., the presence or absence of other controversial issues (or candidates) on the ballot.

Conclusion

I have found, in an examination of 50 major ballot questions, that the high-spending side won fully 80% of the time in the 1976-80 period. This has been true whether the source of revenues was corporate or individual, and whether the spending exceeded $500,000 or was less than $50,000. There is, however, only one case in this period in which spending exceeded $1 million where the potential economic impact was low; the remaining 12 high-spending issues were also high-impact controversies.

In 17 of the 32 cases where poll information is available, voter preferences were reversed in the high-spending direction during the campaign: in all but two this was enough to change the outcome. I have inferred a causal relation between spending and outcome in these campaigns, mainly because of the lack of powerful alternative cues (e.g., partisan) available to the voter.

It is also clear that money does not simply go to the side endorsed by major newspapers or prominent political figures: for issues where such endorsements were made, there was a 67% level of agreement between spenders and editors and a 58% level of agreement between spenders and political actors when those actors agreed and took a stand. Nor does the public blindly follow press recommendations: there was agreement between editors and the final outcomes only 68% of the time.

Yet an analysis of the ten deviant cases shows a number of conditions under which high spending may *not* produce a victory. One (in the case of rent control and the bottle bill in Michigan) is the development of a skillful grass-roots organization with strong campaign arguments. Another seems to be the existence of strong norms on the part of the majority, where no amount of spending can offset the voters' original preferences (Michigan drinking age; Oregon death penalty). A third, most interesting condition is the ability of supporters to narrow the scope (and thus the opposition) of a previously defeated proposal (nuclear regulation in Oregon; coastal bonds in California).

In the next chapter I shall examine some of the hypotheses of other scholars about the effect of high-spending media campaigns on the opportunity for rational information gathering activities by voters. I shall be particularly concerned, as well, with the question of whether high spending by *both* sides in a controversy over ballot issues leads to a focus on central issues and correspondingly less emphasis on deceptive and/or peripheral arguments.

Notes

1. For a comprehensive survey of the literature on campaign finance, see Adamany (1977). Among the 14 works covered are studies by Herbert Alexander, Common Cause, Delmer Dunn, John Owens, Howard Penniman and Ralph Winter. In addition, three important studies have been published on spending on ballot issues. These are Lowenstein (1982), Shockley (1980), and Lydenberg (1979). The excellent Lowenstein and Shockley studies are limited to one state each; Lydenberg focuses exclusively on corporate spending. Magleby's (1984) work also deals with campaign finances, notably in chap. 8. His work appeared, however, after our initial presentation on this subject was made in 1983, and thus we do not discuss his results in any detail here.

2. A search of the literature cited in Note 1 failed to unearth comparative figures for winners and losers, other than the statement by Herbert Alexander that incumbents spent 50% more than challengers. See Alexander (1979: 177).

3. The mean expenditure per ballot question studied was: California, $2,326,000; Massachusetts, $405,300; Michigan, $321,400; Oregon, $287,000.

However, since very few of the 91 questions not included exceeded $50,000, mean expenditures based on all questions in the four states should be much lower.

4. John Mueller (1969) points out that while the parties can be important in shaping opinion on propositions, their influence is limited by the fact that few endorsements are made. Norman Thomas (1968) takes a similar position.

5. Magleby (1984: 129) refers to these cases as "standing opinions," using capital punishment, marijuana legalization, and gun control as examples.

6. Another key element in the rent control campaign was the coordination of campaigns on Proposition 10 (rent control) and Proposition 11 (income tax cap). Both were supported by Howard Jarvis, who headed a rental property owners group; both were opposed by a liberal coalition including Governor Brown, tenants groups, and Hayden's Coalition for Economic Democracy. This is one of the few cases we have found of conscious issue linkage by groups active on more than one campaign.

7. Source on spending is Lydenberg (1979). Newspaper totals (before the final reports) were lower. These were "about $100,000 vs. $800,000" for Michigan; $27,689 to $1,195,263 for Massachusetts.

5

THE CAMPAIGN:
MEDIA-INTENSIVE CAMPAIGNS

The crucial importance of campaign funding was established in the preceding chapter, where it was shown that victory went to the high-spending side on ballot issues fully 80% of the time. Yet the uses to which such funds were put varied from logistic support for canvassing and grass-roots organizing to full-scale media blitzes, direct mail, and the like. Then too, after noting some rare cases—ten of the 50 studied here—where the less affluent side won at the polls, winning underdog strategies were briefly considered.

In this chapter and in Chapter 6, I shall take a closer look at campaign resources and strategies from a somewhat different perspective, namely, that of the voters. What difference do strategies make for the citizens whom contenders want to activate and convert? What is the relative effectiveness of professional media campaigners and amateur grass-roots efforts in providing information? In arousing fear, anger, or cynicism? In totally obscuring the issues?

This chapter begins with an expansion of the earlier discussion of the electoral context of these campaigns, examining not only the legal arrangements and informal norms on the mechanisms of direct democracy (introduced in Chapter 2) but the differing roles played by party organizations, interest groups, and candidates in our four states. The next step is a comparison of campaigns subject to one-sided versus two-sided spending at high levels, with attention to problems of deception or oversimplification of issues. After raising similar questions about the impact of grass-roots campaigns in Chapter 6, I will then be able to tackle the complex problem of voter rationality in the chapters that follow.

Legal and Contextual Differences in Campaigns

First, it should be noted once again that California laws differ markedly from others, and especially Oregon, in regard to voter registration and the collection of signatures for ballot questions. Oregon law forbids payment for collecting signatures, California's does not. California allows ordinary citizens to serve as voting registrars after a brief training program and to enroll new voters in their own homes or in public places like shopping centers. Oregon (as well as Massachusetts and Michigan) limits registration to public officials working in regular municipal offices (town halls, fire stations, etc.). Thus the much higher level of expenditures at the petition-drive stage and the more frequent use of voter registration drives in California are partially explained on these legal grounds. California's population size, and thus the enormous number of signatures needed, is also a factor.

Another key legal difference, however, does not seem to encourage readily discerned campaign differences. Michigan has no voter's pamphlet. Massachusetts and California do but carry no campaign advertisements. Oregon, in contrast, prints a large number of individual and group advertisements at the low cost of $300 per half-page (a tremendous bargain since the pamphlet is mailed to all registered voters). A greater reliance in Michigan than in other states on media advertising might thus be expected to compensate for the relative lack of information in a voter's pamphlet. And following the same logic, less funding for commercial advertising should appear in Oregon. Yet this does not seem to be the case, judging from the cost per campaign adjusted for the population of each state. It can be seen instead, in Table 5.1, that *Oregon* campaigns are the most expensive (per campaign, per resident) while *Michigan* campaigns are the least costly. In fact there is little difference between Oregon, California, and Massachusetts spending, using the average cost per resident per proposal. (California costs seem exhorbitant primarily because of the population size.) It is only in Michigan (the one state of the four where the lack of a ballot pamphlet might serve as an invitation for advertisements to fill that vacuum) that average expenditures are markedly lower. The pattern not only persists but is sharper if average costs per resident for only the 21 high-spending campaigns ($500,000 or more) are isolated: Oregon leads with 40.6¢ per resident, while the Michi-

TABLE 5.1: Average Spending on 50 Major Campaigns in Relation To
State Population 1976-80

State	(A) Total spending	(B) Number of ballot questions	(B/A) Cost/ campaign	(C) State population	(B/A)/C Cost/ campaign/ resident
California	$39,017,000	16	$2,438,562	21,520,000	11.33¢
Michigan	5,061,000	15	337,400	9,157,000	3.68¢
Massachusetts	5,473,000	10	547,300	5,809,000	9.08¢
Oregon	2,379,000	9	264,333	2,288,000	11.55¢

gan figure is lowest at 8.36¢ per resident (averaged per campaign).
The corresponding figures for California and Massachusetts are
18.03¢ and 22.29¢ respectively.

I do not argue that per capita expenditures on either the relatively small number of high-spending proposals or the large number of major propositions are likely to remain constant in any one
state over the long haul or even over another sequence of three election years: the extremely high cost of the two nuclear power campaigns may have distorted the Oregon pattern, to choose an obvious
example. But these 1976-80 findings preclude the easy assumption
that legal arrangements automatically determine campaign strategies, even on spending.

During the 1976 campaign in Massachusetts, corporate spending was legally prohibited except in cases where a direct interest in
the outcome could be shown; the *First National Bank of Boston v.
Bellotti* decision in 1978 (435 U.S.), however, struck this down,
and in fact it had been argued that such a law only invited evasion
(e.g., "private" contributions through family members of executives and the like). Yet the states seem to differ on their informal
norms in regard to spending: Californians appear to be more toler-
ant of spending by out-of-state corporations than do Oregonians,
except in cases where the amount is totally out of line with earlier
years' campaigns, or the origin of funds is concealed from public
view (as in one of the nonsmokers' rights campaigns).

In many ways too, California campaigns appear flamboyant by
Eastern or Midwestern standards: endorsements by movie and
rock stars, for example, abound on many issues. The location of

the movie industry may account for the fact that with the exception of John Denver and Lily Tomlin appearances on behalf of the nuclear power issue in Oregon, no entertainers were prominent in campaigns outside of California. It does not explain, however, the large number of academic endorsements—especially by economists and scientists—in California as opposed to Massachusetts campaigns. The relatively greater California use of such publicity techniques as superstar endorsements—as well as concerts, mass rallies, marches in major cities and the like—may be tied to general differences in tolerance and lifestyle; or it may be related to a point made by Daniel Lowenstein (1982: 530-31), who argues that "it is doubtful whether a statewide volunteer campaign can be of more than marginal significance in California, a large state without rooted and stable neighborhoods." Certainly California's extremely large and geographically dispersed population makes traditional precinct work time-consuming in comparison with, e.g., Massachusetts.[1] (Its weather, however, makes it easier!)

Another contrast between states becomes apparent when party and interest group activities are examined. Only one intensely partisan issue arose among our 50 in the sense of a proposition where one party stood to gain at the other's expense. This was on constitutional revision in Michigan. But party organizations were occasionally active in endorsing and working for ballot issues, as were candidates for party nominations, in California and Massachusetts and to a lesser degree in Oregon and Michigan. Traditional interest groups—notably organized labor, teachers unions, and business associations—were active on a wide range of issues in California, Massachusetts, and Michigan and, again, relatively rare in Oregon either in bringing initiatives to the ballot or in endorsing and working in the campaigns. My sense is that the original Progressive ethos on direct democracy—as an amateur, individualistic, antilobbying mechanism—may even today be taken more seriously by Oregonians than others, and that expensive, flamboyant, or highly organized lobbying (as, for example, in the nuclear power campaigns) may more often than not be seen as counterproductive in regard to Oregon ballot questions. While several scholars have characterized group efforts on referenda as simply an extension of their lobbying the legislature, I doubt if this judgment applies in quite such an automatic way to Oregon.

Finally, we need to take note of the variations in the specific electoral context of ballot issues already discussed in Chapter 3. My most important finding was that an issue which might normally attract attention and support in a year when it was the only controversy, or one of two, will obviously suffer in a year of intense competition for resources. Thus the 1976 campaign in Massachusetts was unusual in that five controversial issues competed for the attention of liberals (i.e., gun control, ERA, the bottle bill, etc.). At the other extreme, the 1978 tax classification issue in Massachusetts—like the June 1976 nuclear power issue and the November 1976 farm labor issue in California—stood almost alone in the news. A more frequent pattern saw two or three major issues battling with several minor ones (e.g., most Michigan campaigns). And in the case of both Michigan and Oregon, participants in most multiissued campaigns did *not* compete for the same scarce resources, since the different ballot questions were rarely sponsored or opposed by an overlapping set of ideological bedfellows, as they were in the Massachusetts and California cases discussed earlier.

Media-Intensive Campaigns

We have seen, in the last chapter, that the vast majority of ballot questions with high economic stakes attract a very high level of campaign spending (i.e., total spending over $500,000). This was true for all seven style issues where major industries saw themselves threatened (nuclear power regulation, bottle bills, and the two California campaigns on smoking), and it was true as well for 11 of the 19 high-impact position issues (taxes, rent control, the Massachusetts flat electric rate, and the agricultural labor relations act in California). Most of this funding is used for media coverage—primarily as paid advertising, but to a lesser degree in the form of newsworthy events such as publicizing endorsements by prestigious figures. At least since the 1952 presidential campaign, professional campaign managers have recognized the importance of media exposure for candidates and issues alike. In the (only slightly overstated) words of two highly successful campaign consultants, "the contender with the heaviest and most professional propaganda barrage usually emerges the winner" (Baus and Ross, 1968: 299).

Daniel Lowenstein, in a study of campaign spending and voting outcomes in California from 1968 to 1980, has defined "significant one-sided spending" as existing when either side exceeds $250,000 and when one side spends at least twice the amount of the other (1982: 511). He then goes on to demonstrate that for his 25 cases, one-sided spending is far more effective *in opposition* than *in support of* a ballot proposal, in the sense that the result probably would have been different had spending been more equal. And finally—perhaps most important for our purposes—he demonstrates that the content of messages disseminated by one-sided spending "has characteristically been deceptive, superficial, irrelevant" (1982: 517, 563-65). This is particularly problematic, Lowenstein asserts, since low-spending opponents lack the resources to publicize counterarguments effectively.

By Lowenstein's standards 16 of our 21 "very high-spending" issues (i.e., over $500,000) plus two more that involved slightly lower spending levels (property tax caps, Oregon-1980 and Michigan-1978) were characterized by "significant one-sided spending"; seven others (five tax issues, the agricultural labor relations act, and the homosexual teachers issue) were two-sided high-spending issues. It is my intention in this section to discuss the kinds of campaigns associated with high spending and to argue that Lowenstein's description of "deceptive, superficial, irrelevant" messages seems to apply to at least one side of most of the high-spending campaigns studied regardless of the balance of spending abilities. Nor is an effective response to deceptive arguments made in two-sided high-spending campaigns.

But first, let me note that the data confirm Lowenstein's first finding that one-sided spending is more effective in opposition than in support of ballot measures. Table 5.2 shows the 16 cases that fit his definition (six from California, four from Michigan, three each from Oregon and Massachusetts).

There are only four deviants out of 16; it might also be noted that fewer than one-third of these cases involved high spending in support of propositions. The two cases where opposing one-sided spending was ineffective were the 1980 Oregon nuclear power issue and the Michigan bottle bill, discussed at length in the preceding chapter. The two high-spending victories, in cases of supporting campaigns, were the Massachusetts property tax cap and the California death penalty campaign. Strictly speaking, the latter, as a low-impact style issue, does not belong in the table. It did not

TABLE 5.2: Relation between Support or Opposition by One-Sided High Spenders and Election Outcome on Ballot Questions[a]

| | High-Spending Side | |
	Opposes	Supports
Election outcome:		
Victory for high spenders	2(40%)	9(81%)
Loss by high spenders	3(60%)	2(19%)

a. Limited to 16 cases where one side spent at least $250,000 and outspent opposition by at least 2-1 (Lowenstein definition).

involve the sort of self-interested *corporate* spending Lowenstein was discussing. (Note that death penalty proposals in Oregon and Massachusetts did not attract this level of spending.) The death penalty campaigns will be discussed in the next chapter.

Now let us examine a few examples of three kinds of campaigns: (1) those where one-sided high spending occurred, mainly by business interests, *on behalf* of ballot proposals; (2) those where one-sided high spending arose *in opposition* to ballot questions introduced by public interest groups or general citizens' coalitions; and (3) those where high spending characterized both sides of the campaign.

ONE-SIDED CAMPAIGN SUPPORTING BALLOT PROPOSALS

One of the most expensive ballot issue campaigns of all time was the 1980 California proposal to limit local rent control. This issue provides the first example of a one-sided campaign *on behalf* of a proposition favoring business interests. Supporters outspent opponents by 37:1, but they lost decisively, in part because their campaign strategies backfired.

Proposition 10 was designed to revoke local rent control ordinances unless local referenda were called to uphold them; it also prohibited state rent control laws and exempted single-family dwellings from control. Its major supporters were the Building and Construction Trades Council and several banks. The intensive radio campaign of supporters, characterized by the *Los Angeles Times* (May 1, 1980) as "a classic case of false and misleading advertising, deliberately contrived," implied that the proposal would *establish* rather than eliminate local rent control. The editorial concluded that "a solid no vote . . . would help keep political advertising in California honest." The opponents of course cried "fraud" and surprisingly enough—in spite of a poorly organized shoe-string campaign (which included two gala events that had to be canceled at the last minute)—forced supporters to switch tactics. Smooth commercials urging support of "fair rents and reasonable controls" were replaced by a strident attack on Tom Hayden, former anti-Vietnam activist and a major opponent of the measure. The change in tactics came too late, however, and Proposition 10 was handily defeated, in part, we believe, because a misleading and high-spending campaign caused resentment among both opinion leaders and initially confused voters.[2]

Another example of one-sided spending in a media campaign *supporting* a proposition was the 1980 fight for the Massachusetts property tax cap (Proposition 2). Supporters, who spent $430,500 to opponents' $101,200, won easily by a 58.6-41.4% margin. This campaign is thus one of the "deviants" in Table 5.2 above, where one-sided spending *on behalf of* a proposal was successful despite the vocal opposition of the *Boston Globe* and other major newspapers as well as much of organized labor.

Proposition 2, very similar to California's Proposition 13, was the brainchild of two organizations: Citizen's for Limited Taxation (CLT), a six-year-old, 4,000-member citizens group whose sole purpose was opposition to taxes and government spending, and the High Technology Council, which was the political action arm of 100 Massachusetts electronics and computer firms. The opposition consisted of a loose coalition of labor organizations, the League of Women Voters, the Massachusetts Teachers Association, and organizations for the elderly. In contrast to California, neither the realtors nor industry groups were active in the campaign.

The major argument for Proposition 2 was the need to "send a message" to the legislature to reduce government waste and reform the state's tax structure. (Despite 1978 passage of the tax classification proposal, Massachusetts property owners still felt outrage at high tax rates. The legislature had been thwarted in several efforts at reform, including the voter-rejected proposal for a graduated income tax and a tax cap on local spending which was subsequently overridden by many towns and cities.) Opponents expressed concern over the impact on schools and services of tax cuts, the implication of charging fees for public services, and the question of whether any genuine reform would result from this drastic approach.

The campaign was waged on two levels: a media blitz by supporters, unmatched in recent Massachusetts campaigns by any but the bottle bill, and a statewide combination of public forums, press conferences, and leafleting by the less affluent opponents, who ran only a few media spots. By mid-October supporters had allocated or spent about $300,000 on the media, roughly divided between radio and television. Since only one Boston TV channel accepts paid advertising on ballot questions, this made sense.[3] The first pro-Proposition 2 radio ad, in late September, featured a soothing voice asking, "Do you know about Question 2?" followed by promises of tax relief and lower spending. (The opponents' response, first aired *a month later,* began with a fast pitch for Proposition 2 in a used-car salesman voice followed by a second calmer voice warning the "buyer" against glib promises. This same technique of caricature and warning was to be used again very successfully, it should be noted, by bottle bill supporters in 1982.)

Neither side placed much emphasis on the sort of newspaper advertising which had been used heavily in the 1978 tax classification campaign. Supporters did run a full-page advertisement in most major newspapers just before the election. This one was captioned "Time for Another Boston Tea Party" and again stressed the need to force the reluctant legislature to cut taxes.

There is no question that the media campaign on behalf of Proposition 2 was simplistic, particularly in its wholesale indictment of the state legislature and in its blithe assumption that the California experience applied to Massachusetts, thus ignoring both the lack of an existing state surplus and a more diversified tax structure in California. And it is clear that the opponents' response was "too little and too late." At the same time, we doubt very much if more equitable campaign funds would have changed the outcome. Two other (related) factors instead seem to have made a major difference in Massachusetts. One was the lack of opposition from major political figures or members of the business community. While junior Senator Paul Tsongas had expressed strong opposition, neither Boston Mayor Kevin White nor Governor Edward King made more than lukewarm statements in opposition.

The second factor was a last-minute event parallel with what happened in Los Angeles. In late October Mayor White delivered to Boston voters what he privately termed "the most persuasive advertisement possible for Proposition 2 $1/_2$"—the 1981 tax bill (*Boston Globe,* October 31, 1980). As in California, previously confused voters were suddenly mobilized (though perhaps still confused): between October 13 and November 2 the polls shifted from finding 25% pro, 34% con, and 39% either undecided or never having heard of the measure, to 47% pro, 44% con, and 9% undecided. Many Boston property owners, at least, probably agreed with one *Globe* interviewee: "You bet I'll vote for Proposition 2 $1/_2$. My wife says I should call somebody up about this tax bill. Who are you gonna call?" (*Boston Globe,* October 23, 1980).

I suspect that Proposition 2 would have passed—given White's tax bill timing—even if a stronger campaign had been waged by opponents. What is of real concern to us as observers of ballot campaigns, however, is whether crucial issues were indeed discussed in the campaign. (For example, the validity of the California parallel, a realistic assessment of the impact on schools and public safety personnel, and most important, viable alternatives to an excessive reliance on the property tax for funding major local expenditures.) The author found very little discussion at this level, even among academic friends, scientists, and other professionals. And very little appeared in the infrequent and simplified media arguments of the opponents.

ONE-SIDED MEDIA CAMPAIGNS AGAINST BALLOT PROPOSALS

Two California media campaigns that aroused intense public indignation because of massive spending—in this case by several out of state tobacco companies—involved the November 1978 and November 1980 proposals for a Clean Air Act. Spending figures for 1978 set the highest all-time record for California initiatives: $6,411,300 for the opposition to $700,600 for supporters (a 9:1 ratio). In 1980 a somewhat more carefully drawn proposal involved $2.7 million for the opposition and $1 million for supporters. In both cases the proposal was rejected by voters, in large part because of a media blitz which transformed the debate from the question of whether restaurants, bars, and places of employment should provide nonsmoking areas to a question of government infringement on personal liberties at a very high cost for enforcement.

The campaigns strongly confirm Lowenstein's point that heavy one-sided spending is associated with distortion and oversimplification of the arguments. Authors of the Clean Air Act of 1978 stressed the probable harm of second-hand smoke and the resultant costs to business and taxpayers in sick leave, disability payments, and hospital costs. Instead of answering this argument directly (i.e., by questioning the medical evidence on second-hand smoke), opponents (1) cited extravagant cost figures for no smoking signs, namely, $20 million (later acknowledged to be, in fact, only $20,000—a misplacement of three decimal points!) and (2) mounted a simplistic billboard, radio, and television ad campaign to raise fears that the government was attempting to control people. Billboards and radio spots in early October used the slogan "they're at it again," implying a sinister force at work rather than the thousands of California citizens who had signed the petition. This slogan, in fact, prompted Los Angeles station KFWB to refuse to run the radio spots; the theme of infringement on rights, however, was convincing enough to help inspire opposition endorsements from every major newspaper in the state. The *Los Angeles Times* editorial of September 29 ran under the title "Cool it Ralph." Opposition advertisements carrying a similar message appeared on newspapers across the state: one full-page ad, for example, carried the banner headline "We Have Enough Restrictive Laws Already. Read the Fine Print," followed by a long list of organizations opposing the law.

The disparity in advertising funds became obvious by September 23, when opponents reported an allocation of $2.9 million for advertising, telephones, office space, and direct mail, to the supporters' $287,853. Supporters, having spent most of their budget on direct mail—as well as the earlier costs of the signature drive— were unable to begin radio advertising until mid-October. In response to their campaign for free time to air their commercials under the FCC's "fairness doctrine," nine TV and 17 radio stations (in both northern and southern California) granted limited time for airing commercials by such notables as Carol Burnett, Gregory Peck, and Ed Asner. Nothing like parity, either in amount of time available or quality of time slots, was reached, since the FCC doctrine simply requires a "fair" exposure for those who cannot pay. The opposition, however, complained that a campaign which could afford to mail a full-color brochure had no right to plead poverty, and perhaps they had a point. (In 1980 Howard Jarvis, who ultimately raised $3.6 *million* to support his proposed income tax cap, requested free time in midcampaign because he had used most of his campaign funds.)

The 1980 campaign was, in many ways, a rerun on a slightly more modest scale, as well as one in which supporters were not so heavily outspent. Despite supporters' efforts to tighten the proposal and to guarantee that costs of no smoking signs would be minimal, opposition advertisements again stressed the difficulty and costs of enforcement and the threat to personal freedom. The theme of the campaign was "This Time It's Sneakier Than Ever." One early commercial featured a man in a police uniform saying, "Us police should spend our time looking for burglars, not smokers"; another showed a bartender talking about his economic fears if the measure passed.

While the supporters of the proposal had planned a modest television and radio campaign on the theme "It's new, it's reasonable, and it's only fair," they found themselves unable to proceed, on any significant scale, early in the campaign because the bulk of funds raised by September 23 had gone into the cost of the petition drive. A month later they announced a complaint to the FCC over opponents' failure to identify the tobacco companies as their major contributors. (The complaint was dismissed. The controversy continued to rage, however, over early concealment of the source and extent of opposition funding, since early reports had indicated a very low level of opposition expenditures, which supporters argued concealed large advance pledges by the tobacco firms.) By campaign's end they had raised and spent just over $1 million; however in the view of Lowenstein (who was active in this campaign as well as authoring the law review article we cite) and other scholars, certainty and early availability of funds are essential for planning an effective media strategy (see Shockley, 1980: 43; Baus and Ross, 1968: 243, 299). For supporters it may have been a case of "too little, too late" in a relative sense.

I have already discussed additional examples of one-sided media campaigns in the previous chapter in contrasting winning and losing campaigns on the nuclear power (Oregon 1976 and 1980) and bottle bill issues (Michigan and Massachusetts). But in that discussion the focus was on the strategy of the low-spending side. Thus I shall expand that analysis briefly in order to include four non-California examples of cases where one-sided media campaigns were mounted by corporate interests *in opposition* to proposals by citizens, coalitions, or public interest groups. (I stress the non-California examples because Lowenstein's findings were confined to 25 cases in that state only.) In all cases I will focus on the high-spending media campaigns, which it will be noted include the remaining two deviants in Table 5.2—cases where one-sided spending *against* a proposition did not result in electoral victories.

In 1976 the beverage and bottling industries faced bottle bill proposals in four states. They found it worth their while to concentrate a great deal of personnel and funding in Michigan and Massachusetts, two key industrial states, spending $2,587,000 (to supporters' $56,500) in Massachusetts and $1,316,000 (to supporters' $117,000) in Michigan. They won by an extremely narrow margin (50.4-49.6%) in Massachusetts but lost overwhelmingly (63.8-36.2%) in Michigan. I have argued in Chapter 4 that the major difference was the superior Michigan campaign, both strategically in utilizing the safety argument and financially in going beyond a minimum critical mass needed to mount an effective grass-roots campaign. At this point I want to describe the opposition tactics in a little more detail.

The Michigan Committee Against Forced Deposits faced a strong array of organizations supporting the bottle bill, including the United Conservation Clubs (who handled the campaign and raised most of the funds in support), PIRG in Michigan (a Nader research group run by students), the Farm Bureau, and the State Police. The supporters argued mainly in terms of litter, hazards of broken glass, and the need to help the tourist industry by controlling those problems. Facing a colorful grass-roots campaign and some media advertising, as well as a majority of newspapers endorsing the bill, the beverage industry hired a professional agency and made an initial allocation of $800,000 for advertising. (This amount would more than double before November 2.)

Beginning in mid-September, opposition time was purchased from every major radio station in the state, beginning with 200 minutes from WJR, the Detroit station with the largest audience. Commercials featured, among others, a jingle which criticized the proposal for punishing everyone just because a few "slobs" couldn't stop littering. (Supporters, in contrast, were forced to request free air time in response, under the FCC Fairness doctrine. They indeed were given 100 minutes by WJR on the last Sunday in September and, in addition, were able to purchase time during the campaign's final weeks after raising the funds to cover it.)

Newspaper advertising was heavily dominated by the opposition. For example, while one or more daily opposition ads were run on five days in the *Detroit Free Press* during the final two weeks, I was unable to locate a single ad in support. Another form of advertising (also used in Massachusetts) caused considerable controversy. These were political decals pasted on soft-drink and beer bottles. On September 1 the State Liquor Commission banned the decals, arguing that political advertising was forbidden in state liquor stores. The Committee on Forced Deposits, having purchased over one million decals, appealed and won on October 8 at the level of the U.S. District Court on grounds of free speech.

One final opposition tactic that is worth noting because it occurred on an even greater degree in Massachusetts was what Baus and Ross called the "rougher, negative approach"—in this case, on the question of economic costs. Baus and Ross, who ran several ballot issue campaigns as well as the successful Goldwater primary in California in 1964, argue:

> The basic strategy approach to an issue is set by whether a "yes" or "no" vote is sought. Those managing the "yes" side are trying to change the status quo by selling something new to the voters. Their general approach therefore must be one of persuasion and affirmative interpretation. The "yes" strategy must be soft and smooth. . . . The confused voter votes "no", thus a campaign of enlightenment with affirmative psychology is imperative to pass the "yes" side of a position.

> In campaigning on the "no" side, the situation is reversed. Here a rougher, negative approach is strategically indicated. The campaign strives to point out the pitfalls of the contested measure, and sometimes just one is enough to do the job. [1968: 61][4]

Thus in newspaper ads as well as in radio and TV spots, the Michigan opposition hit hard at the theme of lost jobs, health hazards (from unsanitary conditions in bottle storage areas), and increased consumer costs. One advertisement, for example, asserted that a six-pack of beer would increase from $1.80 to $2.35. The tactic may have helped in Michigan, but it didn't save the election. Massachusetts, however, was another story.

As mentioned earlier, Massachusetts groups spent considerably less than their Michigan counterpart. Nevertheless, the opposition had already collected $1.195 million by October 15, spending about 80% on a host of media ads similar to Michigan's, as well as billboards, subway posters, signs in retail stores and on beverage trucks, and finally, on decals for bottles and cans, not protested in Massachusetts. (At this point in the campaign, the Committee for a Bottle Bill had only raised $27,689, allotting a scant $18,000 to media advertising.) And following the kind of strategy advocated by Baus and Ross, one early opposition ad (*Boston Globe,* October 12) hit very hard at "pitfalls" in the proposal, in what purported to be a factual presentation of the proposal's impact on jobs, litter, grocery stores, and consumer costs.

Within a few days a furor arose over "EPA figures" cited in the ad (along with others from the bottle and can industry) showing an expected cost of $100 per family per year if the measure passed. The EPA characterized the figures as "false and misleading," while Evelyn Murphy, State Environmental Secretary, issued a critique of her own. Finally, Ian Menzies, a *Boston Globe* columnist, used the opportunity to denounce high business spending and out-of-state money:

> Gentlemen, did you ever blow it last week with that great big ad against the bottle bill. . . . Now I know for sure that you guys are from out-of-state. . . . But Question 6 goes a lot deeper . . . this is a people's bill. This is a chance to realize that they are not so helpless as they are wont to say . . . an opportunity for people who are weary of business fighting every effort to build a clean America. [October 17, 1976]

The opposition advertisements nonetheless continued, minus the offensive copy but hammering the same theme, on three of the last four days preceding the election in the *Globe,* in other major newspapers, and in a continuing barrage on the radio. Despite the controversy, the scare tactics apparently paid, for as discussed in the preceding chapter, public opinion on the bottle bill (as on so many other issues) shifted from an initial favorable stance in June (73% approval) to a small majority in October (56% approval) to a loss by 0.4% on election day.

I would argue, as earlier, that a key reason for the difference between Michigan and Massachusetts results on the bottle bill—given an almost identical media strategy by opponents—lay in the magnitude of the spending ratio (11:1 in Michigan, 46:1 in Massachusetts) and thus the lack in Massachusetts of a critical minimum of funding on which to mount even an effective grass-roots campaign ($56,500 does not provide even a minimum of staffing or leaflets for a large volunteer operation).

The final pair of opposition campaigns in 1976 and 1980, over nuclear power proposals in Oregon, need only be touched on. Opponents outspent supporters by $985,200 to $238,100 in 1976 and by $600,000 to the astonishingly low figure of $34,800 in 1980. Yet a 42-58% defeat changed to a 53.2-46.8% victory in four years. As pointed out in the earlier discussion, I believe that the narrowing of the scope of the proposal (from what opponents charged was a "ban" to something more like "regulation"), coupled with national concern over the incident at Three-Mile Island in 1979, accounted for the shift in the electorate.

In the 1976 elections the opponents of nuclear regulation ran a nearly flawless campaign from a strategic perspective. By mid-October 1976 over $80,000 had been spent on newspaper ads, with an almost equal amount for radio and television. One hundred eighty-seven billboards had been plastered about, as had 5,000 lawn signs. Then in the final week of the election, not only were three large ads placed in all major Oregon newspapers, but an attractive eight-page supplement called "The Oregon Energy Review" was distributed with the final Sunday newspaper. (This contrasts with two tiny ads and a final full-page ad featuring Jacques Cousteau on the part of supporters.)

The contrast in advertising *content,* however, is probably more important than sheer magnitude. Almost every major opposition ad stessed the views of prestigious Oregonians that nuclear power was safe and was essential for future economic well-being. The first listed 100 Oregon scientists, engineers, and educators; the second repeated and expanded the point under the head "400,000 Oregonians Say No." The fourth featured photographs of prominent opponents, including the U.S. Representative Edith Green and several labor leaders, in addition to listing organizations that covered the business, farm, educational, and scientific spectrum.

Probably the only opposition mistake in the 1976 campaign was an effort to activate stockholders of the many out-of-state utilities involved in the struggle. Some unfavorable publicity resulted when a few recipients of a letter from Union Carbide publicly voiced their displeasure at the effort. The tactic was not repeated (or at least it did not surface) in the 1980 campaign. In fact, the 1980 campaign was extremely low-keyed in comparison. No scientific stars were brought in this time, either as speakers or in advertisements; only five opposition ads were run in the *Oregonian* during the entire period (three full-page, with one featuring a letter signed by Oregon legislators, and leaders of organizations like the Grange, the Portland Chamber of Commerce, and the State AFL-CIO).

One senses that although the negative theme was the same ("Measure 7 Would Pull the Plug on Future Sources of Electricity"), the opponents may have seen the handwriting on the wall, in the form of a far more moderate proposal and a public no longer unquestioningly enchanted with nuclear power. The outcry over mammoth out-of-state funding which arose in the earlier campaign (although not strong enough to save the 1976 proposal) may also have entered into the new strategy. At the same time, $600,000 is still a huge expenditure by Oregon standards: it is possible that the opponents, given the almost universal success of defeating nuclear power elsewhere in recent years, were simply overconfident about their cause and genuinely expected to win.

Whatever the reason for the less strident 1980 campaign, we should not lose sight of the fact that in both 1976 and 1980 the opponents of nuclear power regulation ran a strong negative campaign and indeed managed (for the most part) to avoid the major argument of supporters, nuclear safety. The supporters spoke out about accidents, about nuclear plant vulnerability to sabotage, about hazards for employees and nearby residents, all of which were inadequately covered by federal liability insurance. The opponents brought in their scientists who said—briefly— "nonsense" and then went on to spell out the dreadful things that might happen to an increasingly beleagured Oregon economy if nuclear energy were not developed in the state (loss of industry, loss of jobs, rising electrical rates). These again are exactly the sort of strong negative tactics that are recommended by consultants like Baus and Ross, while deplored by Lowenstein or by Shockley (1980: 14-18) in describing similar events in Colorado.

TWO-SIDED HIGH-SPENDING MEDIA CAMPAIGNS

David Lowenstein raised the question of whether propositions that attract high spending on both sides fare as poorly (in terms of both electoral results and an informative discussion of the merits of the case) as do those that attract one-sided negative spending. (His California data were inconclusive.) He also suggested that an examination of Massachusetts Proposition 1 in 1978 (the tax classification proposal) might prove instructive about the quality of two-sided campaigns (i.e., the degree to which voters were well informed, the presence or absence of deception, etc.). In this section I intend to examine the media campaigns on that Massachusetts proposition and of one other—the Agricultural Labor Relations Act considered in California—to see if opposition *and* supporters' campaigns follow the tactics we have thus far observed in one-sided campaigns. But first, I note in passing that there are three propositions (outside of California) that meet Lowenstein's criteria for high two-sided spending (one-side spending at least $250,000; neither spending double the other). These are the Massachusetts tax classification proposal (passed), the Michigan 1978 tax compromise (passed), and the Michigan voucher-for-education proposal (defeated). Combining these with the four "two-sided" California measures in our own study (Proposition 13 and Proposition 8 in 1976, the Agricultural Labor Relations Act, and the homosexual teachers issue) yields a total score of three victories and four losses. Again, inconclusive evidence. I shall, however, show, in some detail in my chapter on voting behavior, that when *all* of the measures in the present study are counted (including low-spending style issues), the voter is not nearly so negative as pictured by some observers.

The tax classification proposal (Question 1) was the dominant issue for most of the 1978 election in Massachusetts, receiving almost as many votes and often more media coverage than the hotly contested U.S. senatorial race between Paul Tsongas and Edward Brooke. A forerunner of the property tax cap that was to be approved two years later, Question 1 was a proposed constitutional amendment to allow the legislature to classify real property in four different categories for tax assessment purposes. The goal was to allow residential property to be taxed at a rate lower than commercial or industrial land—a practice that was common in Massachusetts before a 1974 State Supreme Court forbad it. To avoid asking voters for a blank check, the legislature passed a bill the summer before the election setting forth specific rates to take effect if the amendment passed.

Two broad coalitions faced each other in the election campaign. Supporters included all candidates for statewide office, Senator

Kennedy, and all but two of the Congressional delegation, the Massachusetts Mayors' Association, most of organized labor, the Catholic archdiocese and the Council of Churches, senior citizens, and over 60 other groups. Mayor Kevin White of Boston and his statewide Mayor's Committee were the driving force behind the coalition. Opponents, almost as formidable, included most local chambers of commerce, the Farm Bureau, several suburban taxpayers groups, and the Massachusetts Selectmen's Association, which saw the proposal as benefitting older cities at the expense of suburbs.[5] Supporters argued that tax classification would bring much needed tax relief for urban homeowners; opponents argued that this perpetuated overreliance on the property tax and simply delayed an overhaul of the entire tax structure. They feared creation of a climate that would drive away (or fail to attract) business, particularly since the proposed tax rates were not written into the amendment itself and thus not binding for the future.[6]

Aspects of the campaign were quite colorful. Supporters, for example, sponsored an old-fashioned "Whistlestop Rally" in a 1916 railroad car that traveled across the state after a gala sendoff from Boston by the governor and lieutenant governor. Opponents brought in California's Howard Jarvis for a major press conference and reception. But most of the effort of both sides went into gigantic media campaigns, which eventually were dominated by legal and political arguments over both the funding itself and the content of advertisements. Voter confusion was probably inevitable in any case, given the technical nature of tax assessment, but the legal and fiscal controversies that dominated the campaign so clouded the issue that as late as a week before the election fully a third of the voters were undecided. I would argue, in fact, that the ultimate decision for many boiled down to the question of which side to trust rather than any real understanding of the factual argument.

I shall not review the extensive legal controversy over the mayor's funds. Suffice it to say that most of the $975,000 appropriated by the City of Boston was not available to the classification campaign until after an October 20 court decision; before this date the supporters' coalition was forced to borrow from the unions for a direct mailing and to rely on free air time (under the Fairness Doctrine) from about three-quarters of the state's radio stations to counter the opposition's advertising. But it was the *advertising* by both sides, rather than the merits of the proposal, that grabbed the head-

lines and the voter's attention, if by now voters had not thrown up
their hands.

Accusations of deception erupted early in the campaign. In early
October the mayor of New Bedford sought (and failed to get) an
injunction against radio spots being aired by the opponents. On October 19 the field coordinator for opponents admitted that a prepared news release was misleading in its claim that business taxes
would rise by $270 million if the amendment passed. His justifica-
tion, in a *Boston Globe* interview, speaks for itself:

> How do you explain such a complicated issue to people? The quick
> way is often the cheap way, but how else can you be sure of getting
> your point across?[7]

Then, beginning on October 23, charge began following counter-
charge in a series of eight full-page ads placed in the Boston, Wor-
cester and Springfield newspapers.[8] The first ad by supporters,
under the heading "What Will It Cost You If Question 1 Is Defeated?" presented a list of all Massachusetts cities and towns, with
two lists of alternative tax figures for passage or nonpassage. On
October 28 the opponents' Committee Against Tax Discrimination
countered by repeating the same advertisement, revised in red, to
show their own very different computations. This ran under the
caption "What It Will Cost You If Question 1 Is Passed: Why Didn't
The Mayors Tell You If You Vote For Classification Your Taxes
Will Go Up?"

Subsequent ads by supporters featured line drawings, photographs of the elderly, lists of sponsors, and simple messages. Two
further ads of opponents, however, continued to hammer at the
disputed figures. One, on November 3, was headed "Don't Play
Mayor White's Property Tax Shell Game: Don't Let Them Do Anything To Your Taxes But Cut Them!" By now the *Boston Globe*
was editorializing about both sides' tendency to oversimplify, the
Cambridge city manager accused "the big corporations who are
financing the anti-classification campaign" of causing the confusion, and Ralph Nader issued a statement from Washington on
November 1 endorsing the proposal and questioning the opponents'
figures.

The point in detailing this long controversy—which of course
had its counterpart in the simultaneous radio and TV campaign—is

to show that high two-sided spending does not necessarily prevent campaign deception (especially through advertising). In this case it resulted in debates on peripheral and indeed *distracting issues about the conduct of the campaign itself* and massive voter confusion. The *Boston Globe,* many other papers, several radio and TV stations, and the League of Women Voters did their best through editorials and forums to clarify the issues for voters. This may have helped, but I suspect that many had "tuned out" of the whole controversy by that time.

Another problem for the voter—a problem shared by Californians three months earlier in June 1978 during the Proposition 13 battle—was the very large number of local and state officials and agencies who issued *contradictory statements* on the probable impact of the proposal. Who was to be believed? Most voters apparently resolved the confusion (there were only 108,811 "blanks" on Question 1 out of 2,044,076 people voting, or about 5%) by believing the mayors, but one is led to wonder if some of the strongly cynical feelings about government which erupted two years later over the property tax cap found sustenance or even their roots in this earlier battle about taking "the cheap way . . . of getting your point across." Tax classification, approved by a two-thirds majority, in the end only served as a stopgap that gave way to the meat-ax approach of Proposition 2½.

If the two-sided high-spending battle over Massachusetts taxes degenerated into confusion and deception, it nonetheless looked like a formal English tea in comparison with the 1976 campaign in California over the Agricultural Labor Relations Act. The two fights had much in common: technical issues clouded by arguments and litigation over campaign tactics, set against a background of public officials taking opposite sides on both the facts and the merits of the argument.

Expenditures on the Agricultural Labor Relations proposal (Proposition 14) broke all California records prior to November 1976, with supporters spending $1.36 million to opponents' $1.90 million, for a total of $3,257,000. Voter interest was also high, with an overall election turnout of 81.5% of registered voters and all but 5% of these expressing a choice on Proposition 14. (More people voted on the proposal than did on the hotly contested battle for U.S. Senator between John Tunney and S. I. Hayakawa.) There was, in fact, only one other major controversy over a proposition in this election, on the legalization of betting on greyhound racing.

In a sense this is the campaign that had everything: massive voter registration drives, fund-raising rallies by supporters, a TV debate between Cesar Chavez and the spokesman for opponents, an extraordinary amount of precinct work by both farmers and farm workers. But the points that stand out are (1) an extraordinarily long and complex proposal that almost *forced* oversimplification in both the campaign and voters' minds, and (2) a campaign marked by more litigation and more arguments about deception than any others encountered in this study, with the possible exception of the 1980 California debate over rent control.

I begin with a brief historical summary as an aid to understanding the 1976 controversy, which was in some ways a referendum on Cesar Chavez and the United Farm Workers (UFW). Chavez's work in the 1960s in organizing the UFW with the assistance of national union funds, a nationwide boycott of grapes and lettuce, and a great deal of personal charisma led to an agreement by major growers to recognize the UFW as bargaining agent for migrant farm workers. Peace did not come to the fields, however, in part because growers then encouraged the Teamsters to compete for worker support. As a next step, both Chavez and Governor Jerry Brown pushed for an Agricultural Labor Relations Act to oversee and certify union elections, to enforce fair labor practices, and in general to do for farm labor what the NLRA (Wagner Act) had done for industrial workers since 1935.

The Original ALRA was *passed as a statute* by a divided legislature which controlled all appropriations for the election supervision of the newly established board. Growers, who had reluctantly acquiesced under pressure, assumed wrongly that most union election under the ALRB would in fact go to the Teamsters, with whom they preferred to negotiate. Instead, the UFW won about two-thirds of the first year's elections, almost one-third went to the Teamsters, and 7% of the 400 elections opted for no union. As a result, growers called for changes in both the law and the makeup of the board itself, and a legislative coalition of conservative Republicans and rural Democrats cut off funding for the fledgling ALRB. Thus no new union certification elections were held between February and November 1976.

At this point Chavez and his followers began collecting signatures in order to force an election on the issue. Despite a hasty compromise by the growers and the legislature in regard to funding,

Chavez (who now had 700,000, or more than double, the signatures required) continued the petition drive, since an ALRB established by an initiative could not be rescinded or amended without another referendum. The new proposal included a minimum 12-month waiting period between union elections (to prevent constant growers' pressure to reverse decisions to unionize), provided stricter requirements for decertification, and included a highly controversial provision on the *access* of union organizers to farm workers. It was this provision that brought forth subsequent campaign arguments over private property rights.[9] At the outset of the campaign, most Californians probably saw the issue as one of strengthening the authority of both the ALRB and the United Farm Workers.

Two major arguments arose in the campaign. One centered on the private property rights issue, the other on the propriety of law-making by initiative. On this latter point, for example, the *Los Angeles Times* (October 29, 1976) went so far as to argue that "the extreme measure of going to the initiative process should be reserved for occasions when the legislative process has broken down." The private property issue was raised to an inflammatory level by opponents. For example, Janice Gentle of the Central Valley Women for Agriculture Group, asked: "How long will it be before gun registration and insurance coverage is subject to house to house inspection?" (*Times* Sunday Forum, October 24, 1976). A similar theme in the growers' TV and radio commercials led Chavez to label them "misleading and fraudulent."

The campaign was characterized by heavy litigation and pressure on the FCC and broadcasting industry in regard to advertising. In addition, very early in the UFW drive, the growers sought injunctions against pamphlet distribution and voter registration in several southern California shopping centers on the grounds that solicitation by outside groups was forbidden on such property. The California Supreme Court, however, upheld the UFW argument that a statutory right existed for such activities.

A second move against the Farm Workers was made by the Ganin Company of Salinas (a vegetable grower), which on October 16 served a $1.5 million libel suit on Chavez while he was celebrating communion preceding a rally at the University of San Francisco. This suit was over UFW posters linking Ganin with child labor. On October 20 a superior court judge ordered the Ganin name blacked out of the poster photograph showing a young child picking onions and placing them in a discarded pesticide can after Ganin claimed he didn't use child labor, didn't use pesticide cans, and didn't grow onions at that time. Two days later, after the UFW presented further evidence on child labor, the decision *was reversed* on appeal. (Note that it was now less than two weeks before the election.)

In the meantime, the UFW made a series of complaints to the Los Angeles District Attorney, the FCC, and the California Fair Political Practices Commission, all of which received more attention in the news than the contents of the proposition. One set of complaints alleged "false and misleading statements" in the opponents' radio and TV advertisements. This centered on the opponents' claims about a violation of property rights in spite of the fact that the "access" rule had been upheld by the Supreme Court. In addition, the UFW objected to the false implication (in commercials) that the ruling also applied to nonagricultural property. The district attorney concluded that he could not act under the state penal code because of uncertainty over whether it applied to political advertisements. However, ABC did temporarily order its six California affiliates to suspend all anti-Proposition 14 commercials that discussed property rights.

The UFW complaints to the state FPCC charged that opponents were not reporting campaign contributions (from 16 growers' associations) in accordance with state law. A week later (on October 28), Governor Brown charged at a press conference that several major oil companies had also secretly joined the growers' campaign. The next day the growers labeled these charges "misleading" since the oil companies had only contributed $8,100. Relations between the growers and Brown had deteriorated to the point where they were both staging demonstrations in his Sacramento office and running two full-page newspaper advertisements that questioned his veracity.

One of these ads (October 28), captioned "The Truth Test," challenged readers to telephone the ALRB about the accuracy of Brown's description of the law, prominently displaying the governor's phone number; the other (October 31) challenged Brown's television statements about property rights. A third ad (October 29) shifted the attack to Chavez instead. It featured a photograph of the Chavez compound, "La Paz," with a "Private Property" sign visible on the gate and a caption reading "Cesar Believes in Property Rights Too." (To my knowledge there was no resolution of the campaign contribution issue before the election.) We should also mention that both sides continued to air a barrage of TV and radio spots right up to election day. The supporters, however, only ran one newspaper ad, a full-page "Open Letter from Governor Brown," which appeared in the *Los Angeles Times,* but not in the San Francisco *Chronicle,* on election day.

What are we to make of all this from the perspective of campaign deception and voter confusion? It must be noted that far more than media advertising (and litigation) took place in this campaign: the amount of grass-roots activity on both sides was at least as extraordinary as the campaign expenditures. Thousands and thousands of homes—especially in the large urban areas—were visited by precinct workers on one or both sides. The UFW also registered well over 200,000 new voters, many of whom may have voted for Senator Tunney as well. (It should be noted, however, that Tunney—who, like Brown, actively supported Proposition 14 and also received UFW endorsements—lost his campaign for reelection. His defeat is sometimes mentioned as an example of why many California politicians are wary about endorsing ballot issues.)[10] But I *assume* that all the "media blitz"—including the headlines that seemed to focus more on the latest injunction or libel suit than on the merits of the argument over procedures to protect farm union organizing— had some impact on the voter as well.

The Field Poll reported that in late September *54% of the public* had neither heard nor seen anything on Proposition 14. A month later the figure was 18%. Apparently the opponents won the publicity battle, since the percentage favoring the proposal shifted from 51% (of those who had heard of it) to 35% in the same period—a reasonably accurate forecast of the final 62-38% vote against the proposal.

Conclusion

I began this section by suggesting that Lowenstein's charge of media campaign distortion applied to a number of cases that involved either two-sided high spending or one-sided support, as well as to the more common negativism and deception of the one-sided opposition campaign. I have concentrated on only two cases of two-sided high spending, deliberately contrasting one where business interests lost and the other where they won, in the conviction that in these cases as in others (e.g., California's Proposition 13 and 8 in 1978—the tax cap battle), *neither* side in a two-sided high-spending campaign seems to be wearing a white hat. While it is tempting to castigate the growers for their distortion of the property rights issue in the Proposition 14 campaign, the reverse Lincoln's-mother's-doctor's-dog tactic of the UFW poster showing not just a child but a pesticide can is hardly to the point when the issue is putting teeth and funding into the ALRB. Once again, one wonders on just what basis the voter was able to reach an "informed" decision on a complex issue—or whether the decision was made, instead, on a "gut" basis.

It has been shown thus far, in this first chapter on campaigns, that one-sided high-spending campaigns are indeed associated with deceptive advertising and voter confusion. This seems to occur because there is no strong and visible opposition to keep the high-spending campaign honest or to provide strong counterarguments for the voters' consideration. When I examined two-sided high-spending campaigns, however, I found, contrary to Lowenstein's expectations, that far from serving as an effective check on each other, *both* sides simplified or sidetracked major issues, indulged in endless arguments and litigation over the truth of the opponents' claims, and in general simply compounded the confusion for the voter. While high-spending media campaigns can be very effective in winning elections, on the whole they do not appear to be enlightening at any very profound level, whether managed by one side or both of the contenders.

It is thus important to examine grass-roots campaigning, again from the dual perspective of electoral victory and the adequate presentation of major issues to voters. I will then present a more detailed conclusion about the findings in both chapters on the campaign.

Notes

1. This of course depends on the size of the volunteer organization and whether the campaign is rural or urban in focus. Public transportation facilities in California cities are less convenient than in, e.g., Massachusetts. However, I think the point is overstated.

2. This point is made in the *Los Angeles Times* editorial cited and amply demonstrated by letters to the editor and *Times* interviews with voters toward the campaign's end.

3. While most Massachusetts stations run brief editorials on ballot issues or reports on genuinely "newsworthy" events, all but the CBS affiliates argue that 30-second and 60-second spots do nothing but distort and simplify complex issues.

4. They go on to argue that opposition forces go into elections "with the solid and stolid 20 percent advantage of people who will vote 'no' on anything because they are frightened, confused, or resisting change" (p. 62). I shall demonstrate that Baus and Ross have exaggerated this tendency, at least outside of California. But clearly many professional campaign managers act as if it were true.

5. Most Massachusetts towns (and a few cities) are governed by a board of selectmen and a representative or full town meeting form of government.

6. Under the legislature's program, residential property would be assessed at 40% of market value, commercial property at 50%, industrial at 55%, and open land at 25%.

7. *Boston Globe,* October 20, 1978, interview with Oliver Ward, field coordinator for Committee Against Tax Discrimination.

8. Sponsorship alternated between the Mayors' Committee and the Citywide Neighborhood Committee, both coordinated by White. Opponents accused White of using the latter as a "front." The ads appeared October 23, 29, 30 and November 1, 2, 3, 4, 5, 6.

9. The initiative would give statutory status to a ruling already made by the ALRB that allowed organizers to enter a farm before an election for three hours a day (before and after work and during lunch hours). Since most agricultural workers seldom leave the farm, the ALRB reasoned that there could be no ready union access to workers other than on the farm itself. Most meetings were held in outdoor parking areas, since the ruling prohibited disruption of farm work.

10. Pierre Salinger, who opposed the 1964 anti-open-housing proposal (Proposition 14) and also lost his bid for the United States Senate, is another frequently cited case. He was defeated by actor George Murphy (see Baus and Ross, 1968, p. 266).

6

THE CAMPAIGN:
GRASS-ROOTS ACTIVITIES

In the concluding part of his study of the six Colorado initiatives defeated in 1976, John Shockley (1980: 41) discusses the disappointment of many liberals who felt that shoestring campaigns organized behind such issues as the bottle bill, nuclear power regulation, and the repeal of a sales tax on food only served to mobilize the opposition *because inadequate attention was given to organizing support for the measure.* He goes on to cite a very provocative statement from the *Straight Creek Journal* (November 18, 1976):

> The lesson is that it is politically irresponsible for a group to put a measure on the ballot without having the resources—financial and organizational—to conduct an adequate campaign. When heavy opposition is expected, it is even more essential that adequate resources be lined up in advance.

I take strong issue with this view, which sounds remarkably like "blaming the victim." In Colorado opponents (overall) outspent supporters 10-1; and even in the face of the seemingly well-financed nuclear power battle (supporters spent $135,000), opponents managed to raise three-quarters of a million dollars of out-of-state money. Does this mean that those who chose to fight tobacco companies, the beverage industry, or the utility companies in the four states considered here were somehow obligated to line up literally millions of dollars beforehand?

There is, however, one important point in the statement. Usually a tremendous organizational effort and the funding to provide a small research and supervisory staff, vast amounts of printed material, and at least minimal media exposure are necessary in a campaign that seeks important changes. In addition, as shown in the earlier chapter on campaign finances, victories over well-financed vested interests are not always won via grass-roots organizing. Well-drawn proposals (sometimes less ambitious in scope than initiators would prefer), issues that match the values of the voters, a focus on arguments designed to broaden support—these factors too have made a difference in the deviant (i.e., low-spending side) victories discussed. But careful organization, an army of volunteers, the occasional use of colorful, newsworthy, even bizarre events and/or endorsements by prominent or charismatic leaders can make a major difference, even if they don't inevitably guarantee victory.

I shall begin, in this chapter, by expanding on some of the brief allusions made earlier to the grass-roots efforts by supporters involved in some campaigns just considered: the Chavez proposal in California and the bottle bill campaigns in Michigan and Massachusetts.[1] I shall also add a word about the opponents in the California campaign on hiring homosexual teachers, a controversy that along with the bottle bill campaigns, was a pioneer in developing newsworthy campaign techniques—and the one low-impact style issue that involved exceptionally high levels of spending. Then, in the second part of the chapter, I shall consider grass-roots efforts on some relatively low-spending style issues like the ERA, abortion, and the death penalty.

Union-Style Organizing Strategies

Cesar Chavez began the campaign for the Agricultural Labor Relations Act with one asset possessed by very few authors of ballot initiatives: more than 16 years of experience in California in labor organizing and in attracting funds for the cause. Thus he had a veritable army of people trained on the picket line and experienced in addressing ordinary citizens, organizing rallies, and raising money from good liberals.[2] (He was also one of the few genuinely charismatic leaders involved in the campaigns studied here.) Thus it is not surprising that his organization was able to collect 700,000 signatures in only a few weeks and later to register over 200,000 new voters over the summer.

The UFW also collected a large number of public endorsements from Governor Brown and Senator Tunney to Jimmy Carter, Alan Cranston, and the mayors of Los Angeles, San Francisco, and Oakland. By the end of October they also were supported by the state-level conference of Catholic Bishops, Board of Rabbis, and

several other religious groups. What is important about these endorsements is that many prominent individuals not only gave their
names but their time and efforts in fund-raising rallies or other
public appearances. (Opponents too had important support, including the speaker of the General Assembly, several state representatives, and 16 major farm organizations.)

Much of the summer was concentrated on voter registration in
the large coastal cities (Los Angeles, San Diego, San Francisco);
but by late September volunteers moved into the central valleys as
well, where population was not so dense, but more Mexican American farm workers lived. In mid-October farm workers and their
families attended a huge rally at the University of San Francisco in
preparation for the last weeks of the campaign. (It was here that
they saw their leader slapped with a $1.5 million libel suit in the
middle of a religious service.) These workers stayed in or near the
city to continue their precinct work.

The weekend after the Chavez rally also saw an impressive countercampaign. On October 23-24, 3500 farmers and their families
were bussed into Los Angeles, and during the last week in October
an additional 3000 went into the San Francisco area, both to hold
rallies of their own and to conduct a door-to-door campaign. (This
is one of the few instances in this study where the "business" side
of an issue conducted a grass-roots campaign. The Flat Electric
Rate campaign in Massachusetts is another. The average "farm"
size in California, as in Texas and some other sunbelt states, is
exceptionally large. Hence the term "business.")

I have no detailed information on how these campaigns were
actually coordinated, other than the fact that a fair portion of expenditures on both sides went into organizing and staff rather than
simply to public relations firms (California Fair Political Practices
Commission: 1976). While the Chavez operation might be cited as
a veritable model for grass-roots organizing (despite the election
loss), it also was an experienced, professional, on-going union organization from the start of the campaign. As pointed out above, very
few initiative campaigns begin with this advantage.

Precinct-Style Strategies

One network of organizations that is beginning to collect this sort
of cumulative organizing experience in ballot issue campaigns is

the group of state PIRGs originally organized by Ralph Nader in 1972. These are the public interest research groups that have coordinated bottle bill campaigns in Massachusetts, California, and elsewhere, although they were apparently not the only major actor in the Michigan campaign of 1976. Mass-PIRG's coordination of the successful fight against bottle bill repeal in 1982 was a strategic feat which may portend a future professionalism that approaches the level of the United Farm Workers.[3]

The Michigan bottle bill coalition, Help Abolish Throwaways Committee (HATC), included the United Conservation Clubs, PIRG in Michigan, and the Michigan Farm Bureau. Because of their stress on the hazards of broken glass, they also won the endorsements of the Michigan Chapter of the American Academy of Pediatricians, the State Highway Commission, and the State Police. Both sides in the campaign relied heavily on media advertising. Supporters, however, both because they had less funding ($117,000 to opponents' $1.3 million) and because they saw the campaign as a people's effort, relied heavily on traditional leafleting, public forums, small fund raisers and the like. Direction of the campaign was quite decentralized.

One unique set of activities to be emulated in the 1982 campaigns in Massachusetts and California was a series of well-publicized "cleanathons" in Detroit, Ann Arbor, and elsewhere to dramatize the litter problem. One hundred volunteers in Ann Arbor collected 37,000 disposable cans and bottles from a ten-mile stretch along the Huron River. The six-foot high "mountain" was then duly photographed and publicized. Twelve days later (a week before the election) another cleanathon collected litter on comparable one-mile stretches of Michigan and Oregon roads to compare litter with the state that had enacted the first bottle bill. The *Detroit Free Press* featured the two photographs in a lead article captioned "Michigan Loses Litter Test" (there were 336 Michigan bottles and cans to Oregon's 37).[4]

The first Massachusetts campaign (1976) began with a tremendous disadvantage in comparison with Michigan. First, it had to compete for both funds and volunteers with several major liberal causes on the ballot—gun control, ERA, the flat electrical rate proposal, and the graduated income tax, most notable. (In Michigan the only competition for liberals was the graduated tax.) Second, and related to the first problem, was a critical shortage of funds. By mid-October, when opponents had already spent $871,000 on advertising and on a statewide telephone campaign, supporters had only raised $27,689, of which $18,000 was spent on radio spots. By campaign's end the respective budgets were $2,587,000 and $56,500. Given this minimal level of funding, supporters relied heavily on debates and public forums, (free) press coverage, and leafleting.

While one very effective technique was the use of outside experts—former Governor McCall of Oregon and a three-person "truth squad" from Vermont were brought in to hold press conferences in Governor Dukakis's Cabinet Room to describe the success of the law elsewhere—the Massachusetts campaign generally lacked the color, the intense press coverage, and the broad volunteer support found in Michigan. One problem was a slightly narrower range of organizational sponsorship, in part because the campaign focused almost exclusively on the environmental arguments and on the question of economic impact. But, as argued above, $56,500, especially in a year overflowing with liberal causes, was simply an inadequate amount to provide the support and coordination vital in facing intensely aroused industrial opponents with seemingly limitless coffers.[5]

It is difficult to specify the minimum level of funding for a winning campaign, or even one which succeeds in educating a significant number of voters, when a volunteer effort faces a well-financed opposition. I would guess at about $100,000 in Michigan and Massachusetts, with a slightly lower figure for Oregon, and probably $150,000-200,000 for California, given the usual need in California *initiative* campaigns for high expenditures during the signature-collection period. This estimate is based on the costs of deviant campaigns shown in Chapter 4 and on costs of losing campaigns that seem to have stimulated publicity and discussion, i.e., some of the tax proposals in Oregon and Michigan, the drinking age issue in Michigan. Note the existence of a host of issues where losing grass-roots campaigns didn't even come close to these amounts: gun control advocates in Massachusetts and death penalty opponents in California provide examples of $8,000-12,000 campaigns battling wealthy opponents. The problem of making such an estimate, of course, is that the amount needed will vary with the alternative resources available—willing campaign workers, sympathetic reporters and editors, and even the degree to which an issue readily lends itself to colorful campaign techniques. I would nevertheless argue that a fair amount of hard cash is essential to provide the office space, the staffing, and the visual aids (pamphlets, bumper stickers, buttons, signs, t-shirts, etc.) that will maximize and coordinate the advantage of these free or low-cost resources.

The 1982 "rerun" in Massachusetts was a very different story. There were three major contrasts: (1) industry was on the defensive because they were seeking to *repeal* a bottle bill just passed by the legislature over the governor's veto; (2) an army of volunteers, many from groups who were now enraged at efforts to repeal a bill they had worked hard to pass, was available despite competition from three other causes (the nuclear freeze, control of nuclear power and waste, the death penalty); and (3) a significant war chest was available for the campaign ($652,558 to opponents' $1,430,247).

Baus and Ross (1968: 218-22) have written an almost classic guide for grass-roots organizers, based among other things on their experience with a California initiative on pay TV. In discussing geographic committees, they suggest several stages in organizing: finding 2 or 3 community leaders; asking each of them to invite 2 or 3 contacts to an organizational strategy meeting; sending a "mobilization" committee from headquarters to spell out *in detail* some simple tasks for this group, while listening to them for suggestions. They then go on to list some of these "simple" tasks: contacting other *local* groups for endorsements, assigning specific volunteers to contact the local press, scheduling speaking dates in local churches and before civic groups, organizing the distribution of literature, fund-raising work. They conclude that "busy committees brew victory: give the troops something to do." Conversely, give careful attention to volunteers or they may disappear (1968: 222).

While it is unlikely that Mass-PIRG read Baus and Ross, it is intriguing to find an almost identical strategy in at least the Boston area conduct of the 1982 bottle bill campaign.[6] The initial organizational meeting in Waltham, for example, was called in the early spring of 1982, in a League of Women Voters activist's home which later served as a "drop" for leafleting, for election day work, and for general chit-chat and morale boosting. Most of the 15-20 people at the initial meeting were activists in groups like the Sierra Club, local Unitarian churches, or the Democratic Party and were veterans of earlier ballot issue campaigns. Some, however, were political neophytes, angry over *this* issue, and activated by friends or neighbors. Some were housewives, some students, and some retired people. (Brandeis students were separately organized in a nearby group that cooperated in leafleting and cleanathons.)

Following this initial meeting, to which a Mass-PIRG coordinator presented a detailed timetable for local activities extending over the next six months, all volunteers were asked (somewhat against their will) to participate in an immediate fund-raising drive. Leafleting at the local shopping centers (where liquor stores and supermarkets had already posted anti-bottle-bill signs) came early in June. A fourth of July cleanathon in a local park, followed by a morning parade in the town center, collected more publicity, funds, and volunteers. In the meantime, individual volunteers were given specific assignments like obtaining an endorsement from the town garden club, lining up speaking engagements (for Mass-PIRG professionals) in their home churches, and enlisting more volunteers for the fall.

Activities in the fall began with another meeting with the Mass-PIRG coordinator to plan precinct and polling place activity. During the *September primary* bottle-bill supporters (along with Nuclear Freeze people) appeared at most precinct places with signs and leaflets, even though the vote on the bottle bill would not take place until November. (It was felt that an early amount of high visibility was important.) In the meantime the media campaigns on both sides went into full swing: hardly a drive during commuters' hours was unaccompanied by a 30-second radio spot from one or both sides. Speakers on both sides of the controversy were also frequent guests on radio talk shows.

The last days before the election saw, as well as the more visible press conferences, public debates, and charges of misleading advertising, leafleting of almost every home in the area, highly organized election day signs and "poll cards," phoning of voters who had not yet shown up at the polls, and what looked like a spontaneous letter-writing campaign to the local newspaper. Five people were asked by the Mass-PIRG coordinator to write—all letters were timed to reach the newspaper on a specific final day. All were printed.

The Waltham operation has been described in some detail because it was typical of the several hundred town and city campaigns all over Massachusetts. The Boston (headquarters) operation was, of course, much larger and in the early autumn days was marred at times by confusion over what to do with the literally hundreds of volunteers who poured in from both local neighborhoods and universities. Within a matter of days, however, those who stayed were put to work on the telephone banks, mass mailings and fund-raising activities, or sometimes on research tasks. Leafleting went on in the subways, in the shopping centers, on the Common, and in the end in a number of neighborhoods.

One final point needs to be made about this grass-roots operation. Many of the volunteers and leaders had either been familiar with or active in the 1976 losing campaign. The "grapevine" also asserted that over $2 million would again be spent by the opponents as it had been in 1976. (As it turned out, the beverage industry instead put most of its 1982 energy into its victorious campaign in California.) Thus the campaign was organized early; a strong emphasis was put on fund-raising; events were continuous, simple, and highly structured, making a good use of the Michigan experience; and volunteers *began* with a zeal largely fired by anger that extended back through six years of battling with wealthy opponents. In a sense Mass-PIRG was following the kind of advice (cited above) of the Colorado *Straight Creek Journal* in lining up essential financial and organizational resources in advance. Whether Mass-PIRG (and other state PIRGs) will be able to mobilize similar human and financial energies for future battles that lack this backlog of anger and experience remains to be seen.[7]

Use of the Bizarre: Unorthodox Strategies

The 1978 battle over California's Proposition 6, a proposal to empower removal of any teacher, school administrator, or counselor "who advocates, solicits, encourages, or promotes homosexual behavior" (California Voters' Pamphlet, November 1978: 30), was primarily a high-spending media campaign by both sides, with roughly equal spending that totalled $2.3 million. In any other year it would have attracted enormous attention both as a controversial and as an exhorbitantly expensive proposal, but this was the year in which voters had just seen Proposition 13 and were now confronted with Proposition 5, the proposed Clean Air Act, as well. I include a brief discussion because of the unusual grass-roots tactics of both sides, in what the *Los Angeles Times* termed the "most bizarre" campaign in California's history.

Proposition 6 was one of the two proposals introduced by State Senator John Briggs (the other was on the death penalty), a man who was one of the prominent archconservative spokesmen at the time. The campaign argument began with the premise that "a coalition of homosexual teachers and their allies are trying to use the vast power of our school system to impose their own brand of non-morality" on California's children (California Voters' Pamphlet: 30). The proposition was immediately denounced by almost every political figure in California, from Governor Brown and Cesar Chavez to former Governor Reagan and Los Angeles's conservative police chief Davis. Civic groups, many local school boards and city councils, and almost every major newspaper branded it a thinly veiled witch hunt.

Why then take such a proposal seriously enough to spend countless hours and over $1 million in opposition? In part because opposition was very slow in growing. As is so often the case with new proposals, early public opinion reports were favorable: opposition in August was 31%, in September 43%, and finally in mid-October it reached 58%. Furthermore, it was the very prototype of an issue where supporters might say one thing to pollsters and another in the privacy of the voting booth. Finally, although some church groups or individuals issued strong statements in opposition (notably all three branches of Judaism, the California Council of Churches, and the San Francisco archbishop), others were either in support (the National Association of Evangelicals) or were ambivalent (e.g., the California Catholic Conference could not reach agreement on a statement).

Most of the campaign spending by both sides went into television and radio advertising during the last week of the campaign, as well as a few statewide newspaper advertisements by the opposition. In the meantime the opposition proceeded on two very different levels. On the one hand, opponents worked hard for support (and funds) from traditional groups like the PTA, the League of Women Voters, and party organizations, which they then listed in advertising and campaign literature. At the same time, many avowedly gay volunteers at "No on Six" headquarters in San Francisco focused their leafleting and posters on gay bars and restaurants. One of the fund-raising activities that attracted wide publicity was a massive all-day "clip-in" by San Francisco hairdressers whose normal fees were contributed to the cause.

Two major rallies held on the Sundays before the election capture some of the contrast in style between the two sides. On October 30 Senator Briggs introduced Reverend Jerry Falwell to thousands of *supporters* in successive rallies in San Diego and Cost Mesa (Orange County). According to the *Los Angeles Times,* the audience of about 3500 in San Diego was dominated by Bible-carrying church members bused in for the occasion. On the following Sunday (November 5) an *opposition* rally was held at Hollywood's Greek Temple, featuring singers Odetta and Peter Yarrow (of Peter, Paul, and Mary) followed by representatives from the Southern California Council of Churches, the Council of Rabbis, and individual Catholic clergy.[8]

Lest all of this be taken lightly as trappings in a campaign that wasn't too serious, note that the election turnout was high (70.4%) for an off year in which the incumbent governor was easily reelected, that only 4.8% of the 7.13 million voting left the choice blank on Proposition 6, and that the margin of defeat, 58.4-41.6%, while comfortable, was not overwhelming.

One reason for including the unorthodox grass-roots techniques on Proposition 6 in this discussion is the parallel finding that such oddities are not completely foreign to low-spending campaigns over style issues. It is important to note, once again, that I follow Berelson, Lazarsfeld, and McPhee (1954: 184) in distinguishing "position" issues, which involve major economic interests, from "style" issues, which deal with matters of taste, lifestyle, and (occasionally) with morality. This in no sense implies that "style" issues are trivial or unimportant; they may, in fact, be of major concern to large numbers of voters, particularly if they have been in the public eye for a considerable period of time. (For example, many voters are likely to have well-articulated standing views on the death penalty, limitations on drinking, abortion, and the like.) At least two other analysts of ballot issue voting (Lowery and Sigelman, 1981: 972; DeCanio, 1979: 55-66) continue to find the distinction useful.

It may be recalled that only two other low-impact style issues (besides Proposition 6) entailed total spending over $500,000. In fact three, including a newsmen's shield law, saw no spending; three more involved sums from $13,900 to $17,100. (This seems quite reasonable given the low economic stakes of many of these issues.)

While Buchanan and Bird (1966) have pointed out that the advantage of financial resources is their interchangeability with other resources, i.e., that publicity, people, polling, and the like can be more easily obtained with money than the reverse, a campaign *lacking* in money may nevertheless be able to win free publicity or supporters with a variety of unusual techniques. Especially in a campaign where both sides spend little, volunteer activity with high visibility plus a modest budget may suffice. Let us look at a few low-spending campaigns.

Two 1978 campaigns, in Oregon and California, centered on the death penalty.[9] (The Oregon proposal called for reinstating the death penalty, which had been abolished in 1964, under a separate sentencing procedure after a murder conviction. The California proposal would broaden the coverage of a death penalty statute enacted in 1977 to include murder for financial gain and the use of explosives, torture or poison.) While California supporters spent $657,900, opponents spent $17,100. In both cases supporters won by substantial margins: 71-29% in California and 64-36% in Oregon. And in both cases the campaigns had very little effect on an initially supportive public. What is interesting, though, is the contrast in techniques and visibility of the two low-spending opponents.

Almost nothing happened in the California death penalty campaign after July 1, when the supporters had spent $451,000 on a direct mailing to voters. In fact, the October 7, 1978, *Los Angeles Times* labeled the procampaign as a "classic case" of peaking early. By October expenditures had apparently outrun receipts by more than $100,000 simply in maintaining an office and staff, with little prospect of finding new funds since the polls showed a clear victory ahead. The opponents, at the same time, lacked funds for even a minimal campaign. Thus there were no ads, no press releases, no signs of a campaign other than one article in the October 22 *Los Angeles Times*, written by a board member of the American Civil Liberties Union. Five letters to the editors appeared in opposition in the *Times* and San Francisco *Chronicle* in late October as well. (This compares to 11 in favor of the Clean Air Act and 29 opposing the homosexual teachers proposal in the same period.)

In contrast to the almost inexplicable silence of the California campaign, Oregon opponents were fairly active. (Oregon supporters were not, and they too began the campaign with polls showing a firm majority of the public in favor of the proposal.) The opposition used a combination of inexpensive techniques to gain free publicity. At least three out-of-state speakers were imported to address Portland audiences: Thomas Gaddes, psychologist and author of *The Birdman of Alcatraz;* Hugo Bedau, a Tufts University professor who authored a definitive book on capital punishment and has been active in Massachusetts campaigns on the issue; and finally, the secretary general of Amnesty International. In addition, a highly publicized March Against the Death Penalty attracted 150 people who walked from the State House to the State Prison in Salem on October 25; the following Sunday a noon-time rally in Portland drew 300 people.

Obviously none of these events prevented the ultimate passage of the measure; and surely, given the continuing news about polls showing little shift (three were published in the *Oregonian*), the opponents were not surprised. This issue, however, like fluoridation, state-funded abortions, and gun control, is one which partisans usually recognize as involving *long-term* public education. (And most leaders of involved groups have been around for a very long time, e.g., Hugo Bedau has been active in Massachusetts anti-death-penalty work for over 20 years, as has the American Civil Liberties Union and the NAACP in all four states.) This long range perspective was probably the motivation for efforts like those in Oregon.

A "Covering" Strategy

Oregonians faced another low-impact style issue in 1978, namely, Measure 7, a proposal to prohibit both state funding of abortion and the provision of "programs or services that promote abortions." (The latter point was almost as controversial as the first, since opponents feared it would apply to medical training at the University of Oregon.) The campaign over abortion, however, involved both higher spending and more intensive activity on both sides than did the simultaneous death penalty campaign. The initiative was introduced and supported by an ad hoc committee called Oregonians Opposed to State Financed Abortion. Ten Portland obstetricians joined the campaign as well in a press conference announcing their support. They spent $50,500 on the campaign. Opponents included the Oregon Medical Association, the Oregon State Employees Association, and the American Civil Liberties Union. Their campaign, led by a group called Taxpayers for Choice, cost $81,200.

Both sides ran modest media campaigns, that is, a limited number of radio and television spots. Supporters financed two full-page newspaper ads and four small ones featuring a photo of a smiling baby with the caption "thank you for not buying my abortion." These ran in the *Oregonian* and in other newspapers during the last ten days of the campaign. But the bulk of activity for both sides was a large number of debates before small audiences in almost every part of the state, generally with speakers from the community itself. Both sides apparently were wary about the other's regional strength and concerned about covering every option. Supporters' main strength was in traditionally conservative eastern and southern Oregon, while major opposition strength lay in the cities. But, according to the *Oregonian,* various past campaigns had floundered by concentrating exclusively on Portland and the Willamette Valley, so the opposition followed the supporters' lead in a heavy emphasis on debating, informal meetings, coffees, and old-fashioned door-to-door leafleting, reaching every part of the state but the sparsely populated east.[10]

Apparently opponents were correct in this "covering" strategy. While there was a very small percentage (8-9%) of undecided voters, public opinion did shift in the last weeks of the campaign, from 39% pro-Measure 7 (antiabortion) on October 20 to 41% on October 29 to a final vote of 48.3-51.7% on election day. Portland voters did strongly oppose the initiative but, according to county voting figures, would not have been able to carry the state even with the addition of cities like Eugene without support from other areas as well.

This is the only instance found (although there may have been others where strategy was not discussed as candidly) of what might be called a cautious chesslike strategy that extends over the entire "board." Not flamboyant, certainly very time consuming for many volunteers, but probably one that neither side could afford to refuse. Since the issue is probably not dead in Oregon, given the closeness of the vote, the supporters may take comfort in having at least begun a campaign to change public attitudes on the issue.

Movement Strategies: Building on Affinity Groups[11]

My final example of a low-cost grass-roots campaign on a style issue is the controversy over ratification of the ERA in Massachusetts in 1976. Recall that this was the year when hundreds of bottle bill supporters, gun control advocates, and working-class initiators of a flat electric rate were pounding the streets. Thus it is surprising that ERA supporters were able to sustain a massive volunteer operation over the entire campaign period. The campaign, in fact, began in 1972—and that may have been the secret.

The purpose of the ERA (Question 1 in 1976) was to add one sentence to the state constitution to provide that equality under the law may not be denied on the basis of sex, race, color, creed, or national origin. Supporters argued, throughout the campaign, "It sounds simple—and it is." This slogan was meant to imply that the amendment simply meant *legal* equality. Opponents, in Massachusetts and elsewhere, insisted that it implied a battle between the sexes and raised the specter of coed bathrooms and female army combat troops. These were the arguments repeated over and over, in a loosely structured informal sort of campaign, but one that may have been the angriest battle in the Massachusetts election.

Endorsers included the Fords, the Carters, Senators Kennedy and Brooke, Governor Dukakis and Mayor White, and most of the Massachusetts delegation to Congress. Active organizations included the Boston Teachers Union, Common Cause, the League of Women Voters, the Council of Churches, the Jewish Congress, and the State AFL-CIO. The campaign for the amendment was run by 25 area coordinators who enlisted over 3,000 volunteers in communities throughout the state to raise money, talk to church and civic groups, and push the local newspapers for support and coverage. There were no paid media ads by either side until the final week before the election; instead, both supporters and opponents depended on publicity through their arguments and activities. (It should be noted that the *Boston Globe* coverage was extensive, with three long articles and an editorial endorsement, plus several shorter reports during the last weeks of the campaign. I also found brief coverage of a local forum in one of the two local weeklies I saw in the period.)

Beginning in 1972, the ERA campaign was carried into almost every city and town through coffee klatches, bake sales, wine and cheese parties, and church suppers. Supporters raised over $50,000 of the $66,500 spent by the end of the campaign through these small fund-raising events and by the sale of bumper stickers and t-shirts that carried the ERA message. Activities just before the election varied from informal discussions to large meetings featuring well-known speakers like State Representative Barney Frank, to the designation of October 24 as "ERA Sunday" by eight churches in Harvard Square, with attendant sermons and discussions.

In the last days a modest leafleting and newspaper advertising campaign was undertaken by supporters. Two ads in the *Globe,* on October 30 and November 2, carried the slogan "It sounds simple and it is—vote yes on ERA." The first also listed 60 organizations and individuals who endorsed the amendment. Finally, a visible presence was maintained on election day, with signs and sometimes balloons at most polling places; as far as the author can determine, a system of observers, runners, phone calls, and rides to the polling place was also operating in many precincts.[12]

The opponents, who organized late in the campaign and spent only $2300, were much less visible. Their most publicized campaign event was a talk by Phyllis Shafley, who spoke on October 24 to a meeting of 300 women sponsored by the Catholic Daughters of America. The two ad hoc organizations reporting expenditures undertook no media advertising. Opposition quiescence is somewhat surprising, given occasional *Globe* reports of a quiet and strong undercurrent of opposition, and the frequent anger and vehemence expressed by individuals on radio talk shows. It is possible, of course, given Massachusetts' deviant status in the 1972 presidential election, that opponents felt their money and efforts were best spent in other states.[13] They may have been right, since the amendment was ultimately approved by a 60-40% margin.

Conclusion

In this and the preceding chapter, different kinds of campaigns have been examined, namely those characterized by a high degree of media advertising and other publicity that usually entail high costs, and those distinguished by major reliance on grass-roots activities. (A rare few, like the Chavez campaign on the Agricultural Labor Relations Act, have tried to do both.) My goal has been to assess the effectiveness of these strategies from two frequently contradictory perspectives: winning elections and/or providing information to voters.

At the outset several differences among the four states in legal arrangements, political context, and general norms about the conduct of ballot issue campaigns were explored. California laws on voter registration seem to be important, especially for the allocation of time and funds, for the style of some campaigns in that state, as is the Oregon prohibition on payment for petition signature collection. Differences in regard to ballot pamphlets, on the other hand, did not seem to matter greatly for the conduct of campaigns.

Major attention was then given to Lowenstein's hypothesis that one-sided high-spending campaigns (especially *in opposition* to ballot proposals) lead to deceptive advertising and voter confusion because simplification and distortions cannot be adequately answered by the low-spending side. While the six cases of one-sided high-spending opposition considered in detail here seem to confirm Lowenstein's point, deception and distortion are characteristic of other kinds of high-spending campaigns as well. In only one of these cases—the rent control issue in the 1980 California elections—did the high-spending side's advertising effort to deceive and confuse the voter boomerang to help lose the election for the spenders. (In two other cases, the Michigan bottle bill and the 1980 vote on nuclear regulation in Oregon, the high-spending side lost, but in neither case was the issue of deception or of outrageous levels of spending the major reason for the defeat.)

What about the level of information provided to the voter through the campaign itself? (I am not concerned for the moment with newspaper coverage, which on the more controversial measures, at least, was quite thorough in the major regional papers.) Did these different sorts of campaigns serve to illuminate the issues or to obfuscate through slogans? Here the picture is quite grim. I would argue that with the possible exception on the two bottle bill campaigns where the issue was less complex than most, a voter would need to be a very careful newspaper reader or have some reliable source of information beyond campaign rhetoric and slogans to make an informed decision. Even the ballot pamphlets in three of these states are written at a level beyond the ready comprehension of the average reader. This was also true of two-sided high-spending campaigns, since excessive funds were accompanied by excessive litigation and endless arguments over the other side's veracity, instead of a clear debate on the core issues.

The two California campaigns over the Clean Air Act provide perhaps the best example of an extremely expensive advertising campaign that shifted the debate away from the original issue. In both 1978 and 1980 the tobacco companies succeeded in picturing a proposal to establish separate nonsmoking sections in restaurants, bars, and public places as exhorbitantly expensive, unenforceable, and an unwarranted invasion of privacy. It somehow became an issue of "Big Brother is watching." The supporters, clearly outspent but hardly penniless, colluded in their own defeat, taking a similarly negative stance, by arguing in turn about outside money and fraudulent advertising when they might have done far better with a simple positive slogan on the theme of equal space for clean air. Confirmation that the voters learned very little from the experience (or else have *very* short memories) comes from the marked similarity of the two campaigns in opinion polls, in initial levels of uncertainty or ignorance, and in the shift from initial approval to ultimate defeat. (Opposition rose from 38% in August to 55% in November 1978 and from 33% to 52% in the same period in 1980. It was defeated 54.4-45.6% in 1978 and by 53.4-46.6% in 1980.)

Other one-sided high-spending opposition campaigns tell the same story. Massachusetts bottle bill supporters in 1976 allowed themselves to become ensnared in endless arguments over the economic costs of the measure in jobs, costs to stores, increased costs of beverages instead of stressing their positive environmental themes. The first Oregon campaign on nuclear power also bogged down in technicalities and on whether the views of a singer, comedienne, and thousands of citizens should be preferred to the beliefs of "4,000 Oregonians" and a number of outside scientists and experts. Once again a fight about economic impact (in a state where the unemployment rate was climbing) took precedence over safety, security, and waste disposal.

I have already mentioned one example of one-sided spending in support of a proposal—rent control—which lost. The other instance of one-sided positive spending—the Massachusetts property tax cap—is another example of vastly oversimplified arguments where responses were lost in the combination of a brilliant advertising campaign and taxpayer fury over the eleventh-hour delivery of high tax bills. A cold, hard look at viable alternatives for tax reforms is never likely in the heat of an initiative campaign, but the media hype, playing to mass confusion and anger at the state government (or at the generalized "them"), almost guaranteed that rational debate was impossible.

Even worse is to come. The two examples of two-sided high-spending campaigns (one of which was almost exclusively played out through the media) demonstrate that *two* heavy spenders may simply cause twice the confusion of one rather than one forcing the other to confront the real issues. Both the Massachusetts tax classification controversy and the campaign over the Agricultural Labor Relations Act in California gave rise to so much litigation and so many controversies over the truth of the opponents' claims that each, in the end, degenerated into a referendum on the character and power of the opponents. The argument over the expected change in tax rates never was resolved in Massachusetts, nor was any effort made to place the change in the context of overall, long-range tax reform. It is thus not surprising that the whole issue resurfaced in 1980, in the form of yet another (but more extreme) stop-gap measure, which still failed to address the basics. Did the voters realize this? I rather suspect that in both cases they simply sent a message: "do something; we're mad."

In the case of the Chavez Amendment, once again how could the voter make an intelligent decision on the most lengthy and technical proposal considered here when the opponents reduced the issue to private property rights and the supporters, despite bringing legal allegations of fraud and misrepresentation, never managed to put the lie to the argument? Nowhere in the campaign was there a clear discussion of labor stability in the fields and the mechanisms needed (including consistent and continuous funding for a labor board) to bring this about, while at the same time preventing "capture" of that board by one or either of the contestants. Perhaps the genuinely informed voter would need to be a specialist in labor law to handle this; if so, the campaign (by *both* sides) was of very little assistance.

I am not arguing that issues raised in advertisements are invariably specious or unimportant. On the contrary, concern about government interference with individual freedom or with private property is as legitimate as concern about health hazards or the practicalities of farmworkers' elections. Similarly, unemployment, the cost of electricity, and the health of a state's economy need to be considered in debates over nuclear power safety. These are issues on which honest citizens disagree. My negative stance on high-spending campaigns instead is based on the contrived shift in the debate resulting in a focus on either the conduct of the campaign itself (charges and litigation over deception or statistics) or on just one or two of the many issues that are relevant.

The shifting, of course, makes good strategic sense. David Magleby (1984: 168) puts it succinctly: "the side that defines the proposition usually wins the election." Once the supporters lose control over defining the terms of the argument, they probably lose everything. A distinction must be made, however, between media strategies that are fraudulent (the California rent control issue) and those that simplify, obscure, or shift the debate. While high-spending strategists (and their paid consultants) are usually the initiators of both kinds of problem, in the second case the response of their opponents (e.g., authors of the Clean Air Acts) too often is reactive, unimaginative, and overly defensive. In both cases the resulting confusion and lack of information are the voter's loss.

I thus conclude that intensive, high-cost media campaigns have not been enlightening, even though most of the one-sided negative campaigns have been successful in the electoral sense. This has been so, in almost every case, regardless of whether the high spending was one-sided or two-sided. Thus I went on to assess grass-roots strategies, in both expensive and shoestring campaigns, as a possibly more constructive alternative.

An examination of nine different grass-roots campaigns involving six different issues leads to somewhat more positive conclusions than those reached about media campaigns. Three slightly different styles of grass-roots efforts have been reasonably (or in a few cases, extremely) effective both in informing voters and in winning some elections. One of these, for lack of a better term, could be called the traditional precinct-style operation, typified by the 1982 campaign against repeal of the bottle bill. (I suspect it was also used, perhaps more informally, in the Michigan bottle bill campaign, but had no information on the actual structure of that campaign.) A second could be termed union organizing, combined with a political movement strategy, as typified by the unsuccessful Chavez campaign and some elements in both the campaign against the ban on homosexual teachers in California and the fight for the ERA in Massachusetts. The third is the unusual chess game "covering" strategy of the prochoice forces in the Oregon abortion campaign.

The precinct-style strategy calls for campaign finances that are adequate to provide continuing staff and research help and basic supplies (i.e., pamphlets, posters, voter lists, contacts) throughout the campaign. This implies an ongoing organization (like the PIRGs) or a large number of experienced activists from earlier campaigns. It also implies a degree of pragmatism and a lack of emphasis on nonhierarchical "participant democracy" that may not be possible for those who see ballot issues as ideological battles (for example, supporters of the nuclear regulation proposal in California and in the first Oregon campaign).[14] Certainly one reason for the effectiveness of the 1982 Save the Bottle Bill campaign was the willingness of most volunteers to follow the strategy outlined by the PIRG coordinators rather than viewing the campaign as an exercise in group democracy.

Both the precinct and movement strategies are likely to be most effective with a strong, ongoing, and experienced membership that knows and trusts its leaders and that already has established outside support and sympathy. This was the greatest strength of the Chavez effort in 1976; it probably was also a strength of at least a solid core of the women who worked for the ERA in Massachusetts. A movement strategy may also yield unusual techniques for fund-raising, gaining additional volunteers, and generating publicity.

The "clip-ins" and Indian war paint of the California gays, the ERA emphasis on small group activities, female solidarity, t-shirts, and bake sales, the mass rallies and music of the farm workers, the nuclear power opponents, and later of the nuclear freeze advocates in all four states are examples of movement techniques—some traditional, some new—that can be used in ballot issue campaigns if they are not so far removed from the mainstream that they antagonize the moderate supporters necessary to election victory. The balance between militance and moderation, and their strategic and moral implications, is of course a very old and unresolved problem for political movements in America.

Finally, there is the informal, low-keyed "covering" chess strategy of the Oregon prochoice campaign. This is of course only appropriate as a defensive move when opponents and supporters are relatively equal in resources, strong in numbers and low in funds. (The Massachusetts ERA campaign didn't need to do this, although their campaign also ran on geographically dispersed, small meeting lines, because their opponents ran almost no visible campaign.) This strategy would seem ideal for winning low-impact style issues; more important, it is one technique that can be very effective in informing and perhaps activating voters if the content of the debates or discussion is reasonably thorough and accurate.[15]

I have also considered some campaigns where grass-roots activity was either nonexistent or almost token in nature. In almost every instance this seemed to occur when supporters were highly confident and/or opponents felt they were fighting for a lost cause (for example, the death penalty opponents in Oregon; ERA opponents in Massachusetts). While I would be the last to argue that activitists should continue to pour their time and hearts into such hopeless efforts (having done too much of this myself!), I would argue that allowing an election to go by default renders a disservice to the whole initiative process itself and to the ideal of an informed citizenry. From this perspective, the very low level of activity on some campaigns is disturbing.[16]

One final note of caution is necessary in regard to this assessment of grass-roots campaigns. I have employed two (not always explicit) criteria in this and the two preceding chapters to judge the impact of money, media, and grass-roots activity: electoral success and public education. Since it is clearly necessary to gain the voters' attention before attempting to inform, to clarify the issues, and ultimately to change or reinforce their views, even shallow but flamboyant campaign tactics (Indian war dances, celebrity appearances) might be seen as informational. At the same time, a "successful" campaign, in the sense of electoral victory, isn't always informative. Some of the winning strategies discussed above—notably the "covering" strategy on abortion in Oregon—included a heavy dose of informational work (local debates and discussions). Others— notably the movement-style campaigns—seem tipped toward attention getting. Presumably both the soundest educational strategy and the most colorful consciousness-raising techniques work best when used in tandem. The next chapter will focus on confusion and rationality among voters.

Notes

1. We omit the other issues such as the Massachusetts tax classification proposal and property tax cap or the Clean Air Act campaigns in California in part because there was less grass-roots activity involved, but largely to keep the discussion manageable and nonrepetitious. Nuclear power issues are not discussed for the same reason.

2. By the same token, in those 16 years he had aroused strong feelings of opposition—not just among growers but among "average" people who may have felt he had already "won enough." The author encountered several Californians, in nonrandom conversations, who felt "it was time to redress the balance." This theme also cropped up in occasional letters to the editors.

3. Several state PIRGs have also been active on initiatives involving public utilities, hazardous waste, and other environmental and/or consumer issues. Thus they are gaining continuing experience in ballot campaigns as well as in ongoing lobbying.

4. The success of this sort of effort depends, of course, on the cooperation and interest of the media. Similar efforts in Massachusetts in 1982 met with mixed success depending on local editors and reporters. Another strategic justification for group efforts like cleanathons, parades, or mass leafleting is the positive effect on morale of campaign volunteers.

5. John Shockley (1980: 29-33) tells a similar story about the 1976 campaign in Colorado. The supporters were outspent by $19,283 to $591,398; they faced competition from five other liberal causes including a nuclear power proposal, a move to repeal the ERA, and two proposals on utilities which absorbed the energy of COPIRG, an organization that might have worked for the bottle bill. The supporters, in addition, began with overconfidence, given initial high levels of voter support.

6. I was an active volunteer on the Waltham, Massachusetts, bottle bill committee (while simultaneously working against the death penalty in a campaign that contrasted in every major way). In addition, I was in close touch with Mass-PIRG researchers and with five students who did field work with the Boston headquarters. One of my efforts (which failed) was to convince Mass-PIRG to place more emphasis on the safety argument, using the Michigan experience as a guide. Thus much of the text on this issue is based on participant observation.

7. One problem faced by the PIRGs is a lack of continuity and experience in their (poorly) paid leaders. Within a year of the bottle bill campaign, the three key people with whom the author had been involved had all either returned to college or taken jobs elsewhere. (The organization is staffed by a combination of paid and unpaid volunteer college students, making high turnover inevitable. The Waltham coordinator had been on leave from Princeton during the 1982 campaign.) Subsequent PIRG speakers who came to my classroom in search of volunteers on the hazardous waste issue were relatively inexperienced.

8. A similar rally was held in San Francisco on November 4. Another widely reported (and pictured) event was a demonstration, in war paint and Indian regalia, of 150 militant gays outside a debate held in Healdsburg between Senator Briggs and a gay schoolteacher who had been attacked by name in Brigg's statement in the *Voters Pamphlet*. This occurred on October 25.

9. There also was a successful campaign to restore the death penalty in Massachusetts in 1982, where opponents spent $56,187 to nothing for supporters. There was also very little visible activity by either side in this campaign.

10. This strategy was discussed by the opposition manager at length in the *Oregonian,* October 22, 1978.

11. We borrow this term from the Clamshell Alliance demonstrations at Seabrook, New Hampshire, and other movements using civil disobedience, though we are not sure the ERA supporters would use the term.

12. It is difficult to convey the somewhat unique spirit of this campaign. Many volunteers were political neophytes, sometimes bound together by friendship or affinity groups; many brought small children with them; the mood was at

times angry but generally buoyant. I was not involved (since I was working in a congressional campaign), but friends who were active compared the ERA campaign to the first Massachusetts campaign for Eugene McCarthy's presidency.

13. John Shockley (1980: 8) reports expenditures of $25,219 in a 1976 effort in Colorado to *repeal* the ERA (opponents of repeal spent $38,862; the effort was defeated 61-39%).

14. On this point see Shockley (1980: 17-18). He points out that supporters of the nuclear power initiative in Colorado disagreed on their primary goal: passing the initiative or educating the public on how to take control of their own destiny. Those who favored the former advocated bringing in scientific experts to counter the opponents' arguments; the latter group felt experts already had too much to say in major economic and political decisions.

15. Of course *any* medium—whether television ads, debates, or informal discussions in community centers—*can* be misused (to mislead, simplify, deceive) by skillful speakers. Continued deception or oversimplification would seem to be more difficult, however, at a series of informal, face-to-face meetings with time for questions and discussions as well.

16. Even more disturbing is the complete lack of activity *on either side* of some issues that would seem to merit more than newspaper editorials. These include the ban on school assignments on racial groups (Massachusetts, 1978), the proposed deep water port (Massachusetts, 1976), and the newsman's shield law (California, 1980).

7

VOTING BEHAVIOR:
CONFUSION AND RATIONALITY ON
BALLOT QUESTIONS

The voter's decision on ballot questions is potentially the purest form of "issue voting" that occurs in American politics. In theory, questions about public policy or procedures are posed without reference to long-standing partisan loyalties (and party platforms) or to the personalities, charisma, or rhetorical skills of candidates who espouse a particular position. In actual practice, as well, very few instances where major party positions on ballot questions were widely publicized or seen as relevant by either the campaigners or the media occur in this study. The major exceptions were the proposed constitutional convention in Michigan (1978) and, later in 1982, the series of referenda on reapportionment in California. Similarly, a close and widely publicized association between authors or candidate-supporters of initiative proposals and the arguments over those proposals was rare: Cesar Chavez and Howard Jarvis, and to a lesser extent Governors Brown and Dukakis, are the only cases where the association was striking.[1]

Given the lack of either party cues or spillover from the personalities and oratorical skills of prominent advocates, how do voters go about the potentially massive task of collecting and sifting the information needed to make a decision on ballot questions? What role do reference groups, broad ideologies, or symbolic arguments play in those decisions? And what difference (if any) do the mechanics of the ballot (length, wording, order of the questions, etc.) make for turnout or for voting outcomes? These are some of the important questions to be discussed in this chapter.

I will begin with some of the folklore found, both in campaign manuals and scholarly work, about voter responses in the ballot format, the origin and permanence of proposed changes, and alleged causes of confusion and negativism. I will then consider several explanations (most notably the concepts of "rational choice" and symbolic voting) of two major sets of issues, tax proposals and nuclear power regulations, with a brief consideration of allied economic issues and crime control proposals as well. This final discussion will integrate my findings with those of several major studies that utilized in-depth survey material.

Folklore about Voting on Ballot Questions

Three different kinds of explanations recur in the literature on ballot questions, all of which are addressed to the intense problems faced by voters in deciding on a large number of issues in a political milieu usually devoid of cues from candidates and parties. The first concerns the *mechanics of the ballot* itself, the kinds of proposals (e.g., initiatives vs. referenda) considered, and the context of the election (e.g., candidate races). The second might be termed the voters' reaction to their own (presumed) confusion: negative voting, abstention from voting, different responses to complex as opposed to simple proposals. Finally, a third level of explanation, more akin to the presidential and congressional voting studies, deals with the *substantive* reasons for voting choices in terms of either voter characteristics or (in the case of the few intensive surveys on ballot question preferences) broader attitudes toward, e.g., science and technology, taxes, racial integration, and the like. In this section I will discuss the first two sets of explanations.

BALLOT LENGTH AND POSITION OF QUESTIONS

Baus and Ross (1968: 345) argue, in a narrative that offers advice from their own experience as political consultants in California, that because the *length of the ballot* in itself creates problems for voters, the *order of questions* can be crucial to the decision on specific proposals. Thus propositions 1-3 "have a distinct edge"; by the time the voter reaches number 10, however, he/she "starts to fret, then gets irritated and becomes ever more minded to vote 'no' or to skip it altogether." Hence the jockeying for position that goes on in contacts between authors of ballot measures and the office of secretary of state.

Shockley (1980: 19) makes a related point when he explains voter rejection of a Colorado proposal to repeal the ERA partly in terms of the very large number of negative campaigns being fought (and won) on other propositions. Thus "the fact that the last eight initiatives on the ballot were all defeated probably means that in response to the overall campaigns some people simply voted against all of them." But John Mueller (1969: 1197-1212), in a much older study which included perusal of actual ballots cast in California campaigns, found voter avoidance of uniformity (i.e., yes or no voting) over a long stretch of the ballot. Thus there are contradictory expectations, all of which imply a somewhat thoughtless or mechanical response on the part of the voter.

To test these propositions I segregated the eight elections (out of 15) in which ten or more ballot questions were presented to voters. (This included two from Oregon, one from Michigan, and five from California. Massachusetts voters were asked to decide on only 6-9 questions per election in the 1976-80 years.) First I examined the relationship between passage or defeat of a proposal and the proposal's position on the ballot. Second, in order to check Baus and Ross's assertion that irritable voters skipped questions, I sorted propositions by the number of blanks per question (i.e., nonvoting). Table 7.1 shows that none of the expectations about the importance of ballot order is clearly supported. There is indeed somewhat more negative voting at the end of the ballot, but if this simply indicated voter impatience/fatigue, propositions in the middle position (4 9) would be rejected at a higher rate than those at the beginning. Instead, there is a drop in the middle. One tempting explanation might be to argue that bond issues are usually at the beginning, while initiatives (usually more controversial than proposals offered by the legislature) are usually at the end, hence the high approval rate in the middle. But it should be noted that this is *not* the line of reasoning Baus and Ross followed. Second, the bond-referendum-initiative ordering does not fit either Oregon or Michigan, since neither state voted on bond issues in these years, and in both cases there was some intermingling of initiatives and referenda.[2]

To test Shockley's suggestion that a largely negative mind-set, caused by intense negative campaigns on a series of initiatives, might lead to rejection of an otherwise acceptable proposal, I inspected the pattern for each campaign. While there was one case of six consecutive "no" votes (Oregon 1976), one of four nos (Cali-

TABLE 7.1: Relation between Ballot Position, Rejection of Propositions, and Number of Blanks on Propositions For Eight Elections Involving Ten or More Propositions*

| | Ballot Position of Propositions | | | |
	1-3 (N = 24)	4-9 (N = 48)	10 or more (N = 28)	Total (N = 100)
Proportion of Propositions Rejected	54%	33%	64%	47%
Proportion of blanks cast on propositions				
Highest 3 (# blanks) in election	17%	25%	29%	24%
Middle range	58%	56%	39%	52%
Lowest 3 (# blanks)	25%	19%	32%	24%
	100%	100%	100%	100%

*Oregon 1976, 1978; Michigan 1978; California June and November 1976, June 1978, June and November 1980. The table includes *all* ballot questions for these campaigns, not just the controversial measures studied in other chapters.

fornia, November 1980), and two cases of five consecutive "yes" votes, none of these fit the Shockley pattern since all were on a mixture of relatively uncontroversial referenda and highly debated initiatives, and none of the "runs" was predominantly liberal or conservative in direction.

There were, in fact, two consistent elections in regard to negative or positive voting, both of which involved a relatively small number of proposals. In 1978 Massachusetts voters *approved* all seven ballot questions, while in 1980 Michigan voters *rejected* all seven with equal consistency. In both cases, however, there was no clear ideological pattern to the vote: Michigan rejected tax cuts, prison construction, and a reduced drinking age, while Massachusetts accepted both tax classification and a proposal *forbidding* school assignments on racial grounds.[3] Thus I find no more support for the idea of an overall mind-set, whether negative or positive, than I did for the common myth that voters reject or abstain on the final proposals on a long ballot. (Mueller's suggestion that voters attempt to break "runs" cannot be tested without, of course, examining individual ballots.) Finally, it can be seen that while the proportion of propositions with a high percentage of nonvoting

"blanks" increased among those at the end of long ballots, so did
the proportion of popular (i.e., low blank) propositions. There is
simply no clear trend to indicate that voters skip questions as they
approach the end of a long ballot.

INITIATIVE VS. REFERENDA; AMENDMENTS VS. STATUTES

Another very common scholarly observation is that voters are
more likely to give the legislature the benefit of the doubt on referenda than they are to approve the popularly authored initiative.
Lowenstein (1982: 549), in fact, cites a 73% approval rate for referenda, in contrast to 27% on initiatives, in 1968-80 California
elections. He goes on to speculate, however, that the difference is
based more on the relative *merits* than on the *origins* of the two sets
of proposals. A related observation is made by Eugene Lee (1978:
98) in regard to voting behavior on constitutional as opposed to
statutory change. Lee implies that voters are more reluctant to
change the constitution than they are to enact new laws by popular
means, for the obvious reason that constitutional change is seen as
more basic or more permanent. Since both Lee and Lowenstein
were discussing California, I shall examine the data separately for
the four states to check for regional variations. Table 7.2 shows the
results.

While the information in Table 7.2 supports Lowenstein's (California) finding that voters approve referenda more readily than
initiatives, the trend is by no means consistent across states. In
Michigan, in fact, voters more readily accepted initiatives, but in
the context of the lowest overall approval rate of our four states.
Massachusetts, with the highest overall approval rate, also was relatively more negative about initiatives than was the case in other
states. I am inclined to agree with Lowenstein that while the voter's
relative preference for referenda may be true for some states, the
finding needs to be treated with caution in the context of voter-
perceived merits of specific proposals. Note that two of the rejected
referenda (one each in California and Oregon) represented hastily
drafted legislative alternatives to tax cap initiatives. It seems reasonable that voters are far less likely to "defer" to the legislature in
these circumstances than may be the case with ideas originating in
the legislature itself before a popular initiative forced this action.

In contrast to the partial support given to the Lowenstein argu-

TABLE 7.2: Approval Rate: Initiatives vs. Referenda and Constitutional Amendments vs. Statutes

State	Referenda (N = 78)	Initiatives (N = 42)	Advisory Questions and Bonds (N = 12)	Total (N = 132)
Mass. (N = 21)	86%	17%	100%	67%
Mich. (N = 22)	30%	42%	—	36%
Oregon (N = 32)	44%	29%	50%	38%
Calif. (N = 57)[a]	63%	20%	44%	53%
Total	59%	29%	50%	50%

State	Constitutional Amendments (N = 84)	Statutes, Bonds, and Advisory Questions (N = 48)	Total (N = 132)
Mass. (N = 21)	85%	25%	62%
Mich. (N = 22)	32%	67%[b]	36%
Oregon (N = 32)	50%	28%	38%
Calif. (N = 57)	58%	47%	54%
Total	55%	38%	50%

a. The June 1976 California election is omitted since I did not have access to the full ballot pamphlet and do not know the proposal status of any but the controversial measures.
b. There were only *three* constitutional amendments proposed in Michigan, of which two passed. All other cells in the table contain at least eight cases.

ment on referenda versus initiatives, no such support is evident from the table for Lee's expectations on amendments versus statutes. In fact the only state to demonstrate the expected trend, Michigan, is suspect because the 67% approval rate for proposed statutes is based on a total of three cases. Thus it appears, contrary to Lee's expectations, that constitutional amendments, especially in Massachusetts and Oregon, are markedly more likely to be approved by the voters than statutory changes. One reasonable explanation is somewhat akin to Lowenstein's earlier argument. Given the inclusion in all four state's constitutions of mundane as well as "basic" law, and thus equally mundane proposals for constitutional change (for example, changing state census-taking procedures in Massachusetts), the anticipated awe is probably not universally present in regard to state constitutions. It is likely that voters decide more on the perceived merits of the argument than on the basis of the permanence of the proposed change, even assuming that they are aware of the difference.

THE "CONFUSED VOTER" AND NEGATIVE VOTING

One of the most common assertions in studies of ballot questions stresses the relation between voter confusion and negative voting. Baus and Ross (1968: 61) make the classic statement:

> Ballot propositions, being written by lawyers, have a degree of complexity, and some are Gordian knots of language. This very intricacy interposes a barrier to success. *What the voter does not understand he may reject. The confused voter votes "no".* (emphasis added)

This statement appears, almost verbatim, in several scholarly studies of specific propositions (Lee, 1978: 117; Shockley, 1980: 34; Lutrin and Settle, 1975: 356; Break, 1979: 44) and in editorials in both the *Los Angeles Times* and the Portland *Oregonian*. In fact, almost the only scholar to question the assertion, at least in its simplest form, is Lowenstein (1982: 549ff), who points out (1) that in California, at least, more propositions are accepted than rejected, and (2) that the "confusion" theory only makes sense if it is reformulated to include the idea of fear, i.e., he asserts that confusion and fear can be stimulated by a controversial negative campaign.

I have already shown, in the present data, that at least as many propositions pass as fail even when divided into "long" or "short" ballots. But the earlier chapter on campaign finance demonstrates that a very large number of propositions initially favored by voters (according to polls) have been defeated by negative high-spending campaigns. Thus it seems imperative to break this proposition into its logical components and to test it (if possible) using these same data. I will then be able to move on to a more general consideration of voter rationality.

Most of the scholars and campaign analysts cited believe that voter confusion (and thus negative voting) is caused by the large number of propositions and both the length and complexity of individual proposals on the ballot. Presumably, then, a negative campaign exploits this confusion to induce a "no" vote. I have already cast some doubt on the negative effect of long ballots by showing that placement at the end of the ballot does not imply a high rejection rate (Table 7.1), but what about the overall rejection rate in "long" versus "short" ballots? The answer here is that the length of ballot does *not* predict rejection rate: in fact, voter approval is slightly *more* likely on long ballots than on short ballots. I find, as reported earlier, a 53% approval rate for the 100 measures considered on ballots containing ten or more ballot questions. In the remaining seven campaigns, where ballots contained less than ten questions, only *44%* of the 48 measures were approved.[4] While the difference is clearly not startling, it certainly is sufficient to cast considerable doubt on sheer number of questions as an explanation for negative voting.

The next component in the "confused voter" hypothesis is somewhat more difficult to operationalize. The *clarity* of ballot questions might be computed by a word count of questions or by an assessment of the difficulty of language. It may be recalled from Chapter 4 that Brestoff (1975: 935) cites a Loyola University study of the reading difficulty of 28 California propositions (including 22 at the state level) which found that 18 were at the level of sixteenth grade or above, with none below the eleventh-grade comprehension level. David Magleby (1984: 118-119) reports similar results for descriptions in voters pamphlets from California and Oregon (seventeenth grade level) in contrast to an only slightly easier level for Rhode Island and Massachusetts (fifteenth grade). Neither of these techniques (rating the length of question or reading level), however, takes into account the difficulty of understanding the issue itself, e.g., the inherent complexities of property tax or nuclear regulation issues versus the simplicity of changing the drinking age, *apart* from length or difficulty of language.

Thus I have rated all of the 133 propositions whose full text was readily accessible on a simple 1-4 scale of "clarity," trying to take into account the combination of length, wording, and inherent complexity of the issue, as well as watching for misleading cues on the direction of vote required to achieve the voters purposes.[5] (My assessment was also checked with three nonacademics, one of whom was currently in the eleventh grade.) While this is both an impressionistic and inelegant measure, it may suffice for present purposes, namely, to examine in a rough way the relationship between "clarity" of proposals and rejection of more proposals by voters. Table 7.3 reports the results:

It can readily be seen that the data, *on the whole,* support the "confused voter votes no" hypothesis if it is assumed that the lack of clarity per se leads to confusion which, in turn, leads to the nega-

TABLE 7.3: Relation between Clarity of Measure and Rejection by
Voters

	High[a] (N = 43)	Medium (N = 52)	Low (N = 38)	Total (N = 133)
Percentage voting "no"				
Massachusetts (N = 21)	29%	33%	60%	38%
Michigan (N = 22)	38%	75%	83%	64%
Oregon (N = 32)	54%	73%	63%	63%
California (N = 58)	53%	38%	53%	47%
Total	47%	50%	61%	52%

a. The rating technique is explained in the text. High = 1, Medium = 2, and Low combines 3 and 4, since numbers were too small to permit a separate analysis by states.

tive vote. Massachusetts and Michigan—as well as the overall trend—conform strongly to the pattern. But problems arise in regard to both California and Oregon, where no such linear pattern appears. (In fact, California voters rejected the 15 "high" clarity and the 19 "low" clarity proposals at exactly the same rate, i.e., 53%.) Thus I am somewhat wary about an immediate embrace of the "confusion" hypothesis, *at least in its original formulation.* I am more inclined to agree, instead, with Lowenstein that it is not always confusion alone that produces a negative vote but, rather, confusion exploited by an agressive advertising campaign on the negative side.

An examination of the 38 low-clarity issues in Table 7.3 shows that 14 (or 37%) were high-spending proposals, most of which have been considered at length above: property tax cuts, nuclear power issues, the Chavez Amendment, the nonsmoking proposals, rent control and the like. In fact *13 of these 14 proposals were rejected by voters.*[6] This rejection rate of 93% for 14 high-spending controversial proposals contrasts with 42% rejection for the remaining 24 low-clarity (low-spending) proposals. I thus conclude that the confusion hypothesis is correct—but only because in some cases high-spending opponents are there to take advantage of that confusion. In cases where high spending did *not* occur, fewer than half the low-clarity proposals were rejected.

In summary, most of the folklore about voting behavior on ballot questions that arises from either the mechanics of the ballot or the confusion of voters does not stand up well under close scrutiny. Although I have found some increase in negativism at the end of a long ballot, a consistently higher rate of blanks has not been demonstrated—indeed there are some very heavily voted on propositions numbered in the teens. While the expectation that referenda were approved more frequently than initiatives was confirmed for three states, Michigan failed to fit the pattern; in contrast, Michigan seemed to be the *only* state that showed the anticipated preference for statutory proposals over constitutional amendments. I thus concluded that most of the folklore about the "mechanics" of ballots and ballot measures is better interpreted in terms of specific issues or campaigns.

Finally, I do not find strong support for the frequent assertion that "the confused voter votes no." There is, contrary to expectations, a higher approval rate on long (presumably confusing) ballots than on short ballots. Second, while there seems to be a modest relationship between estimated clarity and approval rate (i.e., low clarity implies negative voting), that relationship all but disappears when the level of campaign spending (and, thus, media attention) on low-clarity measures is taken into account. The negative voting takes place more frequently on high-spending, high-media measures than on the low-profile measures where voters might reasonably be confused. This leads to the conclusion that it is the presence of opponents who exploit confusion, rather than potential confusion alone, that leads to the "no" vote.

It is now time to consider the substantive issues themselves and the long-deferred topics of rationality, self-interest, and symbolic voting.

Rationality, Self-Interest, and Symbolic Politics

I have so far treated the voter as a relatively passive *object*, acted on by money thrown into elaborate and sometimes deceptive media campaigns or by grass-roots activities reaching voters through community contacts, organizations, and informal gatherings. Thus ballot formats, length and complexity of questions, and the likelihood of voter confusion or irritability as well have been considered in a sort of vacuum apart from the voter's substantive preferences and the predispositions or values that led to those choices.

It is now time to examine those predispositions and the knotty arguments over voter rationality, the relative importance of self-interest and symbolic voting, the role of ideology, and the like. I shall do this inferentially, from a combination of sources including:

(1) the aggregate data on the 1976-80 elections in the four states, as well as census data and other information on the state's economies, location of major industries, and general population characteristics;

(2) poll data and interviews with voters reported in major regional newspapers, informed as well by my conversations with voters in Massachusetts and California;

(3) studies, including some intensive surveys, by other scholars on tax and environmental issues.

Let me note at the outset David Magleby's (1984: 123ff) helpful and systematic discussion of the conditions necessary for "voter rationality" on ballot issues: interest, knowledge; multiple sources of information; attentiveness to the major campaign issues; ability to read and use the ballot pamphlet; and ability to translate general policy choices into the vote. It is tempting to settle, at this point, for a reassessment of his somewhat pessimistic conclusions, applying them in turn to the present set of controversies. (Several of these conditions have been considered earlier, particularly in regard to the ballot pamphlet and the question of attentiveness.) I am, however, concerned in this chapter with "rationality" in a slightly different sense: namely, not only the ability but the *propensity* of voters to pursue their self-interest through their choices on ballot questions. Is rationality, in this sense, an important or valuable tool in explaining the campaigns and results observed?

Recent work by David O. Sears and Jack Citrin (1982) found the concept of "self-interest" to be of limited value in explaining voting behavior (and activism) on property tax proposals in California. Quite apart from Sears and Citrin's reservations, I question the applicability of either the concept or the rational choice model itself to voting decisions on ballot questions, even in cases of high economic impact.

I do not want to sidetrack our present discussion by a lengthy explanation of the various "rational choice" models. I refer to the large body of scholarly work, beginning with Downs (1957) Riker and Ordeshook (1968) and others, that postulates something akin to a cost-benefit or marginal utility analysis of the voter not only in voting decisions but in regard to political activities in general. There are several (related) problems with the explanatory value of these models as applied to decisions on ballot questions.

First, there are a multiplicity of *economic* roles that individuals take which may be relevant to specific proposals. For example, the city or county employee of the public works department may be more concerned with taxes on his home in the San Fernando Valley than he is with the possible loss of his job.[7] The homeowner (and consumer of electricity) may worry about the prospect of a cut in salary because a flat electric rate will increase her large employer's costs and neglect possible savings in her own electric bill. Obviously a calculus of benefits and costs is theoretically possible in these and analogous circumstances; I suspect that it is very unlikely to take place for most voters, and it would certainly be complex if the goals/values dictated by these different roles *are in conflict*. I am not arguing that voters more often act as producers than consumers—an inference perhaps implied by the second example—but that most voters do not see the effort involved in making such a calculation as worth the trouble given the easier out of avoiding the dilemma by opting for a simpler or more symbolic answer. In fact, they simply may not be *aware* of a dilemma in the first place.

Second, there is probably sufficient cynicism, especially in Massachusetts, about the probable future behavior of government officials *after* a new tax proposal is approved to make voters wary about even a proposal that seems beneficial. This cynicism may also lead voters to reject the public statements on economic impact that might assist rational calculations of individual or community costs and benefits, particularly if campaign antagonists are arguing about the truth of such statements. Thus the almost universal rejection even by low-income people of the graduated income tax in Massachusetts, arising partly from fear of *any* change in the tax structure. Thus the skepticism in both California and Massachusetts about massive cuts in public services that might result from property tax caps.[8]

Third, rational choice theory seems to ignore the problems most people have in understanding the specific impact of different kinds of economic proposals on their own lives. Sears and Citrin (1982: 117-118) point out that one of the appeals of Proposition 13 was the very *concrete,* immediate tax benefit promised to homeowners, even tabulated in major newspapers in terms of assessed property values. Many other tax proposals that did not pass (including Jarvis II in 1980) lent themselves to no such simple calculations. How many voters understand the differential benefits of a graduated income tax in comparison with, e.g., the more regressive sales tax?[9] (My college students have trouble with the concepts of "regressive" and "progressive" taxes, again complicated by intense cynicism about how tax policy is implemented.)

If it is difficult for individuals to understand the economic impact of many proposals, or even to believe what they are told, issues like rent control, bottle bills, and nuclear power regulation defy the imagination in this regard. Voters are no longer dealing with the concrete question of how much they will pay on an occasional meals tax or twice a year at the town assessor's office; they are now estimating long-range effects on electric bills if construction is halted on the local nuclear power facility or calculating effects on both the grocery bill and the state economy if a bottle bill is approved.

Finally, there seems to be no room in the rational choice model for noneconomic values to be taken adequately into account. I am not referring to the problem of quantifying noneconomic goods. Rather, I am concerned with the question of whether some strongly ideological or moralistic voters even weigh economic costs (for themselves, their community, or society) on some questions, e.g., the nuclear power questions or the nuclear freeze, abortion or the death penalty. Granted, economic arguments may be made in the campaign on defense jobs lost, the high costs of hydroelectric or thermal power, or the cost to the state of life imprisonment versus the lengthy appeals process for those on death row. I doubt very much, however, if these arguments are even *relevant* to those voters while decisions rest on moral imperatives or on deeply held beliefs that have little to do with immediate costs and benefits. It might be noted, in passing, that these are some of the issues about which the recently ballyhooed "gender gap" seems to be relevant; oddly enough, although large numbers of women supported Proposition 13, the gender gap also seems to appear in regard to tax cap as well.[10]

Because of these problems, I am more inclined to seek other sorts of explanations, such as the concept of symbolic voting currently

used by Sears and Citrin, but with antecedents going back at least
to Edelman (1971) if not to Walter Lippmann (1922), and to draw
on some of the debate about issue voting—notably the suggested
distinction by Carmines and Stimson (1980) between "hard" and
"easy" issues. Finally, I shall have occasion to use some of the work
of students of social and political movements particularly in discussing the various nuclear proposals.

The next task is to try to explain *differences* in voting behavior
on some issues that arose in several states, drawing on whichever
model, theory, or partial theory seems helpful, including some
elements of rational choice analysis. I do not believe that an effort
to "test" different theories against the vast ballot question terrain
mapped here is appropriate. It is important to explore, however,
which kinds of explanations are most helpful on what categories of
questions. This is crucial for any future integration of explanations
about voting on referenda and voting in presidential elections.

Property Tax Proposals

All four states had at least one election in the 1976-80 period in
which a property tax cap and a more moderate alternative reached
the ballot; in each state at least one related tax controversy arose in
at least one additional election. But outcomes differed. In both California and Massachusetts voters approved the more stringent measure. In Michigan the tax cap was rejected while the alternative was
approved. Oregon voters rejected both in 1978 and continued to
do so in subsequent elections (although by a very narrow margin
in 1982). In addition, while Californians very clearly saw Propositions 13 and 8 as noncompatible alternatives, there was some doubt
about this in Oregon and Michigan, while in Massachusetts the
alternative, which dealt with educational funding only, was all but
ignored. To understand these differing choices, each campaign
must be examined separately.[11] (Our discussion will concentrate
on the major two-proposition campaigns, only discussing the subsequent or earlier proposals when essential to the explanation.)

CALIFORNIA

California's Proposition 13 (passed in June 1978) came in the
wake of almost a decade of discontent which included three different

defeated ballot measures, including one by then Governor Reagan. The discontent was somewhat analogous to that in Massachusetts: much-needed reform, in the form of adopting uniform tax assessment procedures, had the effect of massively increasing homeowners' property taxes. As if this weren't bad enough, average home prices doubled in as little as five years in major urban areas—Los Angeles, San Francisco, San Diego. Reassessment kept pace: Sears and Citrin (1982: 22) cite increases of about 30% per year for counties south of Los Angeles, while the San Francisco *Chronicle* (May 8 and 17, 1978) gave even higher figures for Marin and Santa Clara counties in the north. The main reason for this extraordinary degree of inflation in the housing market, much higher than in the other three states, seems to be the continued rapid growth of population, particularly in southern California and "Silicon Valley" (the area around San Jose in the north). Finally, the increase in the size of government, especially in public safety and *welfare* functions, was considerably higher than the national average, a fact known and resented by many. One saving grace, not widely recognized by voters, was that the size of the state surplus had also increased along with state spending.

In any case, the confluence of high taxes, high inflation, and increasing awareness of a large public sector that was seemingly wasteful laid the groundwork for an electorate that was, by late May 1978, angry and intensely aware of what they saw as economic wrongs to them, particularly as homeowners. (Over 60% of the population owned their homes.) Their anger was nurtured as well by a legislature which had been unable to agree on a tax reform measure in the 1977 session, and which only "got its act together" in time to offer Proposition 8, a smaller tax cut, with the added provision for classifying residential and industrial property at different assessment rates, in early 1978, at the very time Jarvis was collecting signatures for Proposition 13. This was seen by many as too little and too late.

Were taxes, and especially the property tax, exceptionally high in California? According to most specialists, the answer is yes, although the Massachusetts burden was comparable. (The total tax burden, as a ratio of total taxes to total personal income, was, according to Frank Levy [1979: 77], 9.2 in California in comparison with a national average of 6.3. Only Hawaii and New York were higher. Massachusetts scored 9.1, Michigan 7.0, and Oregon 6.3.) Property taxes provided one-third of the total revenues collected by local units of government, which included not only towns and school districts but counties and special districts handling expensive functions like water, irrigation, and soil conservation. In addition, most voters were probably highly aware of the state income tax and state sales tax, which together provided 67% of the total state revenue in 1978 (Attiyeh and Engel, 1979: 131-141).

The Proposition 13 campaign has been discussed above. What has not been sufficiently emphasized, in all probability, is that it not only involved over $2 million expenditures on both sides but a very large amount of grass-roots campaigning by proponents, especially at the beginning. Simultaneously with the impressive media campaign, a large number of ordinary citizens went out to participate in local forums and debates; Jarvis and other leaders also encouraged supporters to saturate local radio talk shows with their calls. And literally no day passed in the two months before the election without at least one long story, and usually several, in the *Los Angeles Times*.

Despite this intense coverage and involvement by supporters, however, the Field Poll showed a close race through early May with 42% pro, 39% con, and fully 19% undecided. (This was an improvement over April when 48% were undecided.) It is thus entirely possible that Proposition 13 would not have passed, given the traditional erosion of support on so many propositions, if it weren't for the very poor timing of the Los Angeles tax assessor's office in mailing notices of reassessment in mid-May. The average increase of 17.5% (reported by the *Los Angeles Times* on May 16), followed by an announcement of rollbacks in response to the outcry, which were then rescinded after a protest about preferential treatment from those not due to be reassessed until the following year, transformed what might have been a gradually dwindling and relatively narrow "revolt" into what Sears and Citrin (1982: 222ff) call a "surge of recklessness, a period of nearly blind emotion" that rapidly spread to other parts of the state and to some of the least involved. This was probably the single most decisive event of the campaign, and one strongly reflected in the polls: 57% pro, 34% con, and 9% undecided among those interviewed during the last week in May (San Francisco *Chronicle*, June 2, 1978). In the end, Proposition 13 was approved by 65% of the voters; the alternative, Proposition 8, was defeated, 47-53%.

MICHIGAN

In November 1978, five months after California passed Proposition 13, 17 states considered tax proposals, most of which involved either a shift in the tax burden or a limitation on state expenditures. Oregon and Michigan were two of the four considering Proposition 13-type local property tax caps and were the two states to defeat the proposals.[12] Michigan voters, however, who considered other tax proposals in the 1976 and 1980 campaigns, approved a "moderate" alternative in 1978, while Oregon voters rejected three different tax cuts in 1978 and 1980.

The Michigan tax alternative (called "Headlee" after its sponsor) had first been introduced as an initiative in the 1976 election and defeated 57-43%. The major purpose was to limit all state taxes and expenditures (to 8.3% of personal income) and to forbid state expansion of local programs unless state funding was provided for such activities. It received considerable support from the business community (and from Milton Friedman) and initial public support in the polls as well, but opponents, including the governor and the Michigan Education Association, utilized an expensive media campaign against the proposal.

By 1978 Michigan saw itself in increasingly serious economic straits. Unemployment, particularly in the auto industry, was rising (it was to reach 14% by 1980). A large segment of the business community saw the state at a competitive disadvantage with other industrial states because of a very high state budget in comparison with taxable income. Many felt the item-by-item budgetary process to blame, given a strong interest group system in the state (Mariotti, 1978: 15-26). The total tax burden, as discussed above, was not so high as in California and Massachusetts but was well above the national average. Thus the 1978 campaign saw three proposals relevant to the tax and budgetary problem.

The first (Proposal E) was a reintroduced version of the 1976 Headlee proposal, with the limit on state taxes raised to 9.3% of personal income. The second (Proposal J) was a more radical, California-style property tax cap dubbed "Tisch" after its conservative sponsor. The third, providing for state vouchers for both private and public education, also would both require state tax support for education and forbid the use of local property taxes for school expenses. Supported by private and parochial school advocates, it never received the campaign attention of the others.

While campaign expenditures were moderately high (a total of about $500,000 in support and almost $800,000 in opposition to all three proposals), and an extensive media battle was waged, the level of rhetoric and anger never matched the California feelings about Proposition 13. Arguments were very similar on both sides—antitaxes, waste, and inefficiency, plus opposition to a level of government spending that discouraged business investment or expansion, versus the loss of public services and the threat to public education. Tisch urged his supporters to oppose the Headlee proposal as an ineffective measure; the most vocal opponents (led by Mayor Young of Detroit and the Michigan Education Association) opposed all three proposals and frequently attacked either two or three in the same advertisements. The Chamber of Commerce and the realtors, however, strongly supported Headlee, and even such opponents as the governor and major newspapers muted their opposition at least in part because of their fear of the more radical alternatives.

Toward the end, polls showed considerable confusion in the voters' minds about whether to view the Tisch and Headlee proposals as supplements or alternatives, and in fact the *Detroit Free Press* speculated on what would happen if all three passed. It was also clear that while many believed the Tisch proposal to be more effective, they feared its impact. There were no striking campaign errors, no last-minute notices of tax increases, and no colorful/controversial characters like Howard Jarvis. Thus Michigan voters saw neither a sharp choice nor an exciting, vitriolic campaign. In the end they opted for moderation, approving the Headlee proposal 52.5-47.5%, while rejecting Tisch and vouchers-for-education by majorities exceeding 70%.

In an almost anticlimatic, but far more bitter, campaign the Tisch proposal was reintroduced in 1980 and defeated by 74%. The irony, this time, was that the campaign also carried to defeat an M.E.A.-League of Women Voters proposal to shift a portion of school expenses from the local property tax to the state income tax. Patience was apparently wearing thin. Supporters of alternative measures[13] spent almost all of their energy and most of their funds in fighting Tisch, denounced this time by the governor as "perhaps the most pernicious proposal ever put before state voters." Thus the LWV-MEA proposal lost as well, by 79-21%, in an election in which Michigan voters (initially supportive of several proposals) rejected the entire set of seven ballot questions.

OREGON

There were two serious campaigns, in 1978 and 1980, for an Oregon property tax cap almost identical to Proposition 13. The first, Measure 6 in 1978, called for a 1.5% limit on property taxes, with future increases limited to 2.5% per annum. It would provide relief for homeowners and business alike, but not to renters. The more moderate legislative alternative, Measure 11, was proposed in haste as it had been in California—and was seen, by opponents and supporters alike, as a clear alternative, not as a supplement. It proposed a state refund of 50% of property taxes on owner-occupied dwellings (up to $1500); comparable relief for renters; a limit on state spending tied to the growth of personal income; and a freeze on property reevaluation for a year, while the legislature studied possible reforms in assessment practices. Note that this measure did not include business tax relief.

Incumbent Governor Straub, the AFL-CIO, and the Portland School Board were among those supporting Measure 11; Vic Atiyeh, Republican candidate for governor, supported Measure 6. A number of liberal groups and individuals, including the Oregon Education Association, opposed Measure 6 while avoiding a stand on Measure 11; the Association of Oregon Industries remained neutral. Many of these organizations took a "lesser of evils" approach, avoiding too strident an attack on the moderate alternative in their fear of Measure 6. The polls added to their caution, showing 53% of the voters supporting 6 (in comparison with 49% pro 11) in mid-October; by October 29 the figures were 45% for 6 and 38% for 11.

But Oregon's tax circumstances were different from California's and in many ways less conducive to a sense of urgency. While economic circumstances were disturbing (with rising unemployment and a troubled lumber industry), Oregon taxes were about at the national average. Oregon voters had considerable control over school budgets and other local budgets, too, in the form of periodic "levy" elections, a mechanism not present in California. And the Homeowners and Renters Relief Program had returned $90 million to over a million Oregon households, another program that did not exist in California. Finally, of course, Oregon (like Michigan and Massachusetts) did not have a large state surplus to cushion any drastic drop in school (or other vital) funding that might result from a huge cut in local budgets. Thus it is not altogether surprising that Measure 6 was defeated 52-48%; oddly enough, so was Measure 11 by a vote of 55-44%.

The reintroduction of Measure 6 in the 1980 election was greeted with far less alarm and attention than had arisen two years earlier. Despite the opposition of broad coalition of groups, including Associated Oregon Industries, and opposing campaign expenditures double the earlier Anti 6-Pro 11 sum ($300,000 to $153,000), not too much in the way of public speaking, press releases, or even newspaper coverage occurred until after October 20, when a spokesman for the Association of Oregon Cities warned publicly of overconfidence and announced that one of his polls showed Measure 6 leading by 11%. Apparently, he argued, most groups believed "It's So Bad It Won't Pass." The final weeks of the campaigns saw more coverage and more opposition activity. Ultimately the measure was rejected, in what had been a surprisingly quiet campaign, by 63-37%.

MASSACHUSETTS

Massachusetts was the last of the four states to consider a Proposition 13-type tax cap and indeed to adopt it by a strong 59-41% vote. To explain the outcome in this seemingly liberal state, I must briefly review the 1978 passage of tax classification (discussed at length in the preceding chapter) and a subsequent court ruling declaring it unconstitutional.

Passage of tax classification was the result of long-standing efforts by the legislature to provide some relief to homeowners in a state that relied excessively on the property tax and was forbidden by a 1974 court ruling to continue informal preferential treatment for residents in old neighborhoods. Citizens for Limited Taxation, a newly formed Massachusetts organization which was enthusiastic over Proposition 13, had been collecting signatures for a tax cap proposal; the legislature itself favored a graduated income tax (defeated in 1976) and refused to consider a rollback on state expenditures. Thus the classification amendment, which would change the constitution to allow differential rates for industrial and residential property, seemed a heaven-sent answer to the impasse. It was approved by the comfortable vote of 66.4-33.6% in 1978.

Alas, subsequent specific legislation was set aside by the State Supreme Judicial Court, which ruled differential rates unconstitutional in 1979. By this time Citizens for Limited Taxation and its new partner, the Massachusetts Council for High Technology (the political arm of about 100 electronics firms), were ready to take advantage of taxpayer fears and anger, and "Prop 2 $1/_2$" was born. In many ways it was more appealing than its California antecedent, in that it provided direct relief for renters as well as homeowners and also included a reduction of the much-hated annual tax on automobiles.

The campaign involved (by Massachusetts standards) very high spending (over $500,000) and an unusual amount of media coverage. (It should be recalled that California came much earlier to the use of professional public relations firms and expensive media-saturation campaigns, in comparison with any of the other three states. The 1976 bottle bill campaign, the first Massachusetts example of this type of operation, outraged many voters, as indeed did Mayor White's 1978 expenditures and advertisements for tax classification.) In any case, two large and vocal coalitions opposed each other in the Prop 2 $1/_2$ battle, with big business arrayed against a liberal-labor grouping that also included the junior U.S. senator and several mayors. (Real estate interests and the A.I.M. were not active.)

The arguments, advertisements, and campaign rhetoric paralleled that of California in 1976, as did the early polls, where about 40% of the voters reported not having heard of (or having no opinion on) the measure. Then, in a not quite believable parallel, the Boston tax bills were mailed out two weeks before the election, with news of an increase in the rate.[14] There was no official retreat and then recanting as there had been in California, but there was massive anger, not only in Boston but in the surrounding and most heavily populated part of the state. One week after the tax increase a *Boston Globe* telephone poll found 47% pro, 44% con, and only 9% undecided. This translated by election day into approval of Proposition 2 $1/_2$ by a 58.6-41.4% vote.

One brief addendum is needed to complete the story. Massachusetts voters, as in other states, were presented with an alternative to Proposition 2 $1/_2$ which apparently was not taken seriously by anyone but the sponsors, namely the Massachusetts Teachers Association. It proposed a three-year future freeze on property taxes at the 1980 level and a state takeover of 50% of local school expenses by 1984. No provisions for new state funding were written into the initiative. The proposal was denounced by the *Globe* as "nothing more than a symbolic gesture"; it was largely ignored, even by the MTA, which spent most of its efforts in fighting Proposition 2 $1/2$. The electorate defeated the proposal by 64.3-35.7%, apparently undeterred by lack of information on the subject.

INTERPRETATION

Thus there were three different outcomes of tax cap proposals: approval in Massachusetts and California, outright rejection in Oregon, and acceptance of a compromise measure by Michigan voters. My task is to explain this difference, with particular reference to self-interest and symbolic voting and other interpretations of the voter's stance.

At one level the answer is fairly obvious: in the case of both California and Massachusetts, massive resources (in terms of both dollars and large numbers of volunteers) were thrown into campaigns that virtually dominated public debate for the entire election period. No other proposition or candidate (including the presidential aspirants in Massachusetts) came close to attracting the media attention given to the tax cap initiatives. Especially after the ill-timed announcements, in both states, of higher tax bills, large segments of the public itself seemed obsessed with the controversy. This was a marked contrast to the relatively low-keyed, low-spending campaigns in Michigan and Oregon, where a host of other issues (e.g., drinking age and various law-and-order proposals in Michigan; nuclear power in Oregon) as well as hotly contested battles for statewide office competed for volunteers, financial resources, and public attention.

But this is begging the question, namely why the property tax issue came to dominate the electoral scene in two states but was treated less seriously in the others. One part of the answer probably is the higher relative tax burden in California and Massachusetts, as discussed above. A second crucial difference may be the way in which the voting alternatives were publicized and ultimately understood by the voters. And the third critical element was probably the difference between the states in the level of trust in the government bureaucracy itself (i.e., belief in official assertions about the *need* for high taxes and the fairness of the distribution of resources): an already high sense of cynicism and inequity was increased to an intolerable level for many voters by the eleventh-hour mailing of tax bills in California and Massachusetts. These last two points must be examined more carefully.

Consider first the question of voting alternatives in the four states. In California supporters and opponents apparently agreed that Proposition 13 and Proposition 8 were diametrically opposed. The No on 13-Yes on 8 funding was merged; the campaign slogans mirrored this dual concern. The Proposition 13 voter apparently received and acted on the message that Proposition 8 was a watered-down compromise to be defeated at all costs, while Proposition 13 opponents succeeded in convincing a more modest number of like-minded voters that support for Proposition 8 was the only way to defeat the more extreme measure. The message came through clearly in the advertisements, and polls indicated little or no confusion among voters about the meaning of their options. It did not seem to occur to many voters to vote against both proposals.

In Massachusetts there was similar clarity, but for different reasons: the Teachers' Union proposal for a tax freeze was never publicized as a serious alternative, was ultimately ignored by the media, and apparently was not treated as an option by moderate but economy-minded voters. Thus in the end opinion simply crystalized around the pros and cons of Proposition 2 $^1/_2$ alone.

The Michigan and Oregon campaigns were far more complex. According to polls, a significant portion of the Michigan public apparently saw nothing inconsistent in supporting both the Tisch and Headlee proposals; and although the badly outspent Tisch forces argued against this view, the Headlee proponents did little to dispel the confusion. In Oregon (in the 1978 campaign) major tax cap opponents apparently felt sufficiently confident to try yet another approach, i.e., to run a strong opposition campaign to Measure 6 (the tax cap) while remaining silent or neutral on the moderate alternative (Measure 11). Their confidence was rewarded with the defeat of both proposals.

But such contrasting campaign strategies (and outcomes) did not operate in a vacuum—thus the relevance of the third explanatory element mentioned above. I would argue that the either-or strategies used in California and Massachusetts were successful largely because they played on, and indeed had their roots in, the considerable latent anger and cynicism of the voters, a great many of whom cared less about the complexities of tax policies than about their perceptions of government waste and legislative indifference to the plight of the homeowner. In Oregon and Michigan, in contrast, concern over the survival of an already beleagured school system (Michigan) or of a proud park and forestry service among other public functions including higher education (in Oregon) seemed to argue for caution, in spite of some voter dissatisfaction with the level of taxes. Hence a campaign on alternative proposals culminating in the passage of the compromise measure in Michigan, but the defeat of both proposals in Oregon.

One of the most persuasive explanations of the success of California's Proposition 13 is James Buchanan's (1979: 692) application of the "free rider principle" to that campaign. That principle, derived from public finance theory (and long used as well by political scientists in studying incentives for organization membership), argues that:

> If the benefits of an action are concentrated and well-defined while the costs are diffused and generalized, we can predict that individuals will, in many circumstances, act without due regard to the costs involved . . . conversely, if the costs of an action are concentrated and well-defined while the benefits are diffused and generalized, we can predict that individuals will, in many circumstances, refrain from taking certain actions . . . because of a failure to take the benefits sufficiently into account.

Buchanan's main point in regard to Proposition 13 is that this proposal, in contrast to earlier (defeated) efforts to limit taxes, was formulated in a way to enable voters to concentrate on concrete benefits without much regard for costs (1979: 693). I would add, however, that the reality of *costs* were precisely what the opponents were attempting to drive home to the voter via literally dozens of statements about anticipated cutbacks in school and park programs and the like. The puzzling factor is why the Oregon (and to some degree Michigan) opponents succeeded in this effort while failing abysmally in California and Massachusetts.

The contrasting outcomes certainly cannot be explained by interstate differences in the skill and expenditure levels of opposition campaigns since the California and Massachusetts opposition was *more* vocal or, at any rate, more successful in publicizing prospective cuts in services. I believe, instead, that public attitudes toward their state government are probably most crucial. To wit, both California and Massachusetts voters had experienced a rapid rise in assessed property values, a frustrating lack of action by the state legislature, and a high degree of dissatisfaction with some public programs, notably welfare and (to a lesser degree) public education. As Musgrove (1979: 701) puts it, with regard to this latter point in California, "the image of the bloated powerthirsty bureaucrat has become a standard feature of political cartoons . . . and it is argued with a straight face that public expenditures could be cut by one-half without lowering public service levels one inch."

A CONCLUDING NOTE ON INDIVIDUAL DEMOGRAPHICS

My discussion has been directed to questions about differing outcomes on the property tax issue among the four states in the present study rather than to differences among individual voters. This is an appropriate focus given my "macro" level data, as well as the widespread agreement among scholars that individual demographic differences do not have much explanatory power for the tax issue. I have, however, computed correlations (by county) between major demographics and the voting outcome in three states and a city level correlation for Massachusetts. My findings conform to those of Sears and Citrin (1982) and of Lowery and Sigelman (1981), both of whose studies use individual responses. There is a weak positive relation, in all four states, between both the percentage of homeowners and the percentage of registered Republicans in the county and the vote for a property tax measure; the only other consistently strong relationship was with education (% of high school graduates), where the correlation was negative.

I did not pursue the subject at length both because of inferential problems in using county data, and because I am convinced by the existing studies that demographic explanations neglect some of the more interesting campaign phenomena, notably, the ability of public relations experts to transform "hard" issues into "easy" issues or to capitalize on symbolic discontent and thus to provide a convenient shortcut for some voters who might otherwise become involved in determining their economic self interest.

I do note, however, that a county-by-county correlation of the vote on tax reduction *alternatives* (e.g., Proposition 8 and 13 in California, Propositions 2 and 3 in Massachusetts, etc.) is consistent with the preceding conclusions on that point. While there is a *very high* negative correlation between the California votes on Proposition 8 and 13 (-0.81) the corresponding correlation was moderately positive in Oregon (+0.40) and very weak in the other two states. (Scattergrams confirmed the strong linear nature of the relation in California and Oregon as well.) This finding supports the idea that voters in California indeed saw Proposition 13 and Proposition 8 as clear alternatives without giving much consideration to opposing both, in contrast to Oregon where tandem opposition or support was common.

Voter Rationality on Nuclear Power and Other Ballot Issues

NUCLEAR POWER REGULATION

Only two of the issues included in this study have been widely researched in the recent scholarly literature. These are the property tax proposals just discussed and the issue of nuclear power regulation. (Fluoridation referenda, widely studied in the past, have received little recent attention; the Oregon proposal, in any event, was not paralleled recently in the other three states.) Three studies seem particularly relevant to understanding not only the voting outcomes on nuclear power but of the whole question of the voting public's ability to deal with complex, technical issues. Those are Benedict et al.'s (1980) mail survey in 1976, of voters in four states, including Oregon; Hensler and Hensler's (1979) intensive panel study of California voters for the Rand Corporation; and the analysis by Kuklinski and others (1982) of alternate explanatory modes, using the Hensler data. Both the Benedict and Kuklinski articles cite and draw upon an even more extensive earlier literature as well.

All three studies are clear on the important point that arguments over the development of nuclear power are not readily reduced to "easy" issues, in the sense that Carmines and Stimpson, for example, use the term. The nuclear issue is new to the agenda, it concerns means rather than ends, and (most important) it is a highly technical problem. Kuklinski and associates, using the Rand data that is reported in the Hensler study, test three different decision-making modes of voters (1982: 619): (1) an instrumental approach using cost-benefit analysis; (2) use of reference group cues to reduce information costs; (3) a reliance on "core values" from the past, notably general attitudes toward technology and/or political ideology.

They find, basically, two sharply contrasting ways of reaching a voting decision, dividing the "more knowledgeable" 20% and the "less knowledgeable" 80% in the sample, defined by cumulative responses to an information scale on the workings of nuclear power. The knowledgeable voters rely relatively heavily on political ideology, which also colors their *cost-benefit calculations;* the less knowledgeable draw on their general attitudes toward technology and upon group cues insofar as those are available and accurately perceived. Kuklinski argues that the ability to apply political ideology to a new issue requires a degree of informed sophistication not characteristic of most unknowledgeable voters, who instead fell back on more general attitudes toward technological development, the role of experts, the importance of efficiency as a value, and the like.

Kuklinski's findings are consistent with both the Benedict work on a four-state sample and the more intensive (but less theoretically oriented) work of the Henslers. The Benedict study found a very strong relationship between approval of technology and opposition to nuclear power regulation. They also found a more modest relationship between opposition or support and self-identification as conservatives or liberals. While no effort was made to divide the Benedict sample on knowledgeability, both studies seem to support the idea of two rough clusters in the population, one of which is conservative, protechnology, and pronuclear power, in contrast to a less scientifically knowledgeable, antitechnology, liberal antinuclear group.

It is impossible to do justice, in a brief fashion, to the highly complex results of the Hensler (1979) study. The most important findings for present purposes are:

1) Beliefs about nuclear power and other energy issues were far more important in explaining the vote than either general political orientations or social background characteristics;
2) Most nuclear power support came from the belief that the country needed more energy, and *not* from a belief in economic or environmental advantages of nuclear plants;
3) Most opponents (75%) cited safety concerns (plant accidents, meltdowns, plant explosions); some were also concerned about radioactive waste;

4) Some indirect explanatory power was found in group orientations, i.e., individuals who trust environmental groups were
more likely to oppose nuclear power, while those who trust scientists, the Republican Party, or business leaders were likely to
support nuclear power; but the effects of group orientations of
voters were not as strong as their beliefs about energy, the environment, and safety issues;

5) Similarly, while self-identified liberals and Democrats were
more likely to oppose nuclear power, ideology and party orien-
tation had less explanatory power (for the individual's vote) than
beliefs about safety, energy, and the like;

6) While California nuclear power opponents argued (after the election) that the imbalance in election expenditures, the wording of
the ballot question, and the campaign emphasis on a "nuclear
shutdown" and a loss of jobs created confusion among voters,
the net effect of this confusion or distortion was actually too
small to affect the final outcome of the election.

The Hensler (1979: 10) study is most interesting in what it has to
say about the effect (or lack thereof) of the campaign. The authors
not only find that voter confusion (while a fact) was insignificant
for the outcome; they imply in a continuation of the same discussion, that neither the high-spending opponents nor the grass-roots
supporters of Proposition 15 were entirely successful in bringing
their package of arguments home to the voter. While the opposition
was successful in convincing voters that the election was a simple
choice between continued nuclear development and a virtual halt to
construction, warnings about dire economic consequences (especially the "fewer jobs" argument) apparently "fell on deaf ears."
Similarly, and this seems a crucial point (1979: 7), the authors of
the initiative never succeeded in selling the safety issue to the public.
The Henslers argue, first, that opposition to nuclear power plants
seems "to crystallize only from a firm, coherent conviction that
they are dangerous. People who see them as neither safe nor risky,
or even as a little risky, are more likely to be favorable than unfavorable." They then go on to assert (1979: 10) that:

Had the proposition been construed more narrowly on grounds
related to safety, for example, had it offered the option to invest
additional resources in plant safeguards or in strengthening radioactive waste management regulation, the results might have been
different.

It may be recalled that, in explaining the success of the second nuclear referendum in Oregon (in 1980), I discussed a multiplicity of causes, including the Three Mile Island accident in the intervening years, the more nearly equal level of campaign expenditures by the two sides, and the narrowing of the scope of the proposal as revised. Part of that narrowing removed some of the plausibility of the argument that nuclear power would be *banned* by passage; another element was an intensive focus on safety regulations. Thus the Hensler prediction, if it were possible to remove the confounding effect of Three Mile Island, which of course also heightened national awareness of safety problems, seems to be supported by the Oregon outcome.

VOTING CUES, RATIONALITY, AND COMPLEX ISSUES

Many theory-building efforts on issue voting, and more specifically on voters' decisions about ballot questions, have focused on a set of dichotomies: "easy" versus "hard" issues (Carmines and Stimpson, 1980), "style" versus "position" issues (Berelson et al., 1954), "rational" or "instrumental" versus "symbolic" voting (Sears and Citrin, 1982), or, adding a third possibility, models involving instrumental motives versus reference group cues and "core values" (Kuklinski et al., 1982). Yet my examination of campaigns and voting behavior on two complex issues, property tax caps and nuclear power regulation, shows that such simple distinctions may be misleading, or at least not very useful in explaining the vote. On the nuclear power issue in particular, even those who tried to make instrumental decisions apparently were far from being value-free in the process. As Kuklinski put it (1982: 656, emphasis added), "The subjective probabilities of informed citizens. . . , it turns out, relate strongly to their political ideologies. Liberals and conservatives, *especially when informed,* do not even make the same predictions."

On both the nuclear power and tax cap issues, furthermore, I have argued that campaign efforts tended to capitalize on, and foster, the tendency to transform complex or "hard" issues into "easy" ones. An issue about the safety of nulcear plants became, for many opponents, a vote against technology itself. Similarly, the issue of an equitable distribution of the tax burden became, again for opponents (at least in California and Massachusetts), a vote against government waste and/or welfare fraud, permissive schools, or potholes. How many issues, among the large number considered in this study, demonstrate this phenomenon of hard issues transformed by groups cues, ideology, and simplistic campaigns into either symbolic decisions or seemingly instrumental decisions rationalized by ideology? All of the high impact position issues, and most of the environmental issues, seem to display this mix of the instrumental and symbolic. The 1976 Chavez proposal and the 1980 rent control proposal in California, for example, contained obscure, technical provisions beyond the reach of all but the most patient and expert of voters—provisions, it might be added, whose innate difficulty was further distorted by high-spending campaigns. Both proposals, however, lent themselves to sloganeering about individual rights versus government bureaucracy (or, conversely, about underdogs being hurt by greedy owners). In both cases economic antagonists (growers versus farm unions, owners of rental property versus renters) sought to enlarge the scope of conflict and to bring a previously private controversy into the public sphere—and in so doing, made contradictory claims in the name of the "public interest."

Is it any wonder that in the absence of clear partisan cues or ready tools for performing an instrumental calculation of self-interest (would home owners gain or lose from rent control? would consumers gain or lose from a unionized agricultural labor force? why should they care?), large numbers of voters fell back on vague ideological references, slogans, or their gut reactions to prominant claimants like Tom Hayden, Cesar Chavez, or Howard Jarvis? Or (in some cases) acted on their anger at campaign spending or distortions in campaign advertising?

A strong case can be made that the same sorts of campaign processes took place on many of the seemingly less complex "law and order" issues as well, for example, on mandatory sentencing, capital punishment, and most of all, on gun control. (The 1982 Victims Bill of Rights in California is also a prime example.) In most states capital punishment was probably an "easy" issue for experienced voters in that it was an old and nontechnical issue. If public opinion polls and newspaper interviews over a period of decades are credible, the gut issue was a moral one for many of both sides: the ethical arguments against the state putting people to death versus the belief that convicted murderers deserved the punishment to compensate for the death they had inflicted. Yet the arguments that surfaced in the print media in the three states in this study[15] stressed ends and means of a far more sophisticated nature: the effectiveness of deterrence, the relative cost to the public of life imprisonment versus the cost of extended appeals of the death sentence, and the like. While I have known student interns who came to change their views because of such calculations (particularly in regard to deterrence), I strongly suspect that most of the public uses the more complex cost-benefit approach *to rationalize* more affective or moralistic opinions developed over a period of years. The gun control issue, with even more elaborate arguments about costs and deterrence, seems to evoke similar responses, with the added factor of an obvious tie to liberal and conservative ideologies and reference groups.

My argument is that the act of voting on ballot issues may, for many voters on most issues, serve the sort of expressive purposes discussed by Berelson (1954) in regard to "style" issues and by Sears and Citrin (1982) in regard to "symbolic voting" even when public discussion highlights economic positions or rational means to solve complex social or political problems. In some cases the public campaign seems to reduce complex arguments to slogans; in others, the public arguments seem, in contrast, to mask or render respectable the more primitive emotions at work. All of this seems sadly reminiscent of Lasswell's definition of politics as the displacement of private needs onto public objects, rationalizing all the while in terms of the general good.

Does this mean that at least the "less knowledgeable" voters are *irrational* in the one political arena where they are forced to deal with issues per se, with no strong partisan or candidate cues on all but a handful of ballot questions? My answer is a qualified "no." The qualification stems from the earlier findings, detailed in Chapters 4 and 5, that high-spending media campaigns have succeeded in at least 15 cases out of the 50 studied from 1976 to 1980 in shifting voters in the direction of that spending to the degree that the outcome has changed. In too many instances this has been done primarily via tactics designed to simplify, to confuse, and/or to arouse strong emotional responses.

But rational choice theory, at least as modified by Riker and Ordeshook (1968: 25-29), leaves ample room for the motivating power of the *noninstrumental benefits* of information gathering by voters. While ethical (good citizen imperatives) and intellectual satisfactions are stressed in this regard by Riker and Ordeshook, there seems to be no a priori reason to exclude the opportunity for venting feelings of anger, helplessness, or revenge through the vote on provocative topics like property taxes, the death penalty, or abortion. Whether this sort of expressive activity is good for democracy or is what the early advocates of the mechanisms of direct democracy had in mind is another question, to be considered at length in Chapter 9. The point here is one of concurrence with Kuklinski et al. (1982) and Weatherford (1983), among others, that the dichotomy between symbolic and instrumental voting (at least on ballot issues) is both unhelpful and false.

Conclusion

In this chapter I have examined two kinds of information about the behavior of voters in regard to ballot questions. The first concerns voter responses to the voting situation itself: the kinds of propositions considered (initiatives vs. referenda, proposed amendments vs. statutes), the order and length of the ballot, and the complexity of questions. The second centers on questions of self-interest, rationality, symbolic voting, ideology, and group cues, particularly in regard to complex questions on issues like tax reduction, the environment, and the control of crime.

Because my data do not provide direct answers about voter motivation, consistency, intensity, and the like, I have utilized the work of others when available (notably on tax and nuclear power issues) to supplement my own sources. Thus my conclusion on voters' attitudes and behavior are presented as inferential statements which seem to make sense in the context of my related strong findings about campaign spending, media advertising, and grass-roots activities.

My examination of responses to the voting situation itself provides very little evidence for most of the common pessimistic lore about voter confusion or negative voting. Long ballots do *not* seem to cause consistent patterns of either negative voting or a drop in participation at the end of the ballot. Nor do "difficult" propositions (in substance or in wording) invariably evoke negative reactions. Contrary to earlier scholarly expectations, there is no consistent preference for referenda over initiatives or statutory change over constitutional amendments, despite the logic of voter preference for less drastic change or for voter deference to the judgment of legislators.

These findings on voter reactions to the mechanics and context of the voting situation are reassuring in that they cast considerable doubt on the almost universal assumptions about the negativism and apathy of voters in very demanding situations, i.e., making decisions on a large number of issues where few ready cues are available.

An examination, however, of the more complex question of voter rationality—used here in the Downs-Riker sense—leads to a less comfortable conclusion. First, while it is clear that some "knowledgeable voters" perform a sort of cost-benefit analysis on issues like nuclear power regulation, it is not at all clear that such calculations are much more than rationalizations for long-standing ideological preferences. There seems to be a pervasive tendency to mix instrumental and affective choices and to reduce "hard" or complex and technical issues to "easy" issues, amenable to decisions on the basis of reference group cues, attitudes toward technology, or just plain fear, anger, or cynicism about government. This same explanation seems to hold in less researched areas as well—for example, on issues like capital punishment and gun control—where no amount of arguments about the failure of the deterrence effect of the death penalty or the massive expense of the appeals procedure has much impact on those who (underneath all of the rationalizations) are concerned about retribution.

While this use of the ballot for expressive purposes is not inconsistent with the Riker-Ordeshook version of the rational choice model, it is a far cry from what the historic advocates of direct democracy had in mind. The proliferation of media campaigns—with simplistic slogans that further nurture this reductionist-expressive tendency on the part of many voters—can also be defended as providing at least a minimal level of information to non-newspaper-reading voters, following the reasoning of Patterson and McClure (1976), discussed in Chapter 4. But again, multimillion dollar campaigns financed by corporations and groups directly affected by ballot proposals are polar opposites to the hopes of the early Progressives. One major purpose of the initiative, in fact, was to circumvent the close alliance between the legislature and corporate interests. The concluding chapter will thus be devoted to a summary discussion of both my major findings and their implications for both Progressive and pluralist conceptions of democracy. This discussion will, however, be preceded by a brief detour to consider the results and trends in the 1982 elections on ballot questions.

Notes

1. A case might also be made for the importance of Tisch and Headlee as authors of the major property tax proposals in Michigan. There was, however, little media focus on the style or personalities of these men, in contrast to widespread publicity about Howard Jarvis.

2. In Michigan initiatives were in positions 2 and 4-8; in Oregon in 1978 two referenda followed six initiatives. The 1976 Oregon ballot carried all initiatives after the referenda.

3. In the Massachusetts election the remaining five questions were relatively routine proposals by the legislature; all but two passed with sizable majorities.

4. The eight campaigns involving long ballots included five from California, in contrast to only one among the seven with short ballots. The latter set of campaigns included all in Massachusetts, Michigan in 1976 and in 1980, and California in November 1980.

5. The 1976 Michigan election and the June 1976 California elections are omitted since I do not have the text of the noncontroversial measures for these elections. The classic case of misleading cues is California's 1964 Proposition 14 on open housing, where a yes vote meant *disapproval* of open housing. Raymond Wolfinger and Fred Greenstein (1968: 753-69) argue, however, that very few "wrong" votes seem to have occurred.

6. The one exception was California's Proposition 13, *which was not a negative one-sided campaign.* I do not wish to imply, however, that all 13 cases were won by the high-spending side. In two (rent control and the ban on homosexual teachers in California) the low-spending opponents, who had substantial funds of their own, won a majority of votes.

7. Interview with two street workers (on the job) in Pacific Palisades, about May 25, 1978. They were not, in fact, concerned about job security at all.

8. Sears and Citrin (1982: 230) speak of "the doomsday predictions that seem to anger voters rather than intimidate them." Magleby (1984: 111-115), however, argues that low-income voters are unable to see and pursue their self-interest because they cannot *understand* highly technical measures like the graduated tax.

9. Citrin (1979: 115) cites a variety of national polls on the "fairness" of taxes, including one in 1978 that found the social security tax "most fair," followed closely by the sales tax.

10. See, e.g., Deborah and Carl Hensler (1979: 97) for a survey-based discussion of male-female differences on nuclear power. Sears and Citrin (1982: 222-223) explain the sex difference on Proposition 13 in terms of (1) women's support for government services, and (2) the greater appeal of angry, rebellious styles of politics (characteristic of Howard Jarvis) to men in contrast to women.

11. Here I agree with Frank Levy (1979: 66) that "the circumstances of individual states provide interesting and important variations." Levy contrasts this "micro" view with the "macro" school of analysis which sees the tax revolt as "a series of similar responses to a few root causes" such as rising inflation and taxes and the growth of government.

12. Idaho and Nevada approved tax caps.

13. Still a third proposal would have shifted from the property tax to an increased sales tax. It too was defeated decisively.

14. The increase was $19.80/$1,000 evaluation, bringing the total rate to $272.70/$1,000.

15. None of these campaigns involved television advertising or coverage to any great degree. It should be recalled that the California campaign was over an expansion of the death penalty already enacted by the legislature.

8

THE 1982 ELECTIONS:
HIGH SPENDING, OLD ISSUES REVISITED,
AND THE NUCLEAR FREEZE

In 1982 California voters considered a total of 27 propositions, while the Massachusetts, Oregon, and Michigan electorates voted on another 18, for a total of 45 in the four states. Twenty-two issues were of sufficient analytical interest to be included in this study. (The three reapportionment questions put to California voters in June 1982 are considered as one issue, since campaign rhetoric and spending were combined, and the outcome was almost identical on the three propositions.)

Voter turnout in the June 1982 election was the lowest of any California primary since 1946, in spite of the presence on the ballot of the highly controversial issue of the Peripheral Canal. Turnout in November was about average, in the neighborhood of 70%, for all four states. Newspaper coverage, except in California, was exceptionally light. The most noteworthy element in these elections was the occurrence, in three states, of ten separate campaigns where more than $1 million was spent, with an additional three involving expenditures of between $600,000 and $975,000. Thus over half of the campaigns considered in this chapter fall into the "high-spending" category and were conducted primarily as high-saturation media efforts.

But why not simply combine the 1982 campaigns with those discussed in earlier chapters? Partly because 1982 provides an unusual opportunity to review some of our earlier conclusions about spending and media impact (there are *six* deviants where the high-spending side lost; there are 13 high-cost campaigns) and to check some of our earlier explanations. This can be done in an economical fashion because several important "old" issues (tax caps, bottle bills, gun control, the death penalty) reappear in 1982. Second, I am convinced that lifting issues out of the across-the-board campaign context—although essential for some analytical purposes—leads to a partial neglect of some contextual variables, most notably the problem of competition for scarce campaign resources and public attention in many multiissue elections and the variation in state political norms on spending and strategies. A separate and broad chapter on one year's campaigns may give readers a "feel" for these and other missing elements.

Finally, 1982 was chosen in preference to 1984 for three reasons. There were more replays of old issues, voters in *all four* states were involved (in 1984 there were no proposals on the Massachusetts ballot), and the nuclear freeze issue reached the ballot in all four states in that year. The presence of a *foreign policy* question (unique at the *state* level in this study) almost demands attention, and the fact that campaigns were loosely coordinated by a new national movement is also of analytical interest.

Table 8.1 presents information on spending and outcomes on the 22 issues in the same format earlier followed in Chapter 4. Once again, a distinction is made between position and style issues: the former involve a conflict of *interests,* while the latter involve projective *self-expression.* As earlier, both official estimates and campaign arguments are used to assess the probable economic impact of measures. The only unusual feature of the table that demands comment at this time is the large number of low-impact style issues that attracted high campaign spending. In contrast to only three issues in this category in the 1976-80 period, each of five low-impact style issues cost over $500,000 in a single year. All five were in California; the $9.9 million campaign on gun control broke all previous spending records for that state.

This chapter will begin with a brief state-by-state contextual summary. I will then compare spending, campaign strategies, and voting outcomes on most of the controversial issues encountered two or more times, i.e., in both 1982 and earlier campaigns. Finally, after a brief contrast of the four nuclear freeze campaigns, I shall reopen some of the questions raised in earlier chapters about the relative effectiveness of media and grass-roots campaigns in light of the obviously increasing professionalism and coordination across states of both kinds of campaigns.

TABLE 8.1: Expenditures and Voting on 22 Major Ballot Issues in 1982 Elections

| Ballot Question | Spending (in thousands) | | | Vote |
	Pro	Con	Total	
Position Issues, High Impact (N = 7)				
*Eliminate automatic utility rate hike (Mich.)	$38.8	$4,400.5	$4,439.3	50.7-49.3%
Water resources (Cal.)	1,024.8	2,028.8	3,053.5	35.2-64.8
Peripheral Canal (Cal.)	1,006.4	1,742.8	2,749.2	37.3-62.7
Elected public service commission (Mich.)	22.2	1,699.4	1,721.6	36.7-63.3
Utility rate hike, compromise (Mich.)	1,209.4	38.8	1,248.2	59.6-30.4
Property tax cap (Ore.)	258.1	448.9	707.0	49.5-50.5
*End land use planning (Ore.)	206.8	135.4	342.2	44.9-55.1
Position Issues, Low Impact (N = 1)				
Lake Tahoe Bond Issue (Cal.)	49.4	0	49.4	52.9-47.1
Style Issues, High Impact (N = 3)				
Bottle bill (Cal.)	923.2	5,462.0	6,385.2	44.1-55.9
*Bottle bill (Mass.)	652.6	1,430.2	2,082.8	59.1-41.9
Nuclear power/ waste regulation (Mass.)	111.4	100.2	211.6	67.4-32.6
Style Issues, Low Impact (N = 11)				
Gun control (Cal.)	2,608.6	7,287.5	9,896.1	37.2-62.8
Nuclear Freeze (Cal.)	3,483.6	6.0	3,489.6	52.3-47.7

Reapportionment (Cal.)	0	1,783.4	1,783.4	35.4-64.6**
Victims' bill of Rights (Cal.)	973.8	0.3	974.1	56.4-43.6
*Text loan to private school students (Cal.)	595.5	10.2	605.7	38.9-61.1
*Self-service gas stations (Ore.)	164.9	89.8	254.7	42.4-57.6
Nuclear freeze (Mich.)	187.0	0	187.0	56.6-43.4
*Death penalty (Mass.)	0	56.2	56.2	60.2-39.8
Nuclear freeze (Ore.)	53.3	0	53.3	61.6-38.4
Nuclear freeze (Mass.)	32.6	1.5	34.1	73.7-26.3
Aid to parochial schools (Mass.)	7.5	15.9	23.4	37.9-62.1

*"Deviant cases" where low-spending side won election.
**Three separate ballot questions on reapportionment are treated as one, since campaigns and most newspaper coverage did so. The vote given is for Proposition 10; Propositions 11 and 12 were defeated by margins of 62.2-37.8% and 62.1-37.9%.

An Overview of the 1982 Campaigns

MASSACHUSETTS

There were five ballot issues in Massachusetts, all moderately controversial in a year which saw elections of a governor and a U.S. senator by lopsided margins. (In both cases Democrats won by 59.5% and 60.8%.) In an election more reminiscent of 1976 than of later years, there were several hotly contested issues competing for funding and campaign efforts, once again dividing voters on roughly liberal-conservative lines.

The bottle bill and nuclear freeze campaigns attracted the most attention from voters, although neither was heavily covered by the media. Both were decentralized, massive grass-roots efforts, with supporters of both issues highly visible at polling places both in the September primaries and during the actual balloting in November. The bottle bill campaigns were also conducted as expensive media blitzes by both sides, although supporters were once again outspent, in this case by a relatively modest 2-1. The fact that industry was attempting to *repeal* a statute passed only a year earlier by the legislature, after a five-year drive by supporters, undoubtedly contributed to the 59-41% victory of supporters. The nuclear freeze resolution, considered below, was approved by the sizable margin of almost 3-1 in the lowest-spending campaign on the issue in any of the four states.

A constitutional amendment authorizing the death penalty was placed on the Massachusetts ballot, as it had been in other states, to meet the objections of the state and national supreme courts to earlier laws as "cruel and unusual" punishment. It was approved by 60-40% after an underfunded effort by only a handful of organizational and individual opponents in a largely neglected campaign similar to earlier battles in Oregon and California. (It might be noted, however, that a petition to place restoration of the death penalty on the *Michigan* ballot failed to receive enough signatures to qualify in 1982.)

Finally, campaigns on two other issues received surprisingly little attention given the high emotions and massive spending similar proposals had aroused in other states. These were proposals to regulate both nuclear power and nuclear waste disposal and to permit public aid to parochial schools. The first, subject of a limited ($212,000, evenly divided) campaign, passed by a 2-1; the second question, which attracted the lowest amount of spending of any issue considered in the present chapter, was defeated 38-62% with little fanfare in spite of the sizable Catholic population in the state.

MICHIGAN

Michigan voters were presented with seven statewide ballot questions in a year when races for the governor's office, U.S. senator, and several Detroit-area propositions were also on the ballot. Newspaper coverage, while more extensive than that in Massachusetts, was still sparse given the complexity of the issues.

Five of the seven questions touched some aspect of the economic distress Michigan felt in 1982. Two Michigan questions, proposing limits on automatic rate adjustments for fuel costs, broke previous state spending records with combined totals of $5.69 million. The level of advertising slogans, first of the opposition ("D is dumb") and ultimately supporters ("D is dandy"), may also have set a record for simplicity. The passage of both the Michigan Citizens Lobby Proposal D (by 51-49%) and the "compromise" proposal offered by the utilities (by the larger margin of 60-40%) left considerable uncertainty after the election about which law, if either, would take precedence over an eleventh-hour legislative alternative, passed on October 13. The voters' problems were further complicated by an additional proposal, by ACORN, that would have substituted an elected commission for the appointed Public Service Commission, which sets utilities rates. This question (Proposal G) attracted $1.7 million in opposition to a shoestring ($22,200) campaign by supporters. It was defeated 37-63%.

Two other economic proposals (not considered here) dealt with due-on-sale clauses in mortgages and with the impact of shrinking budgets on the state police. Another minor proposal sought to eliminate the statutory immunity of state legislators. Finally, the Michigan ballot also included the nuclear freeze proposal. While somewhat more was spent by Michigan supporters ($187,000) than was the case in Massachusetts or Oregon, this successful campaign was also run in a decentralized fashion by 31 separate geographical committees, with little reliance on media advertising or coverage.

OREGON

Oregon voters considered six propositions, four of which were quite controversial, in a year where only the governor's race attracted much rival attention. (Incumbent Governor Atiyeh won, 61.4-38.6%; there was no race for U.S. Senate.) One of these propositions—a reconsideration of the property tax cap proposal defeated in 1978 and 1980—not only involved expenditures of $707,000 but resulted in a defeat by less than 11,000 out of over one million voters. The only measure to be approved, in fact, was the low-keyed nuclear freeze issue, by 61.6-38.4%.

The two relatively noncontroversial issues (both defeated) concerned the time period for the governor's consideration of bills and the effect of new property construction on the local tax base. There was little coverage of either of these constitutional amendments proposed by the legislature, no campaign spending, and a total of 8% blanks on the ballots.

Almost as controversial as the property tax cap were two other initiatives which involved considerable campaign spending as well. One, which pitted agricultural and real estate interests against environmentalists, was the proposal to end the state's land use planning powers by abolishing the powerful Land Conservation and Development Commission. The voters rejected this measure, for the fourth time in 12 years, by a 55-45% margin. The second was an initiative to permit the operation of self-service gas stations in Oregon. While I shall not discuss the campaign in detail below, since it had no counterpart in other states in the 1976-82 period, it is worth considering briefly as an almost classic case of symbolic politics.

The question was simply put: "Shall persons other than service station operators/employes [sic] be allowed to pump gasoline and other vehicle fuels for retail sale?" Proposed by the state Consumer League, Grange, and Cattlemen's Association, it would have enabled Oregon to join 48 other states (all but New Jersey) in allowing customers a choice between full-service and self-service gas. At the beginning, the campaign was barely visible, with the Gasoline Dealers Association and the Multnomah County Labor Council (Portland area) the only major opponents.

Beginning in mid-October, however, an intensive media campaign was launched by the dealers to convince Oregonians that "Big Oil" was conspiring against individual freedom and convenience in a move that would both raise gas prices for consumers and deprive attendants of much-needed jobs. Over 160,000 comic books on the problems of self-service gas were distributed through gas stations, while a TV ad pictured a well-dressed woman splashing herself in her struggle with a recalcitrant pump. The dealers' unfavorable image of "Big Oil" was supported by publicizing the fact that large numbers of ARCO employees from California had donated their vacation time earlier in the year to collect petition signatures in Oregon.

Thus what had begun as an argument over economics (pricing, employment, consumer preferences) somehow became a pitched battle over both safety and individualism. As the *Oregonian* put it:

It gets adversaries' glands pumping overtime. Perhaps that is because many opponents see self-service stations as the urban equivalent of a clear-cut in the middle of a cathedral grove of redwoods. They view self-service stations not as an extension of their freedom of choice but as another inexorable intrusion into their lives of semi-automated, depersonalized and unchivalrous corporate Goliaths.

Thus, once again, after a relatively inexpensive media campaign, voters who apparently were initially favorable to the proposal were turned around by strong emotional arguments. The proposal was defeated 57.6-42.4% out of 1,038,794 voters—almost 12,000 more than expressed themselves on the nuclear freeze and 18,000 more than those voting on the highly publicized, high-spending issue of the property tax cap!

CALIFORNIA, JUNE 1982

One reason for the record low turnout in June 1982 (35.9%, the lowest in 36 years) might have been the extraordinary number of choices presented to California voters. They were asked to choose among 13 Democrats or four Republicans for governor and 11 Democrats or 13 Republicans for U.S. senator. (Senatorial candidates included Jerry Brown and author Gore Vidal among Democrats, and Pete Wilson, Representative Pete McCloskey, Barry Goldwater, Jr., and William Shockley of race-and-IQ fame. Brown and Wilson received the nominations.) In addition, the hapless voter was expected to pass judgment on 12 ballot issues, five of which involved high-spending campaigns.

These were Proposition 8, the Victim's Bill of Rights; Proposition 9, the Peripheral Canal proposal, and Propositions 10, 11, and 12, legislative proposals for reapportionment brought as referenda to the electorate by dissident Republicans. While Proposition 8 was approved (56.4-43.6%), the other proposals were rejected by margins of almost 2-1. It should also be mentioned that only 6% of the 5.85 million voters "blanked" Proposition 9 on the Peripheral Canal, in contrast to 12% and 14% blanks for governor and senator and 14-15% on the the the other controversial proposals. In other words, the fight on the Peripheral Canal enlarged the number of votes on candidates rather than the reverse.

The Victims' Bill of Rights campaign will be discussed below in the context of several campaigns involving law-and-order issues. It was the most expensive campaign waged, as of June 1982, on any issue of this kind in our four states. The $974,000 spent was, however, exceeded a few months later by the $9.9 million campaign on gun control in California.

As discussed in Chapters 3 and 7, the only proposal fought on primarily partisan lines between 1976 and 1980 was the 1978 Michigan referendum on a constitutional amendment. That proposal, overwhelmingly defeated, was portrayed by Republicans as a Democratic power grab. A very similar argument arose in California in 1982 over the three reapportionment plans, dealing separately with U.S. congressional, state senate, and state assembly districts. Common Cause and the Republican Party argued in this case that the bills passed by the Democratic majority in the legislature had been drawn along blatantly partisan lines. The collection of signatures to allow a popular vote was, in fact, only a first step; in November the Republicans and Common Cause also presented an initiative plan to remove reapportionment from the hands of the legislature and to entrust it, instead, to an independent commission. (This proposal was to be defeated, 54.5-45.5%.) In any case, the June defeat did not occur in time to prevent use of new districts in the 1982 elections, but it did result in a court order for new lines.

The Peripheral Canal issue (Proposition 9) attracted both the lion's share of spending ($2.75 million) and the bulk of the media attention. It is particularly interesting because it is one of the very few environmental-economic battles that strongly polarized Californians on north-south lines. Coastal bond issues and two proposals on Lake Tahoe did not have this effect. While San Francisco liberals were somewhat more opposed to nuclear power than southern Californians, this issue too was not a north-south battle.

The vote actually was a referendum forced by opponents of the plan, passed and signed in 1982, to construct a 43-mile canal linking the Sacramento River to southern California. The canal project, years in the making, was intended to fill increasing southern needs for water, particularly in times of drought. It was opposed by two sets of interests: environmentalists like the Sierra Club and Friends of the Earth, who were concerned about the backup of salt water from the San Francisco Bay into the inland Delta region, and by large-scale San Joaquin Valley farmers who objected to the same safeguards that environmentalists found inadequate. Both sets of opponents argued about costs (estimates ranged from the official

$5.4 billion to a high of $19.3 billion) and also managed to activate the belief of many northern Californians that southerners wanted to "steal" their water. (The San Francisco *Chronicle* charged that canal water would be "siphoned" out of the Sacramento River "to quench the thirst of the people and lawns in Southern California."[1])

While major candidates were divided on the issue, most of the public remained relatively unaware of either the proposal or the candidates' stands until late in the campaign. By the end of May, however, an early favorable stance among knowledgeable voters (50-41-9% in April) had changed to 44-52-4% (*Los Angeles Times,* May 13 and May 27, 1982) and ultimately ended in a 62.7-37.3% rejection of the proposal.

CALIFORNIA, NOVEMBER 1982

In November 1982 California turnout returned to a level comparable to 1978, namely 69.8% of voters. Republicans Deukmejian and Wilson won closely contested races for governor (49.3-48.1%) and U.S. senator (51.5-44.8%) respectively, while voters wrestled with 15 ballot questions, four of which involved multimillion dollar campaigns. Blanks on ballot questions ranged from 18.1% on a little-discussed proposal on local government funds to a low of 5.3% and 5.6% on the gun control and bottle bill proposals.

In addition to the three expensive campaigns on water resources, gun control, and the bottle bill, all of which were defeated by intensive media campaigns, three other propositions attracted considerable attention and/or large expenditures. These were the nuclear freeze proposal, the Lake Tahoe bond issue, and a proposed constitutional amendment allowing textbook loans to private and parochial schoolchildren.

The nuclear freeze campaign is noteworthy because it not only attracted more attention and far more spending ($3.5 million) than did the low-keyed shoestring campaigns in the other three states, but also because it passed by the narrow margin of 52.3-47.7%. The battle was waged at three different levels: in grass-roots forums, discussions, and debates over a period of some years, in public appearances and debates between movie stars (notably Paul Newman versus Charlton Heston), and in debates and endorsements of Nobel Prize notables and others from the scientific community.

The Lake Tahoe proposal also passed by a narrow margin: 52.9-

47.1%. Although it attracted little spending and even less attention, given the large number of explosive issues in 1982, it is of analytical interest for two reasons. First, it was an almost identical rerun of the defeated November 1980 proposal for $85 million to purchase conservation land on the California side of Lake Tahoe. Second, supporters blamed the 1980 defeat on the higher ballot position in that year of the more general parklands proposal (approved by voters) and feared a 1982 repetition because of the presence of four other bond issues, three of which were ahead of the Lake Tahoe proposal on the ballot (*Los Angeles Times* editorial, October 1, 1982).

As I have shown in Chapter 7, voters in fact *do not* vote in accordance with ballot order, measured by either total number of blanks or number of negative votes, but the myth persists. All five bond issues were approved in 1982, with the smallest margin for Proposition 1 (school bonds) and the highest for Proposition 3 (veterans bonds), indicating that voters are more than capable of distinguishing between the subjects of proposed expenditures in spite of excessively long ballots. I shall explore the contrast between the 1980 and 1982 results in a later section of this chapter.

The parochial school texts issue, similar to a 1982 proposal in Massachusetts and the earlier "school vouchers" initiative in Michigan, saw a very high level of spending by supporters ($595,500) and an acerbic debate over constitutionality. While proponents argued that loans to individual students did not violate principles of separation of church and state, opponents hammered at both the constitutional issue and the specter of high costs at a time when voters were only beginning to feel the effects of the 1978 property tax cap. Thus, in spite of a minimal amount of opposition spending ($10,200), the proposal was heavily defeated 61.1-38.9%, with only 10% blanks on the ballot.

I shall continue discussion of the most controversial California propositions, as well as several from other states, and all four campaigns on the nuclear freeze in the remainder of this chapter. It will be noted from the discussion so far that (1) a very large number of repetitions of earlier battles occurred, notably on taxes, capital punishment and gun control, and on bottle bills and other environmental issues, and (2) reliance on expensive media campaigns and/or extensive grass-roots efforts skillfully coordinated by citizens groups increased in all four states.

Earlier Issues Revisited

THE PROPERTY TAX CAP, OREGON

By 1982 two of the four states, California and Massachusetts, had property tax caps in place, while Michigan was subject to the property tax/spending limitation enacted in 1978. Oregon voters, in contrast, had twice rejected an outright tax cap as well as a compromise proposal. But by 1982 the Oregon economy was in serious trouble, with high unemployment, the loss of some relatively new industries, and the shift of corporate headquarters out of state by the state's largest lumber company. Severe cutbacks had also been forced on the state university.[2]

Measure 3 was thus introduced at a time of economic hardship and of the frustration of many property owners over the failure of the state legislature to attempt basic tax reform. In a partial parallel to the earlier Massachusetts and California campaigns, property taxes had increased massively, although Oregon had no state treasury surplus to ease an adjustment to lower taxes. The business community, however, favored a sales tax to diversify the state's tax base.

Despite signs of moderate public support for the measure early in the campaign, including supporters' ability to collect 116,000 signatures for under $500, fund raising of over $100,000 between May and the end of September, and early October polls showing 55% favorably inclined, very little organized opposition surfaced until October. The twice-defeated measure was apparently not taken seriously at the start. In addition, the business community was divided, with Associated Oregon Industries remaining carefully neutral and many small businessmen ambivalent because of their concern about high taxes. This neutrality was in marked contrast to 1980, when business led the opposition from the beginning (*Oregonian,* October 3, 1982).

Yet after a high-saturation media campaign was finally mounted (the opposition outspent supporters $448,900 to $258,100) and a large number of local bodies issued strong warnings about the effect of the cuts, public opinion began the slow reversal so characteristic of other campaigns. By October 6, 50% either intended to vote yes or leaned that way; on October 21-22, the number had shrunk to 37% favorable, with 45% opposed and 17% undecided.

This reversal occurred, however, in spite of another event paral-

lel to those in Massachusetts and California, namely the mailing
of notices of a 32% tax increase in Portland about a month before
the election. While the bad news apparently affected Multnomah
County (Portland) residents to the point where a trend showed in
an October 6 poll and peaked to overall support for the measure by
October 22, there did not seem to be the statewide spillover found
elsewhere. Only 13 (out of 36) counties voted for Measure 3 in
the end. Multnomah County residents favored the measure 54.2-
45.8% with only two counties (also in the Portland area) registering
more support, namely Clackamus (57.6-42.4%) and Washington
(54.8-42.2%). The strongest opposition came from Benton County
(33.1-66.9%) and adjacent Lane County (38.4-61.6%), home of
the University of Oregon. As mentioned earlier, the final vote was
49.4-50.53%, with a difference of fewer than 11,000 votes out of
1.02 million. This was the second closest vote of any encountered
in the four states.[3]

Why was Oregon the only state to reject a property tax reduction? One answer may lie in the fact that major business spokesmen
either opposed or were neutral on the issue, albeit belatedly, in comparison with divided activities in other states. A second reason may
have been the strong environmental arguments put forth by some
opponents, notably by the popular former governor, Tom McCall,
who was dying of cancer at the time, and earlier by the director of
the revenue office of the legislature, who was quoted as saying that
the state park service would probably be "a thing of the past"
under Measure 3 (*Oregonian*, October 3, 1982). Environmental-
ism, while strong in the other three states, takes on an aura of religious orthodoxy for a very large number of Oregonians. Third,
timing may have been all-important: Oregon did not have a large
buffering surplus in the state treasury, as did California in 1978,
and by 1982 the *Oregonian* was publicizing the fact that Californians were paying large fees for services (e.g., parental financing of
athlete's uniforms) once that surplus was exhausted.[4] In addition,
voters may not have been inclined to approve a measure so frequently rejected in recent elections. Finally, anger at the state legislature, coupled with a conviction that no other tax alternatives
were readily available, does not seem to have been as dominant a
theme, even in campaign arguments, as it was elsewhere.

In conclusion, then, I find a combination of somewhat unique
explanations for the third Oregon defeat of the tax cap: the lack of

strong business support, the opposition of environmentalists as well as school officials and local bodies, the moderate electorate, and the timing of the election. The explanation is not, in this case, either vastly superior funding or the use of brilliant or unusual campaign strategies. The well-financed opposition campaign in fact was late in mobilizing and devoid of strong leadership until the end. It should be noted, nevertheless, that strong sentiment for tax reform did exist in Oregon as elsewhere: over 500,000 voters, just a shade under half the electorate, favored the measure in the end.

ENVIRONMENTAL ISSUES

The two 1982 election "replays" on environmental issues that attracted most public attention as well as funding were the bottle bill campaigns in California and Massachusetts. In addition, two other campaigns echoed earlier environmental battles. These were the successful efforts to pass the Lake Tahoe bond issue in California and the regulation of nuclear power and nuclear wastes in Massachusetts. Finally, a major struggle was waged over a water resources proposal in California—not a direct replay, but a campaign involving many arguments and strategies encountered elsewhere.

We have already discussed the successful Massachusetts *bottle bill* campaign in Chapter 6: this deviant case, where supporters defeated an opposition outspending them 2-1, was explained as an example of superb grass-roots strategy combined with a strong media campaign which took advantage of voters' anger over a repeal effort. The losing California effort, where supporters were outspent almost 6-1, closely resembled, in contrast, the 1976 campaign in Massachusetts. There were three major points of similarity.

First, in 1982 California activist liberals divided their efforts among four major proposals (gun control, the nuclear freeze, the water resources plan, and the bottle bill) as Massachusetts voters had in 1976 (gun control, flat electric rate, the ERA, and the bottle bill). With severely limited numbers of people available to mount a large-scale grass-roots effort against a strong $5.5 million media campaign, the 56-44% defeat is not surprising. Second, because this was the first such effort to reach the California ballot, a very large number of voters were initially unaware of the issues involved, as they had been six years earlier in Massachusetts. (By 1982 Massachusetts voters had experienced not only the 1976 ballot campaign

but a vitriolic battle in the legislature, which included a gubernatorial veto and a last-minute legislative override in early 1982.)
Finally, the bottling, union, and retailers' interests ran a brilliant
advertising campaign which diverted the argument to the unfavorable impact of the bill on the existing voluntary recycling program.

I do not mean to imply a poorly run campaign on the part of Cal-
PIRG, other environmental groups, and the farmers organizations
that supported the proposal. California activists, in fact, staged a
series of picket lines at stores in major cities in response to the anti-
bottle-bill signs, leaflets, and grocery bags distributed by grocers
on a far larger scale than similar efforts of Massachusetts groups in
1982. They were quick to respond, as well, to opposition ads claiming Oregonians' dissatisfaction with the long-standing law in that
state, revealing that four out of the five "ordinary people" featured
in ads were in fact beer company employees (*Los Angeles Times*,
October 28, 1982). Supporters also managed to generate a moderate amount of publicity, in spite of the heavy competition from the
hotly contested gubernatorial and senatorial campaigns, as well as
from other major propositions.

But the supporters' campaign was clearly outclassed by a clever
and well-financed opposition campaign that capitalized (in advertisements) on an editorial by station KNBC-TV calling Proposition
11 a "well-intentioned mistake." Opponents argued that the proposal would undermine the existing recycling program, whose 900 centers and 19 curbside collection efforts had succeeded in recycling
60% of aluminum cans in 1981. While opposition advertisements
began in August, supporters were forced to resort to the Fairness
Doctrine to obtain free time, since the bulk of their funding was not
available until late in the campaign.

I suspect that the California campaign was really not winnable,
however, while the Massachusetts effort was, for two major reasons:
(1) on this sort of high-impact style issue, voter awareness may
need to be aroused over a period of years and over several different
battles, (2) industry clearly decided to concentrate its resources in
California ($5.5 million) rather than in Massachusetts ($1.4 million), where stakes were somewhat lower and the victory for the
opposition was more problematic.

Massachusetts Question 3, to *restrict radioactive waste disposal
and nuclear power plant construction*, was the least publicized of
the five ballot questions considered in the state in 1982, in spite of

the fact that it generated \$211,600 in spending.[5] The proposal was supported by environmentalists and opposed not only by utility companies but by the League of Women Voters. The two sides were almost evenly matched financially (\$111,400 to \$100,200) in what was an almost invisible campaign. (I encountered no precinct workers on either side either leafleting or creating a visible presence at the polls during the course of my work on two other campaigns. I did, however, hear opposition radio spots.)

Less stringent in scope and tone than the California and Oregon initiatives of 1976 and 1980, the proposal arose out of concern about the nuclear waste disposal compact being discussed by northeastern states and the fear that Massachusetts would be used as a prime dumping site. It provided for three levels of review, for both waste disposal and the construction of any new nuclear plants. Approval was required first by the state legislature, in regard to safety, environmental, and health impact, second by local officials (re health and zoning codes), and finally by voters, in special, site-specific referenda.

Supporters argued that such safeguards were essential given the poor state of waste-disposal technology and the pressure on Massachusetts from other states as well as from the nuclear industry itself. Opponents argued that existing safeguards were adequate and that passage would delay a regional compact, hinder hospital and other medical research, and impose endless roadblocks, especially for waste disposal. As Robert Turner put it in the October 7, 1982, *Boston Globe:* "voters may want to think twice before they start down a road which has polling booths at every turn."

I am frankly unable to explain the outcome (67.4-32.6% approval) given the almost total lack of coverage, public debate, or polls on the subject. Turner may have been correct in his suspicion that "a large number" of voters may have been confused by the fact that both Questions 3 and 5 (the freeze) dealt with nuclear issues, but our aggregate data provide little information beyond the fact that every Massachusetts county approved both proposals overwhelmingly. What *is* clear is that very little factual help was given by either side or by the media to Massachusetts voters, and that most of the arguments centered on waste disposal rather than on nuclear power per se.

The Lake Tahoe Bond Proposal (for \$85 million) in California is another example of a little-discussed proposal, although this proposition at least had the advantage of a past appearance on the ballot in 1980, when it lost by 1.2%. Only one item, a brief editorial endorsement on October 1, appeared in the *Los Angeles Times*. Only $49,300 was spent in support, with no opposition apparent. The 1982 approval (by a 2.9% majority) appears to be another example of the successful strategy begun in 1980 of breaking the omnibus parkland proposal into smaller parts which then seem less ambitious or potentially wasteful to the voters. Thus most of the goals of the initial proposal, defeated in June 1980, were achieved in two later elections by narrowing both the scope of the funds and the scope of opposition.

It may be recalled that a similar clarification and narrowing of scope was successful on nuclear power in Oregon, where a defeated 1976 proposal seen as a "ban" was transformed into a victorious safety regulation proposal in 1980. This strategy is not always successful, however, as demonstrated by the near-identical margins of defeat for the California Clean Air Acts in 1978 and 1980. In the latter case, an extravagant media campaign seems to have convinced voters that a narrowed scope (and lower costs and penalties of the law mandating nonsmoking areas) was irrelevant in comparison with a perceived loss of personal liberties. Analogous diversionary tactics were not used in the Lake Tahoe case and were not successful in regard to Oregon's nuclear proposals.[6]

Finally, the California *Water Resources Plan* deserves brief attention both because it is another case where environmental and economic interests clashed, and because the two-sided high-spending media campaigns ($1,024,800 to $2,028,800) once again seem to have provided more confusion than enlightenment. This comprehensive proposal, among other things, mandated water conservation measures throughout the state, regulated groundwater management programs in areas where the supplies were decreasing, and provided for a petition process for environmental and recreation interests. It was supported by environmental groups and bitterly opposed by both farm groups and the Los Angeles County Water Board.

Both sides in this controversy engaged in hyperbole and/or distortion reminiscent of the battle over Chavez's 1976 proposal for an Agricultural Labor Relations Act. Opposition advertisements played on fears of high food costs, high water rates, and governmental red tape. One TV ad in particular not only aroused the ire of opponents and the *Los Angeles Times* but was denounced as "ridiculous" and "without proof" by one of the groups on the same side, the Farm Bureau. It showed a child with a carton of school milk; after the milk suddenly disappeared into thin air, a voice-over explained that Californians wouldn't be able to provide low cost food if the proposition were passed.

But supporters' ads were hardly innocent or informative. One commercial denounced the efforts of "a few millionaire farmers . . . who don't care what we want." Once again more newspaper attention was devoted to an analysis of a campaign "more cynical and distorted than any in memory" (*Los Angeles Times* editorial, October 29, 1982) than to a clarification of the proposal's provisions.[7] Predictably, an initial high level of public approval turned to an ultimate 65-35% defeat in November.

AID TO PAROCHIAL AND PRIVATE SCHOOL CHILDREN

It may be recalled that Michigan voters rejected a proposal for "vouchers for education" which could be used by parents in the schools of their choice in 1978 by the overwhelming vote of 74.3-25.7%. That was a year, however, in which the vouchers proposal was linked with two very controversial tax questions, all of which entailed expensive campaigns for a total of $1.4 million. The 1982 campaigns over private school aid in California and Massachusetts differed from Michigan's in that they were not linked to tax reduction issues, and they were both markedly narrower in scope. In addition, they received only infinitesimal coverage in comparison with the Michigan plan.

Supporters of the California proposal massively outspent opponents, by $595,500 to $10,200, in comparison with the modest Massachusetts expenditures of $7,500 to $17,900. Yet both measures were defeated by almost identical margins: 61-39% in California and 62-38% in Massachusetts. This is probably another case of a (relatively) low-impact style issue where even high-spending campaigns have little success in changing long-standing attitudes among voters. (The drinking age and death penalty proposals are other examples of this phenomenon.) Despite the fact that California opponents stressed the cost element in the proposal, the limited amount of editorial and other coverage, coupled with the one-sided results, leads me to believe that a great many voters in both states saw the issues as one on the separation of church and state.[8] On issues of this sort, voters' attitudes (which Magleby, 1984, calls "standing opinions") are somewhat stereotypical and not easily changed in the short run.

LAW-AND-ORDER ISSUES

Four law-and-order issues had reached the electorate in three of these states in 1978. These were the death penalty proposals in California and Oregon and the bail and mandatory sentencing proposals in Michigan. All four were passed by huge majorities ranging from 64 to 83% of the voters; and with the exception of the California death penalty, which cost $670,300, all were low-spending and moderately low-visibility campaigns. The 1976 Massachusetts handgun campaign was the only earlier proposal to fail (by 69.2-30.8%), in part because both police organizations and gun manufacturers opposed it, and it was the only one as well to attract heavy (even national) attention from the media.

Voters in both Massachusetts and California were asked to decide on three law-and-order proposals in 1982. In Massachusetts the effort took the form of a proposed constitutional amendment, approved by the legislature in 1980 and 1982, to authorize enactment of the *death penalty*. Because of a 1980 ruling by the State Supreme Judicial Court (*Suffolk County v. Watson*) that the death penalty constituted "cruel and unusual" punishment, Massachusetts was the only state in 1982 where capital punishment was constitutionally prohibited. The amendment was thus a simple declaration that "no provision in the Constitution shall be construed as prohibiting the imposition of the penalty of death," leaving specific conditions for later action by the legislature.

Proponents spent no money and little visible effort on the campaign. Armed with overwhelming support in the legislature (votes of 123-62 in 1980 and 125-62 in June 1982) and exit polls at the September primary showing a majority desire to "send a message" to criminals, they relied primarily on ballot pamphlet and word-of-mouth arguments about deterrence, retribution, and protecting society from released convicts who might kill again. Opponents, including church groups and civil liberties and civil rights organizations, were led by a committee of anti-death-penalty activists who dated back to a 1968 nonbinding referendum. (In 1968, 61.34% of 1.9 million voters favored retention of the death penalty. Supreme Court and state court decisions, however, rendered the question moot.)

Opponents, who organized well in advance of the campaign, had a strong grass-roots plan on paper: speakers' bureaus, local committees, a fund-raising telethon aimed at lists of earlier activists and current members of sympathetic groups. They argued, via well-researched fact sheets, press releases, small rallies, neighborhood and church meetings, and the like, about discrimination against minorities and the poor, the failure of deterrence, the high costs of capital punishment, and ethical and humanitarian considerations. But the opposition campaign only succeeded in raising $56,200 and in activating a very limited number of precinct workers, although it attracted the endorsements of the victorious Democratic gubernatorial candidate (Dukakis) and of major newspapers including the *Boston Globe*. There was never a strong, visible presence of anti-death-penalty leafleters and poll signs, as well as advertisements, as there were in both the nuclear freeze and bottle bill campaigns.[9] Thus, while the heavily black areas in Boston and in liberal communities like Cambridge, Newton, Lexington, and Provincetown opposed the measure, the majority of Massachusetts voters approved the amendment by a 60.2-39.8% margin.

My view that this is one more style issue where attitudes are likely to change slowly, if at all, is strengthened by the fact that this outcome differed by only 1% from that rendered 14 years earlier. It might be noted, in conclusion, that it took less than six weeks for the legislature to draft a strong bill, enacted in haste to enable the outgoing (and supportive) governor to sign the bill before his successor took office.[10]

The California ballots included two more law-and-order proposals in 1982: a June proposal given the ballot title of a *"Victims' Bill of Rights,"* and a November initiative for *gun control*. The former passed by 56.4-43.6% while the gun control initiative was decisively defeated 62.8-37.2%. Both were high-spending and extraordinarily one-sided campaigns, with Victims' Bill of Rights supporters spending $973,800 to opponents' $300, and gun control opponents setting an all-time record of $7,287,500 to supporters' $2,608,600. Coverage was extremely heavy on both issues as well.

The most controversial features of the complex Victims' Bill of Rights, initiated by Paul Gann, co-author of the earlier property tax cap, were an easing of the "exclusionary rule" that prohibited court use of evidence that is illegally obtained and a repeal of the prohibition in the criminal code against victims appearing in sentencing procedures.[11] Opponents, including the state bar association, the ACLU, the state Probation, Parole, and Correctional Association, and the Organization of Police and Sheriffs, warned that "legal chaos and staggering costs" would result from passage. Supporters (consisting primarily of conservative lawyers and legislators) insisted that the law would restore the balance between the rights of victims and criminals. Senatorial candidates Jerry Brown and Pete Wilson took opposite sides; a great deal of attention was devoted to Los Angeles Mayor Bradley's refusal, in contrast, to take an unequivocal stand in the course of his campaign for governor. (He supported some parts of the proposal but sidestepped endorsement of the package as a whole.)

Despite eloquent and prominent opposition, and dire predictions, there was never much doubt in the polls. While almost 80% of the electorate had not heard of the proposition in late April, the 75% support rate among the knowledgeable was impressive. A month later the *Times* reported considerably more knowledge and an 82% level of support. Only the Peripheral Canal proposal captured more media attention.

I believe that this proposal was in perfect tune with a widespread public mood concerning criminals and victims. While one prominent opposition leader denounced the proposition as "a coldly calculated attempt to cash in on public fear and hysteria in order to foist numerous changes which have been rejected by courts . . . upon an unsuspecting public,"[12] it is clear that the California electorate simply anticipated a similar stance of the U.S. Supreme Court two years later on the exclusionary rule.

The *gun control* proposal, initiated by liberal organizations in California as it had been in Massachusetts six years before, was an entirely different matter. As in the Massachusetts campaign, liberal activists were dividing their attention among a host of ballot proposals in November, in contrast to the single-minded opposition of most of the gun lobby. This did not, however, prevent the supporting coalition (which included state medical and legal associations, religious groups, and a few police chiefs) from raising about $1.1 million early in the campaign (to opponents' $3 million in the same period), demanding free media time under the Fairness Doctrine since they were clearly outspent, and ultimately running an active and aggressive media campaign of their own. Total spending by election day was $2.6 million by supporters and $7.3 million by opponents.

This campaign differed from the 1976 battle in Massachusetts in several key ways: (1) the details of the proposals differed (the Massachusetts question was a ban on handguns, the California proposition provided for handgun registration and restrictions on further sales); (2) the level of spending differed by several orders of magnitude ($102,300 total in Massachusetts, with opponents outspending supporters more than 10-1); (3) the California campaign was a high-spending two-sided media campaign, albeit uneven, while the Massachusetts campaign was a case of grass roots versus media; (4) the public mood on law-and-order issues was much tougher in 1982 than in 1976.

The problem, both for the voters and for our analysis, is in specifying the relationship between public revulsion at crime and a rational choice on the gun control issue. *Both sides* made contradictory, and highly emotional, claims in this regard, using law officers to support their arguments. The opposition ad receiving most attention showed an old woman in bed, with a background sound of breaking glass. She then picked up the phone, dialed the police, and received a busy signal. As the closing picture focused on the look of paralyzed fear on her face, while the bedroom door slowly began to open, a voice-over explained that if Proposition 15 passed, the police would be kept so busy administering gun regulations that phone calls would go unheeded.

The supporters, lacking either the early financing or the army of volunteers available to opponents from California's 1000 hunting and gun clubs, resorted in late October to counterpropaganda that was also designed to arouse fears. Footage was shown of the slain Robert Kennedy, lying on the floor of a Los Angeles hotel, with the statement that "this candidate for President was murdered with a California street gun." Another ad supporting Proposition 15 featured the police chiefs of San Francisco and San Jose (two of only three chiefs in California to support the proposition.)[13]

My point is that the scare tactics used by both sides, as advised by polls they had taken to determine effective arguments, were unlikely to help the voter to reach a calm or detached decision. One side argued that restrictions on the anonymous availability of handguns would prevent criminals from carrying concealed weapons, would cut down on gun use in crimes of passion, and would generally lower the number of murders and armed robberies. The other side argued that Proposition 15 would disarm innocent citizens while encouraging criminals to remain armed, and that it would consume time needed elsewhere by police. But the visual imagery of the TV campaigns, for the most part, stressed blood and gore or people in terror.

Thus it is not surprising that the high-spending side (even in a campaign where both sides had millions) managed to turn an initial 2-1 approval (in June polls) into what was reported to be a very close race by mid-October (with pollsters disagreeing on which side led[14]) and then into a final victory (that is, defeat of the proposal) in November. While this turnaround is not *inevitable* as a result of high spending, it is extremely common where voter confusion exists or *has been created* in the course of a campaign.

Nuclear Freeze Campaigns

The 1982 nuclear freeze campaigns in all four states are of special interest for several reasons. First, this is the one case where voters in all four states (as well as in eight others, the District of Columbia, and many cities) made simultaneous decisions. Second, it is my only example of a state-level vote on a foreign policy issue. Third, with the exception of California, these campaigns were exclusively low-spending, grass-roots efforts, attracting little opposition spending. Finally, they represent examples of long-range low-visibility efforts that attract large numbers of activists with little or no previous referenda campaign experience. (Other examples of this type are the nuclear power referenda and the Massachusetts campaign on the ERA.)

Campaigns in all four states were part of the effort of the national freeze movement, which had begun as an attempt at self-education by concerned citizens and then moved on to lobbying at the level of Congress, before taking the form of ballot questions. In 1982, in fact, it had already begun to move into congressional and senatorial campaigns as well.

The freeze proposal, worded identically in all four states, took the form of a nonbinding resolution in favor of a mutual, verifiable nuclear weapons moratorium and reduction to be negotiated with the Soviet Union and others. Since all four freeze campaigns shared certain structural characteristics (a large number of decentralized geographic campaign committees which collected signatures and funds in their own territory and ran separate grass-roots activities), I shall begin with just a brief description of the campaigns and outcomes. I will then concentrate largely on the California and Massachusetts efforts, both of which involved some opposition spending as well.[15]

Table 8.2 shows first that while opposition spending was nonexistent in two states and minimal in two others, supporters' expenditures varied considerably from a low of $32,600 to a high of $3.5 million. Second, the magnitude of victory seems to vary *inversely* with spending—not in the common-sense direction (i.e., amount spent leads to victory or defeat) but in this case because supporters in California and Michigan anticipated more opposition than did those in Oregon and Massachusetts and adjusted their strategies accordingly.

Oregon supporters indeed had good reason for confidence, since petition signatures were apparently gathered with ease, and broad organizational support included groups like the Portland Gray Panthers, the Nurses Association, the Japanese-American Citizens' Association, and the League of Women Voters. The *Oregonian,* in fact, reported on October 5 that Secretary of State Norma Paulus had to seek out the three authors of the opposition statement in the voters' pamphlet in the absence of the usual volunteers; in addition, late September polls reported favorable attitudes of three out of four voters interviewed, crossing age, racial, educational, and other lines. Almost the only negative views reported (in a low-keyed but moderately well-covered campaign) were those of officials from Washington, like Defense Secretary Casper Weinberger, who called a last-minute (October 28) press conference to oppose the freeze proposals in all nine states where it appeared. This was countered, on the national level, by four retired government officials, including a former CIA director and a former secretary of defense, who issued a letter in support.[16]

Michigan supporters were somewhat more cautiously optimistic, despite a lack of any registered opposition group. According to the October 4 *Detroit Free Press,* which actively supported the measure in five editorials between September 18 and November 1, 30 geographical freeze groups sprang up early in 1982 to collect signatures and then proceeded to hold a series of benefit concerts, church dinners, and small meetings to collect the funds for what was primarily a grass-roots publicity campaign.[17] Some opposition letters, citing arguments from a *Reader's Digest* article that linked the freeze to a KGB plot, appeared in the *Detroit Free Press,* while a late October telephone poll reported a 60-25% margin (with 15%

TABLE 8.2: Spending and Outcomes on Nuclear Freeze

	Pro	Con	Total	Vote
California	$3,483,600	$6,000	$3,489,600	52.3-47.7%
Michigan	187,000	0	187,000	56.6-43.4
Oregon	53,300	0	53,300	61.6-38.4
Massachusetts	32,600	1,500	34,100	73.7-26.3

undecided) in contrast to the stronger showing in Oregon. The final outcome, as noted in Table 8.2, was 56.6-43.4%.

Thus I find a relatively strong margin of victory in the two states where campaigns by both sides were relatively low-keyed, although well covered and supported by major newspapers. Note that the attention of newspapers was simultaneously occupied by controversial ballot questions on high-impact economic issues (the utility rate proposals in Michigan, the property tax cap and land use battles in Oregon) as well as by candidate races. In Massachusetts and California, where freeze coverage was more sparse and activist attention was painfully divided among a veritable host of high-spending style issues (gun control, bottle bills, and the like), opposition was also somewhat more visible.

In Massachusetts, where small community groups had been studying weapons reduction since 1980 and whose activists had joined others in large numbers in Washington in August (1982) in an unsuccessful effort to push the freeze proposal through the House of Representatives, opposition surfaced early on in the state legislature. It may be recalled that Massachusetts, unlike the other three states, employs an *indirect* initiative, requiring prior legislative approval for an initiative petition to reach the ballot. In the case of the freeze petition, the powerful state speaker, Thomas McGee, had delayed appointing a conference committee to find common language for the slightly different versions approved by the two houses. He acceded to last minute pressure (including a September 20 mass rally at the State House, which drew several thousand irate citizens) too late for the proposal to be included in the ballot pamphlet but in time to reach the ballot itself.

Well-organized local citizens groups, forewarned by this initial opposition roadblock, took no chances in the six weeks remaining before the election. Informal meetings, forums, films, folk concerts—and the ubiquitous pins, t-shirts, bumper stickers, and information tables in local churches—appeared to blanket many areas in a low-cost activist campaign rivaled only by the bottle bill supporters. In the end the resolution passed by a stunning margin of almost 3-1, without a single city or town voting against the measure.[18] (The voters of Cambridge, representing as always the extreme, approved by 25,925-4,828. Even traditionally conservative cities turned in 2-1 margins.)

THE CLOSE RACE IN CALIFORNIA

The California campaign, like so many before it, was carried on at several levels. As in Massachusetts, study groups had sprung up, largely from a religious base, as early as 1980. (The Pasadena-based Interfaith Center to Reverse the Arms Race, for example, coordinated much of the activity in southern California, including massive volunteer work in the petition drive.) Alerted early by the formation of an opposition committee, Californians for a Strong America, and by the Field Poll's January 1982 report that while 60% favored the freeze, 32% were opposed, supporters also embarked on fund-raising for a large-scale media undertaking.[19]

To be fully appreciated, the volunteer signature-gathering effort must be recognized as the massive contrast it was to the more orthodox activities of paid professionals. Individual denominations in many cases set concrete numerical goals for their own congregations and fanned out to shopping malls, campuses, and any other place where pedestrians might be found. One UCLA faculty wife collected more than 1000 signatures by "camping" at the Hughes Supermarket in Pacific Palisades to glean perhaps 100 signatures a day; others were solicited at meetings where slide shows and/or prominent speakers were featured. By May 15, 741,900 signatures were filed—about 400,000 more than needed to qualify the initiative.

Then throughout the spring and summer, meetings, peace walks, candlelight vigils, and public galas were held in preparation for the autumn campaign. Petra Kelley and other members of the West German Green Party, William Sloan Coffin, and Bishop Matthiesen (of Amarillo) were only a few of the featured speakers. In the meantime the *Los Angeles Times* (on April 19 and May 1, 1982) was carrying sporadic news of endorsements, for example, by the Los Angeles City Council and by Archbishop Quinn, and a few opponents, e.g., the Republican candidates for governor and lieutenant governor.

On October 1 supporters launched what began as a relatively modest broadcasting campaign with a 30-second spot during a Dodgers-Giants game. (By mid-October three different ads had appeared in all nine major media market areas, at a cost of $200,000.) Some network stations expressed concern, from the beginning, that the opponents—who had raised almost no money—might request free time under the Fairness Doctrine. This in fact happened, and thus by the end of October viewers in at least three major areas (San Francisco, Fresno, and Los Angeles) were treated to the spectacle of Paul Newman and Charlton Heston raising doubts about each other's expertise on arms strategy.

At another level a host of serious debates were held (some on the air, some as public forums) between such notables as Hans Bethe and Edward Teller (both major figures in early nuclear development) and, in Northern California, between Daniel Ellsberg (*Pentagon Papers*) and John Bunzel (President of San Jose State). Bethe and Teller, in fact, authored the lengthy pro and con articles on the freeze for the Sunday *Times* on October 17. One major publicity coup by supporters surfaced in mid-October, when a press conference held at Cal Tech's Jet Propulsion Lab announced freeze support by 900 Cal Tech scientists, including Richard Feynman, a highly respected Nobel Prize winner who had worked at Los Alamos as a young man. A full-page advertisement signed by the group, printing all 900 names, appeared in the *Los Angeles Times* on October 20, as well as in other major papers. Finally, mention should be made of the fact that most major newspapers endorsed the freeze. A lengthy *Times* editorial appeared on October 24. In addition, coverage of the more prominent events was more comprehensive in the *Times* than it was in other states' major newspapers, despite the many heated campaigns in California.

Why then did the *Times* poll find a 48-42% split in mid-October and ultimately the exceptionally close (winning) election outcome? The question is particularly intriguing given California's status as the only state where a multimillion dollar supportive campaign was run, with final opposition spending reported as only $6,041. Three factors seem relevant. First, the Washington administration's last-minute well-publicized opposition (i.e., Weinberger's announcement that well-intentioned freeze supporters were acting against

U.S. strategic interests) may have especially impressed Californians as Reagan partisans. Second, it should be recalled that parts of southern California (particularly Orange and San Diego Counties) have been traditionally conservative on foreign policy. Finally (and this is a related point), I suspect that a good deal of unreported "educational," as opposed to direct campaigning, activity may have been undertaken by the opposition. This indirect work need not be reported as campaign spending, in a situation directly analogous to educational work by lobbying groups, also exempt from official reports.

To check my second point—that freeze opposition came most heavily from traditionally conservative areas in southern California—I have examined voting returns on the freeze issue by county. I indeed find that the four largest opposition counties, providing 27% of the opposition vote with 23% of the state's population, are the traditional areas of conservativism south of Los Angeles. Three other populous counties, Kern, San Joaquin, and Ventura, are inland agricultural areas. In contrast, six counties in the Bay area, with 19% of the population, average 59% *pro* votes, or 22% of the total support. (San Francisco County itself led the state in support, with a 73-27% split; Los Angeles was closer to the state average with 54.7% support.)

It should be pointed out that the four most populous southern California counties at the negative end of the freeze spectrum (San Bernardino, San Diego, Orange, and Riverside) are all mixed urban and farm areas, frequently registering conservative views on both foreign policy and style issues. (It was here that Reverend Falwell spoke to large rallies on behalf of the 1978 proposal against homosexual teachers; it is also here that the John Birch society bases its West Coast strength, having sent one of its avowed members to Congress for years.) These were *not* the counties, however, with the highest *percentage* of opposition: that instead came from three inland and sparsely settled counties: Modoc (70.0% opposed), Sutter (63.1%), and Colusa (63.0%), also traditionally conservative.

The vote cannot be labeled either an urban-rural split (since the southern counties include large urban populations, and some of the Bay area population is the wine country) or a pure north-south split, given the high level of support in Los Angeles. I believe, instead, that the configuration is a reflection of the historical strongholds of conservatives and liberals in the state, whose present leaders took action to mobilize their own.

I am not able to analyze the educational activity undertaken by conservative groups in the area other than by examining the arguments that surfaced in opposition ads and in the Teller article in the *Times*. All of these argued that the freeze would weaken the country's strategic and negotiating position. I do know, however, that one letter sent out to the clergy by the California Committee of Americans for Peace with Liberty characterized freeze advocates as "being duped into becoming propaganda assets for the God-hating Soviet empire" and enclosed a 14-page pamphlet by John Rees of *American Opinion,* the John Birch publication.[20] This was a markedly less subtle version of the argument put forth in the October *Reader's Digest* article that surfaced in the Michigan campaign as well as in statements by Administration officials.

This is not an argument that a majority of opponents were swayed, or even reached, by direct mail or other efforts of ultraconservative groups, since I do not know how active or effective these groups were. I do argue, however, that a plausible explanation of the narrow margin in California, even after an expensive media campaign coupled with more than two years of community activism by supporters, may lie *in part* in such activities. The geographical distribution of the vote lends support to this interpretation.

High-Spending Campaigns

Table 8.1, summarizing campaign expenditures and outcomes earlier in this chapter, showed that a total of ten campaigns cost more than $1 million, with an additional three over $500,000. Thus almost 60% of the 22 major ballot issues in 1982 evoked high-spending campaigns, in contrast to 42% of the 50 campaigns in the 1976-80 period. The more striking shift, however, is in the proportion of *low-impact style issues* that involved high spending: five (gun control, the freeze, reapportionment, the victims' bill of rights, and aid to private schools—all in California) in 1982, in contrast to only one (homosexual teachers) in the $1 million category, and two (California death penalty, Michigan drinking age) over $500,000 in earlier years. This trend toward high-cost media campaigns on style as well as position issues seems part of a general professionalization of battles on ballot questions, a phenomenon not foreseen by the original Progressive advocates of direct democracy.

Once again, the high-spending side was victorious in the majority of cases: 72.7% of the time (16 out of 22 campaigns) in 1982, in contrast to the earlier figure of 80% (40 out of 50). Thus the overall rate of high-spending victories for the entire 1976-82 period (72 issues) is 77.78%. This includes four of the five cases in 1982 where expenditures were under $100,000 as well as eight out of ten that exceeded $1 million. Eight of these ten were lopsided campaigns where one side outspent the other by at least 2-1 (it was 5-1 for the California bottle bill, 11-1 on the Michigan utility rate proposal, and 80-1 in the case of the Michigan Public Service Commission.) Two of these campaigns, however, involved two-sided high spending where neither side had double the other's resources. Thus we return to two questions raised in earlier chapters: Lowenstein's (1982) hypothesis about the deceptive and oversimplifying nature of one-sided versus two-sided campaigns and our own interest in explaining deviant cases where the low spenders won.

Table 8.3 simply summarizes data already given in Table 8.1 on the one-sided high-spending campaigns. At the outset it should be noted that the spending history of one campaign is unique enough to remove it from the present discussion. The funds raised to force a referendum on the California reapportionment measures were spent almost entirely by the state Republican Party (only $250 was spent by a separate referendum committee), and all but $21,075 of the $1.8 million was spent on the *signature drive* rather than on a media campaign to influence the electorate.

Second, note that the high spenders in two cases were *supporters* of proposals and that both groups were victorious, but again, both were unusual. The California freeze drive, as we have seen, involved money raised by activist citizens groups and churches rather than by corporations. (About $120,000 of the $847,000 of donations from large contributors came from corporate sources, with an additional $80,000 from Norman Lear, but this is a far cry from spending by tobacco companies or gun manufacturers.)

The utility company spending on the two proposals on rate hikes in Michigan defies simple categorization because expenditures *for* the compromise proposal would never have occurred without the fear that the more extreme proposal by the Citizens' Lobby would pass. Thus in a situation parallel to Proposition 13 and the legislative compromise measure in the 1978 campaign, both the $4,400,500 against the stronger bill and the $1,209,400 in support of the com-

TABLE 8.3: One-sided High-Spending Campaigns in 1982

Issue	Pro	Spending (in thousands) Con	Total	Vote
Eliminate automobile rate hikes (Mich.)	$38.8	$4,400.5	$4,439.3	50.7-49.3%
Elected public service comm. (Mich.)	22.2	1,699.4	1,721.6	36.7-63.3
Automobile utility rate hike compromise (Mich.)	1,209.4	38.8	1,248.2	59.6-30.4
Bottle bill (Calif.)	923.2	5,462.0	6,385.2	44.1-55.9
Bottle bill (Mass.)	652.6	1,430.2	2,082.8	59.1-41.9
Gun control (Calif.)	2,608.6	7,287.5	9,896.1	37.2-62.8
Nuclear freeze (Calif.)	3,483.6	6.0	3,489.6	52.3-47.7
Reapportionment (Calif.)	0	1,783.4	1,783.4	35.4-64.6

promise should be considered opposition spending. The difference between the Michigan outcome and the Proposition 13 case is, of course, that the Michigan strategy backfired and both bills passed.

Thus there are only four separate issues that are "pure" cases of high one-sided corporate spending: the composite of three related utility issues in Michigan, the two bottle bills, and the gun control proposal. Seen in this light, all were "negative campaigns," in contrast to the positive/supporting noncorporate nuclear freeze campaign. And, in light of the advertising strategies described earlier in this chapter (and in Chapter 6 on the Massachusetts bottle bill), it is fair to say that all four campaigns involved simplistic or deceptive advertising. Recall the "D is dumb" versus "D is dandy" arguments in Michigan or the California gun control commercials giving the voter a choice between a frightened lady about to be robbed (opponents' ad) and the slain Robert Kennedy (supporters' ad).

The Massachusetts bottle bill opponents brought the same arguments about jobs, consumer costs, and sanitation into the 1982 campaign that were used successfully six years earlier. As argued above, the difference in 1982 seems to have been a combination of increased grass-roots professionalism on the part of supporters, who were able to use their sizable funds ($652,600) to counteract the arguments of opponents, plus public anger over the issue of repeal per se. Thus this case seems to be deviant in two ways: first, because the low-spending side won, and second, because it followed a pattern that Lowenstein (1982: 511) hoped would be characteristic of *evenly matched* high spending campaigns.

In California, however, opponents not only outspent supporters by more than 5-1 but used their media blitz to argue that the bottle bill threatened the existing voluntary recycling program. Supporters, despite a $923,200 treasury enabling them to present counterarguments through the media, never managed to convince a majority of voters that the proposal was more than "a well-intentioned mistake." Part of the problem was the timing of fund raising and thus of the advertisements (most money was raised at the end of the campaign); another problem may have been the difficulty of mounting an effective door-to-door effort in the sprawling metropolitan areas of the state, especially given so many grass-roots campaigns in the same election. But this seems to be another instance where initially favorable opinion was eroded through a high-saturation media effort that stressed an essentially peripheral argument.

The two two-sided high-spending campaigns in 1982 were the battles over the Peripheral Canal ($1,006,400 to $1,742,800) and the Water Resources proposal ($1,024,800 to $2,028,800) in California. Both proposals were defeated almost 2-1 by the high-spending opponents, and both were examples of the occasional issue that seemed to divide the interests of many northern Californians from those of the south. This contrasts with an issue like the freeze, which was ideologically divisive instead.

The Peripheral Canal campaign found wealthy business interests on opposite sides: two large San Joaquin Valley farm corporations (Boswell and Salyer) contributing $1,032,000 of the total opposition funds in comparison with oil companies ($141,000), utilities ($15,000) and other industries providing over half of the funds of supporters. Supporters relied heavily, at the beginning, on television and radio ads, with a disproportionate amount going to southern California markets (i.e., building on strength), while the opposition relied on both a small army of volunteers and a $500,000 media campaign at the end of October.

Once again, opposition forces were able to reverse initially favorable sentiment (46% pro, 39% con in March) to disapproval by late May (44-52%) and finally to overwhelming rejection at the polls. As discussed above, this became a regional issue, but opposition ads also made it into an economic issue by insisting that taxpayers (as opposed to users) would need to pick up the tab and by arguing that the water diversion would be more extensive than it in fact was. The "hidden" cost factor was apparently a telling issue for many at a time when the state was beginning to feel the effects of the property tax cap: while there was clearly a strong regional difference in the vote (Bay Area opposition ranged from a high of 97% in Marin County to 89.4% in Santa Clara County, in comparison with 30% in Los Angeles and 26.6% in San Diego counties), it should be noted that 1,007,395 votes *were* cast against the measure in the combination of Los Angeles and the four large southern counties.[21] This represents 29% of the 3.4 million opposition votes, implying that supporters were not completely successful in dispelling the confusion caused by the ads.

The defeat of the state water plan is an even stronger example of a high-spending positive campaign failing to refute the deceptive negative arguments of a wealthy opposition. This was the case (discussed above) where early opposition ads claimed that inexpensive food would virtually disappear if proposed environmental safeguards on water use were enacted. The supporters' countercampaign, however, was scarcely more enlightening, focusing as it did on big contributions from "millionaire farmers."[22] Given the complexity of the measure, which dealt not only with water conservation but groundwater, the flow of streams and rivers, and the filling of the New Melones Dam, it is not surprising that the cautious (if not confused) voter said no.

Thus I find in all six cases that entailed one-sided high spending involving economic interests, and in both cases of two-sided high spending on high-impact economic issues, simplistic and deceptive campaigning was the norm. In only two instances were the low spenders able to win (the limit on utility rate hikes in Michigan and the bottle bill in Massachusetts), and in the first case there is prima facie evidence of voter confusion in the fact that two conflicting measures, meant to be alternatives, were passed.

Deviant Cases: Basic Values and Political Symbolism

I have already discussed two deviant outcomes among the ten high-spending campaigns. Brief consideration must also be devoted to four less costly campaigns where the low-spending side won. These were the proposal to end land use planning and the issue of self-service gas in Oregon, the textbook loan proposal in California, and the death penalty amendment in Massachusetts. My argument here is a simple one and in part a repetition of a point made in Chapter 4. In the case of both the death penalty and aid to private schools, I believe that the proposals aroused such strong emotions, related to beliefs or values of long standing, that no amount of campaign spending, clever publicity, or brilliant logic was likely to change them in the short run.

Thus the textbook loan opponents could spend a mere $10,200 in the face of supporters' $595,500 and still capture 61% of the California vote. Death penalty advocates in Massachusetts reported *no* spending, against $56,200 from opponents, and watched a similar victory in a climate where angry voters wanted to "send a message" to criminals. While the shoestring campaign against the death penalty was not helped by its perpetual state of confusion, I nevertheless remarked at the time that probably a campaign by the Trinity itself, with Apostles running the regional offices, could not have prevented the amendment's adoption given the voters' mood.

The two Oregon campaigns were perhaps a little different. Many Oregonians were proud of the state's record of "firsts" on environmental laws, such as the bottle bill and, in this case, of the establishment in 1973 of the State Land Conservation and Development Commission. Voters had three times rejected efforts to repeal the act. Yet by 1982, when the Oregon economy was suffering from a stagnant housing and construction industry, many businessmen argued that stringent controls on land use and development made Oregon unattractive to new industry. Oregon's farm and industrial organizations were split on the proposal to repeal the LCDA, and public opinion was uncertain. (About 20% of those polled remained undecided in early October.) Indeed, the only major set of interests that were united on the issue were the environmentalists, who opposed the measure as "ill-considered and irresponsible." I believe the ultimate vote against the proposal, by a 55-45% majority, was part of a stubborn, partially symbolic, determination by Oregon voters to remain a progressive, pro-environmental state. In short, environment over economics.

Note that two other propositions also rejected by Oregon voters in 1982 involved the same sort of values. The close rejection of the property tax came about in part because key leaders argued that passage would bring cutbacks in the state park and forest service. The self-service gas measure seems to have foundered on the belief that it represented a step in the direction of faceless automation. (The editorial comparison, cited above, alluded to "a clear-cut in the middle of a cathedral grove of redwoods." This is not an analogy that would have been understood by many in Massachusetts.)

Thus my survey of deviant cases once again leads to the conclusion that there is no single or easy explanation of strategies that can win against high-spending opponents. As was the case in the 1976-80 period, there was at least one example of effective volunteer activity defeating moneyed interests (the Massachusetts bottle bill), another case where the high spenders' strategy of offering a moderate alternative seems to have backfired (the Michigan utility rate proposals), and several campaigns where spenders failed to shift deeply held values on style issues (death penalty, textbook aid to private schools) or on economic issues that were seen partially in symbolic terms (the three Oregon issues just discussed). The addition of 22 more cases to the set of 50 from the earlier period still does not yield any guaranteed winning advice to economic underdogs.

Summary: The Growing Professionalism of Campaigns on Ballot Questions

The spending figures in Table 8.1, earlier in this chapter demonstrate in the most striking way the escalation of costs in the mechanisms of direct democracy. Even outside of California, costs for a large number of ballot questions exceed $500,000. Even more important, this is beginning to happen, with increasing frequency, on issues that would seem to have relatively little direct economic impact on voters. The $3.5 million nuclear freeze campaign in California is a case in point.

This professionalization of the initiative and referendum—and by this I mean the hiring of public relations and media consultants, the widespread use of paid signature collectors, and an ever-increasing reliance on slogans and simplifications of complex issues—has not been without its attendant costs for the voters. If I attempt to apply the standards implied by David Lowenstein's questions (1982: 514-517) about expensive campaigns:

1. would a well-informed electorate have voted the opposite way?
2. did both sides have an opportunity to present their arguments?
3. does the ability of either side to present its arguments more or less reflect the number of people who actually support that side and the strength of their feelings?

it is hard to avoid the conclusion that the increasing professionalism of ballot question campaigns, in the *financial* sense, bodes poorly for the workings of direct democracy. There are too many examples in the 1982 elections, as well as in the earlier period, of initially favorable or uncertain voters turned around by expensive campaigns. There were also several cases where counterfunding became available so late that even relatively affluent underdogs were unable to counter the shift effectively. (Examples include supporting campaigns for the Peripheral Canal, gun control, and the bottle bill in California. Opposition funding for the property tax campaign in Oregon came so late, in addition, that the 11,000 vote margin of defeat appears to be almost an eleventh-hour reprieve.)

In addition, I found in both the 1982 and earlier periods that high-spending two-sided campaigns did very little to dispel voter confusion and in fact may have complicated the voters' task. Scapegoating and deception (the California water plan), fear arousal (California gun control), diversionary tactics (Oregon's self-service gas), and oversimplification ("D is dumb" in Michigan) abound in two-sided campaigns as well as in those that are lopsided.

I concluded in Chapter 6 that grass-roots campaigns, typified by the ERA campaign in Massachusetts, the bottle bill campaigns in two states, and the second campaign on nuclear power in Oregon, held some promise for victories that hinged on enlightenment rather than obfuscation. The 1982 campaigns for the nuclear freeze in California and the bottle bill in Massachusetts are examples from a more recent election, but both efforts involved huge media expenditures as well. The freeze campaigns in the other three states thus come closer to the norms suggested by Lowenstein and envisioned by the early Progressives: low-cost efforts by large numbers of citizens to convince their fellow-citizens of the need for a proposal.

As noted earlier, however, a high degree of *organized* leadership and coordination usually is essential to the success of such citizen activism. Even then it may fail in the face of a well-financed opposition—to wit, the 1976 bottle bill campaign in Massachusetts, and the 1982 equivalent in California, or the Chavez effort in 1976. Or it may drown in the tide of opposing values, as was the case for the drinking age issue in Michigan and the abortion fight in Oregon.

I am, however, encouraged by the increasing professionalism of groups like the state PIRGs and the freeze movement (now organized as Freeze-PACs) in all four states. This is "professional" in the sense of the development of ongoing, relatively stable, highly skilled leadership capable of organizing and coordinating decentralized campaigns and carrying on the long-term research needed to deal with complex problems like environmental wastes, energy costs, and arms control. While skilled fund-raising is certainly essential, and the need for large-scale media exposure is not going to disappear just because of outcries about fraud and misrepresentation, this is not the financially motivated professionalism of the burgeoning industry of political consulting firms. Whether this professionalism of movement and public interest organizations will continue to be a stable counterforce on the campaign scene, and broaden to include a concern with the whole spectrum of issues, remains to be seen.

Notes

1. Quoted in *Los Angeles Times* (June 3, 1982). Typical of the 36 people interviewed by the *Times* in late May was a San Francisco banker who recalled the drought of 1977, when Los Angeles people were reportedly hosing down their driveways "while we suffered."

2. We note the visible impact of economy measures in our own work. The Oregon ballot pamphlet shrank in size and no longer carried advertisements at nominal cost; the statements of vote and financial report on elections are no longer free but are furnished at the cost of xeroxing.

3. The Massachusetts Bottle Bill vote in 1976 was 49.6-50.4%.

4. The *Oregonian* ran lengthy articles on October 24-25, 1982, on taxes in California and Massachusetts, as well as four editorials in opposition between October 14 and 31.

5. I was in fact only able to find one column by Robert Turner and one editorial (in opposition) in the *Boston Globe* on October 7 in addition to material in the

Voter's Information Pamphlet published by the state and a lengthy opposition advertisement.

6. I do not mean to imply a closer analogy than in fact existed. In Oregon the diversionary argument, as in all cases studied on nuclear power, hinged on the loss of jobs and the cost of power to consumers.

7. Information on TV ads comes from an article on October 5, 1982; full-page opposition advertisements appeared in the *Times* on October 28 and 31 and November 1. Another opposition ad on TV, described and denounced in the *Times* editorial, ascribed criticisms of the proposal to statewide candidates who apparently had not made the statements. The ad's producer dismissed numerous complaints about this ad as "trivial."

8. Supporters in both states went to great lengths to avoid this perception. The Massachusetts summary specifically provided that "the grant in aid must be consistent with the First Amendment . . . which guarantees the free exercise of religion and prohibits the establishment of religion." California supporters explicitly distinguished their loan program *to students* from an earlier loan program *to schools* which had been declared unconstitutional. Opponents, however, argued that this was a "distinction without a difference" (*Los Angeles Times* editorial, October 20, 1982).

9. I worked in both the bottle bill and anti-death-penalty campaigns in Waltham, Mass., while several of my students worked in one or the other of these campaigns in Boston. I was one of a tiny group of anti-death-penalty workers (two or three city residents and a small group of Brandeis students), in contrast to about 35-40 bottle bill proponents in Waltham. Students reported a similar difference, except in Boston's black precincts where the situation was reversed. Robert Jordan confirmed this observation in "Boston Black Wards, Against Trend, Soundly Rejected the Death Penalty" (*Boston Globe,* November 5, 1982).

10. Incumbent Governor King, a strong-death penalty advocate, was defeated in the September primary by Michael Dukakis, who was then elected in November. Dukakis was a long-time opponent of capital punishment, although he promised to abide by public wishes after the bill was enacted. There was considerable doubt raised about the bill's constitutionality, however, both because of obscure language and because of its lack of effort to establish guilt beyond all doubt before executions took place (Robert L. Turner, "A Death Bill that Goes Too Far," *Boston Globe,* December 16, 1982). No executions or constitutional tests have yet occurred, as of the time of this writing.

11. The proposal also repealed the right to bail that existed in all but capital cases, banned plea bargaining for serious felonies, permitted the use of a witness's prior felony convictions to impugn that witness's testimony, and provided for rights of restitution of victims. Opponents thus asserted that it violated a provision of the state constitution prohibiting initiatives and referenda from dealing with more than one subject.

12. Statement attributed to Gerald Uelman, a Loyola Law Professor and member of California Attorneys for Criminal Justice (*Los Angeles Times,* May 3, 1982). Uelman also authored a strong feature article in opposition to Proposition 8, which appeared in the April 20, 1982 *Times.*

13. See *Los Angeles Times,* October 8, 12, and 22, 1982; *Detroit Free Press,* October 25, 1982, and a column by Mary McGrory in the October 31, 1982,

Boston Globe for a detailed description of the television campaigns in California. Full-page opposition advertisements were carried in the *Los Angeles Times* on October 25 and 31 and November 1, 1982, in each case featuring statements by police officers and lists of law enforcement groups opposing Proposition 15.

14. The *Los Angeles Times* reported on October 18, 1982, that their own poll found 54% opposed to 42% in favor, with 4% undecided, but the Field Poll found 47% pro, 41% con, and 12% undecided. Finally, Teichner associates reported 44% con, 46% pro, and 10% undecided.

15. A second reason for this focus is the vastly greater amount of information from these states that is readily available to me. As a Massachusetts resident and occasional participant in freeze activities, my information extends back to the origins of the movement. I am also fortunate in having access to the exhaustive files, including some opposition material, of my father, W.D. Hershberger, who has been a long-time activist in southern California freeze activities.

16. The *Oregonian* carried an AP dispatch on November 1 reporting the letter to the *New York Times* signed by W. Averell Harriman, William Colby, Clark Clifford, and Paul Warnke. A strong statement was simultaneously issued by the Federation of American Scientists.

17. We suspect that study sessions, centered in churches and community affairs groups, may well have preceded the petition drive despite the newspaper's report that the campaign "surprised the experts." No newspaper reports covered the extensive groundwork which we know preceded the campaigns in several other states.

18. This was not true in other states. In Oregon voters in five out of 36 counties opposed the freeze, and in Michigan the figure was 51 of 83 counties. The vote in the five most populous Michigan counties (equaling about half the population) favored the freeze by about 60%, providing the winning margin.

19. Poll data are from the *RAR Newsletter* of the Interfaith Center (March-April 1982), since the only poll reported in the *Los Angeles Times* from September 1 to the election was on October 18. The Field Poll also reported 8% undecided.

20. *American Opinion* is published by the Belmont, Mass., headquarters of the John Birch Society. The undated letter was signed by Tom Phillips II, Minister and Chairman of the Committee, which listed a box number in South Pasadena. The letter included the following: "In California, programs paralleling this Soviet peace offensive have already become visible. One such operation calls itself Californians for Bilateral Nuclear Weapons Freeze. Its leaders are claiming formal support from a number of church executives for a program that will benefit the totalitarian objectives of the world's foremost anti-God organization, including a November ballot initiative." The letter is from the files of the author's father.

21. San Bernardino, Riverside, Orange, and San Diego counties.

22. This charge was exaggerated. Only three large farm corporations, including the Boswell Company which had contributed to the anti-Peripheral Canal campaign as well, gave amounts of $100,000 or more, and major donors also included banks, utilities, and oil companies.

9

CONCLUSION

Because there is no compelling reason to repeat the summaries of earlier chapters, this conclusion will not outline or encapsulate major findings. Instead, I will attempt a fresh approach in the five sections that follow, beginning with a general summary of the substance of the proposals studied in four states and the nature of the support, opposition, and coalition patterns found. The second section will review briefly my observations about the role of campaign advertising and then move on to consider the more general questions of media coverage and the quality of information available to voters.

My third task consists of a brief, barebones presentation of the contrasting models of the Progressive reformers and of Robert Dahl's seminal work on "polyarchical" or pluralistic democracy. My purpose, even at the risk of doing violence to these complex and important variants on the democratic theme, is to hold my own discoveries up to the light of some familiar empirical and implicitly normative standards.

Since I find that the campaigns and voting behavior observed fall short, in some significant ways, of both the Progressive and pluralistic norms, my next task is a brief discussion and critique of several proposals for electoral and regulatory reform in regard to campaigns on ballot questions. Attention will be given to the drafting of proposals, the collection of signatures, the regulation of finances and campaign advertising, and finally, the use of the FCC Fairness Doctrine. I then conclude with a brief (and cautiously optimistic) statement about the future of direct democracy.

Substantive Issues and the Bases of Support and Opposition

In preceding chapters several dichotomies were used in regard to the substance of ballot proposals: style versus position, low versus high impact, easy versus hard issues, and the like. Let me now abandon these dichotomies, most of which have only limited value for this work, and instead paint with a broad brush the topics considered by voters. I shall then take a look at the major sources of support and opposition to proposals that reached the ballot.

First, there were four sets of issues that were common to all four states. (All of these reached the ballot elsewhere as well.) These were the property tax cap and its alternatives; proposals that involved economic regulation or other economic activity of the government (for example, the Peripheral Canal and Chavez proposals in California); crime control measures (including gun control); and finally, in 1982, the nuclear freeze. The first three categories, in fact, were the most common of the major questions to appear on the four state ballots, with fully 20 of the 72 proposals studied here dealing with taxes, followed by 11 measures on economic regulation, and nine on crime control.

It is not surprising that taxes and other economic issues occasioned the largest amount of effort on direct legislation, or that issues like bail and mandatory sentencing, a "victims' bill of rights," and the death penalty were frequent questions as well, since these topics also dominated the list of domestic concerns elicited by pollsters during much of the period. In addition, these are policy areas over which states and localities still exercise considerable authority, in contrast to the federal monopoly on foreign policy decisions, immigration, or other issues of national scope.

The nuclear freeze campaigns are thus noteworthy for two reasons. First, with the exception of the ERA in Massachusetts and the balanced (national) budget proposal in Oregon, the four freeze proposals were the only ones of the 72 that attempted to change national or international policy. Obviously other measures like gun control or the bottle bill may eventually serve as models for national legislation, as have a large number of earlier state initiatives dealing with, for example, child labor and the minimum wage. In the case of the freeze, however, the resolution as passed directs state officials to transmit international policy recommendations to national officials.

The second unusual aspect of the nuclear freeze proposal is that it is also one of the few instances encountered here of both parallel *and coordinated* efforts across states by a large coalition of citizens. The nuclear power proposals considered in California and

Oregon, the balanced budget proposal, the ERA, and the bottle bill proposals also fall into this category, although the degree of coordination varied considerably on different subjects. In contrast, property tax campaigns outside of California may have called on Howard Jarvis as speaker, but the four state campaigns were quite distinctive in style, followed separate timetables, differed on details, and were not the product of joint or coordinated activities.

The second most common set of issues involved the environment—most notably the four proposals to regulate nuclear power and the more modest California parklands issues, as well as the environmentally relevant set of bottle bill proposals in three states. Finally, I have studied four measures involving individual rights of women or minorities (ERA, abortion, homosexual teachers, racial assignments to schools) and four more involving a clash of a different kind of rights: proposed limitations on smoking and teenage drinking. The remaining handful of proposals defies easy categorization. All 72 issues are summarized in Table 9.1.

SUPPORT AND OPPOSITION

While considerable corporate funds are spent in opposition to proposals seen as threatening to business, opposition to proposed regulation of nuclear power, agricultural labor, or utilities is by no means confined to corporations. Similarly, I have found some business groups *supporting* major proposals, most notably on taxes. I have not, however, taken a broad look at the kinds of noncorporate groupings that author initiatives, that support the ballot proposals of others, or that oppose these measures.

First, several proposals included in this study were referenda, i.e., measures originating in the state legislature and forced to the ballot by dissidents either inside or outside of that body. Perhaps the most interesting example is the set of three reapportionment bills submitted to the California electorate in 1982 because of the insistence of Republican Party leaders that the Democratic legislature had acted in a blatantly self-serving way. This is one of *only two cases* in the entire study where sponsorship, fund raising, and campaigning *took place along party lines,* thus providing strong partisan cues to the voter. (The other case was the mandatory question of a convention for constitutional revision in Michigan, favored by Democrats as the majority party and successfully opposed by Republicans.)

TABLE 9.1:   Summary of 72 Ballot Questions, 1976-82, in four states,
             by topic and frequency

Tax issues (all but four are related to property tax)	20
Economic planning, land or water use, utility and labor regulation	11
Crime control (including gun control proposals)	9
Bond issues on parklands (California only)	4
Nuclear power/nuclear waste regulation	4
Bottle bills	4
Regulation of smoking/drinking	4
Issues affecting women or minorities	4
Nuclear freeze	4
Constitutional conventions; reapportionment	3*
Miscellaneous (two on aid to parochial schools; newsmen's shield; antifluoridation)	4
TOTAL	72

*California's three reapportionment referenda in 1982 are counted as one issue since they were treated as such in the campaign and the outcomes were almost identical.

Given the near-irrelevance of parties for state ballot controversies, the question of an organizational base for initiative proposals is important particularly for evaluating referenda campaigns in terms of competing theories of democracy. One of the key targets of Progressive wrath was the presumed dominance of organized interests over corrupt state legislatures. Thus in the Progressive utopia, little more than ad hoc groupings of citizens might be expected to play the role of initiators, if indeed any formal organizational base was anticipated. In contrast, modern pluralists place more emphasis on a variety of political elites, including interest groups and elected or appointed officials. In addition, one critic of pluralist thought, Jack Walker (1966), stresses the largely neglected role of social movements in a democracy in performing the dual function of reducing citizen apathy and in forcing political innovation. Thus a very important question concerns the part played by these alternative vehicles for interest articulation—ad hoc groupings, traditional interest groups, and social movements—in initiating, supporting, and opposing ballot questions. A fourth vehicle, the public interest group, which stands structurally between the movement and the traditional economic group, is also important.

Unfortunately, neither sociologists nor political scientists agree on a common definition for a movement: some describe movements in terms that might equally apply to interest groups (citizens working together to bring about basic change), while others insist upon personal life transformation for adherents (a conversion process of some type) as an essential element (Freeman, 1983; Wilkinson, 1971; Gerlach and Hine, 1970; Gamson, 1975; Useem, 1975, among others). If one is willing to accept a loose set of distinctions between movements and groups, namely that movements are loosely organized in comparison with groups, propose an alternative vision of basic societal structures and values (as opposed to simply reforming structures or pursuing values within the existing political system), and may either include some formal interest groups or eventually develop formal structures of their own but are not limited to such structures, then perhaps the role of movements on ballot questions can be discussed.

By these standards I find a moderate amount of movement activity in the 1976-82 campaigns. The advocates of nuclear power regulation are a clear example and in fact, as noted above, lost in California and in the first Oregon campaign in part because pragmatic strategy was subordinated to the overarching "more radical idea that ordinary people should be allowed to participate in and make decisions about technological development" (Shockley, 1980). Many supporters of the ERA in Massachusetts and many of the opponents of the ban on state-funded abortion in Oregon were part of the women's movement. Cesar Chavez's United Farm Workers, initiators of the farm labor relations amendment in California, is probably the clearest example of a full-fledged movement found in this study, and it utilized all of the organizational and highly emotive tactics of the early labor movement to clear advantage, despite its eventual defeat at the polls.

On two other sets of issues, however, it is unclear if I have observed movements per se or skilled, noncentrist political activists. I refer, on the one hand, to the multistate nuclear freeze efforts (termed a movement by members) and on the other to the efforts of California conservatives to promote capital punishment and to forbid public hiring of homosexual teachers. Certainly the busing of Bible-carrying fundamentalists to an antihomosexual rally featuring Jerry Falwell bespeaks Moral Majority involvement in the campaign. The two proposals too were linked together with the same rhetoric in single speeches on more than one occasion. Nevertheless, without more information of a kind not readily available to academic researchers about behind-the-scenes funding and strategic decisions, I am not sure whether the initial idea for the proposals and/or the major sup-

port were provided by the Moral Majority, or whether Reverend
Falwell was simply asked to assist an existing ad hoc conservative
coalition.[1]

The nuclear freeze movement, an outgrowth of a number of small
study groups in Massachusetts and elsewhere, began as a moderate, predominantly middle class, loosely linked network of people
deeply concerned about the arms race. More radical peace activists
questioned, at the beginning, its role in the larger peace movement,
given its commitment to working exclusively through Congress,
local governments, and ultimately the electoral process. Yet shortly
after the 1984 elections (in which various Freeze-PACs had endorsed
candidates) a national freeze convention discussed a wide range
of options including both a broadened study of U.S.-USSR relations and possible direct action (demonstrations, etc.). The degree
to which the movement is willing to adopt radical tactics of course
varies from group to group within its constituency. Thus, while
those who supported the 1982 freeze proposals may have been only
an incipient movement at the time, given their more recent history,
I include them in this census of movements involved in ballot questions. Finally, it should be noted that a number of the older peace
groups, also part of the larger movement, were active opponents of
capital punishment and of some of the law-and-order proposals in
all four states, as well as supporters of the nuclear freeze. These
included the American Friends Service Committee, several other
church groups, and in Massachusetts, Mobilization for Survival.

Public interest groups, according to Berry (1977), differ from
traditional interest groups in that they pursue goals which involve
nondivisible, usually nonmaterial benefits not limited to members.
Many such organizations, like the League of Women Voters, have a
long history; others, like the Nader offshoots and some of the more
militant peace and environmental groups, are newer to politics.
A large number have been involved in both originating and supporting state ballot questions or in opposing some of the proposals
of others. I would estimate that over half of the ballot questions
studied attracted such activity. Most frequent participants included
state chapters of the League (on a broad range of questions including
environmental policy, bottle bills, issues on women and minorities,
and opposition to property tax caps); the state PIRGs (Nader-founded
Public Interest Research Groups relying on student researchers and
coordinators) who took a leadership role in introducing bottle bills

and proposals for utility regulation; and several groups that special-
ized in conservation, civil rights, and civil liberties.

Almost all of these organizations were middle-class and liberal.
Thus two notable exceptions (both in Massachusetts) deserve mention. One is the working-class organization Mass Fair Share, which
has been involved for some years in promoting a graduated income
tax on the state level and has worked for rent control, tenants' rights,
and allied issues on the local level. Mass Fair Share's members carried out extensive grass-roots activity on behalf of both the graduated tax and the proposal for a flat electric rate, which they initiated
in 1976.[2] In contrast, the one conservative public interest group that
I have observed in these campaigns was Citizens for Limited Taxation (CLT), which in partnership with the Massachusetts High Tech
Council was responsible for bringing Prop 2 $^1/_2$ to the ballot. Unlike
its counterparts in other states, most of which either represented specific economic interests like rental property owners associations or
were ad hoc groupings of home-owners and others, CLT spoke for
a variety of economically conservative individuals and businesses
in Massachusetts without hope of exclusive benefits for members.
It predated Prop 2 $^1/_2$ by a few years as well, having cut its electoral
teeth in the 1976 campaign against the graduated income tax. Both
Mass Fair Share and CLT have been blessed with energetic leaders
who serve as interim watchdogs and goads to local action between
campaigns. (CLT's Barbara Anderson, for example, keeps an eye
on proposals for exemption from the stringent requirements of Prop
2 $^1/_2$.)

Another category of groups active on ballot questions in all four
states was, of course, the omnipresent traditional groups representing economic and other tangible interests. Labor unions (especially
teachers groups), educators, the Chamber of Commerce, and various business associations were active on opposite sides of most tax
proposals; the teachers' associations in fact usually both shared in
authoring the more moderate alternatives to property tax caps and
led the opposition campaign, financially and otherwise. The industries most directly affected by proposed regulations, bans, or other
proposals limiting their activities were of course the most active in
opposition to those proposals—for example, the cigarette industry
on California's Clean Air Act, the liquor industry, retailers, and
bottlers on the bottle bills, gun manufacturers on gun control, and
large farm organizations on the Chavez amendment. Frequently

the major contributors were from out of state—and negative publicity resulted. Sometimes (as in the case of the bottle bills and nuclear power proposals) organized labor, fearing job losses, joined with business groups in opposition campaigns.

Finally, one of the most common phenomena found in the less costly and controversial campaigns was the organization of ad hoc groupings around a single ballot question. In a few such cases these groups have continued to operate on a shoestring and have gone on to fight later battles, whether through the legislature or in subsequent elections. Anti-capital punishment, antifluoridation, and pro-gun control groups are examples. In other cases expensive and repeated campaigns have been mounted, as with the California Clean Air proponents. But in most campaigns studied, such ad hoc ventures disappear when the election is over. This is not to say, however, that leaders retire from activism, but rather that the single-issue group as such disappears from the political scene.

It is difficult to specify the relative impact, or even the exact numbers, of these different types of political groups. I have already made the case (in Chapter 6) for the effectiveness of several different organizational styles, including those most characteristic of unions, precinct organizations, movements, and ad hoc groups. What works well in one state may not in others, often because a given style is contrary to local political norms (the flamboyant, high-spending California style would probably backfire in Oregon or Michigan) or because the human resource base is not available (urban precinct-style strategies are difficult in both low-density Oregon and the sprawling cities of southern California). My main conclusion from this brief review is that organizational participants conform exclusively to neither the Progressive nor pluralist expectations. I have found many free-floating citizens' groups, but traditional economic interest groups have been a dominant force in most campaigns. I have found some movements but more frequently observed something that looks like competing elites. No single pattern of organizational structure or activism dominates, even in a given state or on a particular kind of issue.

GROUP COALITIONS AND LINKAGE ON MULTIPLE ISSUES

The effort to coordinate campaign activities of allied groups varied tremendously with such factors as the perceived urgency of issues, past experiences in cooperation, and the compatibility of campaigning styles of allies. It often depends on the participation of groups that have available staff and other organizational resources for the campaign. State PIRGs indeed played this role skillfully on several questions like bottle bills and the Michigan utilities proposals. Activities in Massachusetts included, for example, obtaining lists of active members from groups like the Sierra Club for use as a recruiting source and sponsoring joint events during the campaign itself.

An even closer group alliance exists, on occasion, during the study and drafting phase that precedes initiative submission. One noteworthy example was the joint proposal for educational tax reform in Michigan, drafted after prolonged study by the Michigan Education Association and the League of Women Voters. Such extended work contrasted sharply with the hasty solo effort by the Massachusetts Teachers Association in 1980 to propose an acceptable alternative to Prop. 2 $1/2$. Coalitions on moderate alternatives, or an outright opposition, to property tax caps were commonly encountered in this study. Coordination was undertaken, for example by groups of moderate business and government leaders in both the Portland and Detroit areas.

Another set of issues where considerable cooperation took place included the four nuclear freeze campaigns and several other ballot questions involving church activities (the campaign against the death penalty in three states, the homosexual teachers issue in California). Here existing regional structures like the Interfaith Center in southern California often were able to take the lead because of staff resources and a communications network that predated the campaign.

It is probably fair to say, however, that for most ballot questions where an impressive array of sponsors or opponents is publicized, very little communication and even less coordination occurs, other than occasional joint appearances of group leaders at press conferences or rallies and some channeling of organizational funds through an umbrella committee.[3] In fact, for the vast majority of low-cost or even moderately expensive campaigns, only those groups most directly or historically concerned seem to be more than marginally involved; and in cases where several are at work, there are few slack resources for concerted efforts.

Outside of the property tax campaigns, where support of one pro-posal was usually coupled with opposition to the alternative, link-age of a single group's efforts on more than one ballot question is even less common than multigroup coordination in one campaign. The Michigan PIRG's efforts on several proposals for utility regu-lation and for a shift to an elected commission are one such exam-ple. (PIRG faced a ballot alternative designed to divert support from its own strong proposal.) Only three other examples were promi-nent, and in each case these were proposals that were simply lumped together in press conferences or at rallies rather than paired through-out campaigns. These are the Flat Electric Rate and Graduated Income Tax proposals in Massachusetts, both initiated by Mass Fair Share; the rent control and state income tax cap proposals in Cali-fornia, both pushed by Howard Jarvis and opposed by Tom Hay-den's organization in 1980; and the homosexual teachers and death penalty issues in California, both brought to the ballot by State Sena-tor Schmitz and supported by elements of the Moral Majority in 1978.

My own experience in Massachusetts leads me to believe that group strategists are wise to avoid issue linkage, except in cases where the substantive issues and sources of support and opposition are obviously intimately related. Organizations probably stand to lose more than they gain in peripheral support through such linkage. While many of the same liberal Massachusetts groups supported the ERA, gun control, the flat electric rate, and the graduated tax in 1976 (e.g., the League of Women Voters), clearly working-class constituents of a group like Mass Fair Share would be likely to approach an issue like gun control or the ERA with some caution, and strong linkage might antagonize a member of a local hunt club or the "head" of a traditional household. Similarly, a militant mid-dle class feminist might not want to spend several hours a week on what many saw as a working-class (and nonfeminist) issue on the electric rate. The whole question of issue linkage, with its atten-dant problems of cross-pressures, is in fact one on which movement and interest group scholars and strategists disagree. Should nuclear freeze advocates ally with those opposing nuclear power? With those involved in South African divesture? On which side of the abortion issue? Because there are no simple answers, it is not surprising to find relatively little linked activity on ballot questions.

Money, Media, and the Grass Roots

The single most important finding in this study concerns the crucial role of money in campaigns on ballot questions: in 56 of 72 campaigns studied from 1976 to 1982, or a total of 78% of the time, the high-spending side won the election. In 1982 as in earlier years this happened on low-spending issues as well as high (for example, on the Lake Tahoe bond issue, the Massachusetts fight on parochial school aid, and two nuclear freeze campaigns, all entailing $53,300 or less) and on style as well as position issues.

I have demonstrated that while a goodly number of winning high-spending campaigns also attracted elite and media endorsements, losing campaigns also had their share of elite support. There was not always consensus among elites, and in fact even the business community split on some high-impact economic issues. This fact, combined with the 16 deviant cases where high spenders lost, helps make the case that I have argued about the causal direction: expenditures led to victory rather than initially winning causes having attracted high campaign expenditures. Poll data over time on 32 issues in the 1976-80 period and on a few additional cases in 1982 also strengthen the point by bringing to light a total of 20 cases where an initial majority approval of voters was changed in the direction of the high-spending side to create electoral victory for the spenders.[4] (The change was usually, but not always, from support to opposition.)

There is no question that in the 46 cases where at least one side spent $100,000 or more (and in a few cases where spending ranged from $50,000 to $100,000), a very large portion of the funds was devoted to media advertising, direct mail, and related efforts.[5] The question that has consumed most of my attention thus is the impact of these media/public relations efforts on voters.

As shown earlier, in a large number of high-spending campaigns most voters are—at the outset—either vaguely favorable or undecided on proposals about which they know very little. This seems to be true even in cases of "repeaters" like the California Clean Air Act or the nuclear power issues or in cases where a similar proposal in other states has received extensive national coverage (the property tax cap, gun control, and bottle bills). Then as the campaign progresses, typically the number of undecided voters decreases and voter opposition mounts. This might simply be taken as a sign of highly rational voters who have amassed information about the flaws of the initially favored proposals, if it were not for some rather disturbing evidence that:

(1) There is a high incidence of deliberately misleading or confusing campaign rhetoric and advertising that goes uncorrected in campaigns characterized by one-sided high spending;
(2) The existence of two-sided high spending seems to compound the problem, simply leading both sides to oversimplify by slogans or otherwise to mislead the voter;
(3) Newspaper coverage and the campaign rhetoric in such cases seem to focus as much on the charges, legal threats and actions, and other campaign maneuvers as on the merits of the issue;
(4) Scattered surveys and newspaper interviews indicate a very low degree of voter sophistication (except among a very small group of voters) about complex economic issues like tax caps, as well as on style issues like smoking regulation and gun control;
(5) Invocation of legal or administrative remedies—most notably the Fairness Doctrine—or the existence of official reports on campaign expenditures, prohibitions on paid signature collection (in Oregon), and the like do not seem to make much overall difference. Even the lack of a ballot pamphlet (in Michigan) has not created a markedly different kind of campaign or set of outcomes.

Some of my findings on voting behavior are more positive. While the impact of campaign spending, especially in transforming voter approval to rejection of proposals, might point to the adage that the "confused voter votes no," I have presented considerable evidence that at least the mechanics of the ballot neither confuse nor create negativism per se in voters. I find, for example, no basis for the idea that proposals near the end of a ballot suffer from either neglect or negative feelings unrelated to content. I find no decrease in interest with length of ballot and even find a higher level of interest in some ballot questions than is the case for major candidates. No consistent difference in either number of "blanks" or negativism was found by comparing initiatives to referenda, on the one hand, or proposed constitutional amendments to statutes, on the other, aside from the fact that initiative proposals generally are more controversial and in some cases are less carefully worded than referenda.

Other conclusions about voter attitudes and behavior, drawn largely from either newspaper interviews or the work of other scholars, seem to indicate that the sharp distinction between symbolic and self-interested voting, at least on the range of questions considered here, is more misleading than helpful. For one thing, the "free rider" form of most of the property tax proposals enabled voters to duck the entire question of costs of tax cuts despite the alarm expressed by school officials, public safety officers, and others. For another, several analysts of attitudes on nuclear power point out that it was only the "knowledgeable" voters who attempted a rational calculus, and that there was evidence of considerable ideological bias in the calculations of even these people. Yet in both cases economic reasoning was common among both elites and followers, in public statements and poll responses during the campaigns, and genuine economic *fears* of homeowners combined with anger at the government or others.

I found ballot question coverage by major regional newspapers to be quite comprehensive during most of the campaigns, at least on the more controversial issues.[6] Most of these papers carried extensive background features, pro and con articles, news items on press conferences and rallies, and multiple editorials on key issues, although news of campaign events outside of large metropolitan areas was sparse. However, since only a very small, usually well-educated and politically active, segment of the public relies heavily on newspaper coverage for information about politics, the content of radio and television coverage is crucial. Here the picture is not reassuring. There is relatively little news or editorial coverage per se by most stations, except for colorful or highly controversial events (saturation precinct work by both farmers and farmworkers, a subpoena served on Chavez while he celebrated Mass, large-scale rallies or parades, demonstrations by gays, etc.).

While Patterson and McClure (1976: 117-139) were reassured by the content of 30- and 60-second spots in the 1972 presidential campaign, characterizing them as adequate for voters to judge both candidate capabilities and stands on major issues, I feel no such sense of assurance about the sloganeering spots on ballot issues. It would indeed take far more than 30-60 seconds to provide even partial information on lengthy and complex issues of the type encountered in this study.

Radio talk shows, at least in Massachusetts and California (I have
no information on talk shows in the other states), may have been a
potent source of information on some issues, especially since some
of these shows include lengthy presentations by advocates and opponents as well as the views of callers. I question, however, both the
audience size and the attention span of listeners. In addition, relatively few issues are covered, and some talk show hosts gain their
flamboyant reputations at the expense of objectivity.

In short, while I have found considerable information available
to voters, I suspect that there are markedly different patterns of
consumption, retention, and analysis of such information among
"knowledgeable" and "less knowledgeable" voters. Kuklinski and
associates (1982) found that nearly 80% of the California public fell
below the midpoint on a scale measuring information on the nuclear
power proposal, and that this 80% indeed relied strongly on a combination of television information and group cues in reaching their
voting decision, in contrast to the "knowledgeable" voters' reliance
on newspapers. I have no reason to doubt the generalizability of these
findings, at least on the more complex ballot issues, even though
the exact figure may vary with the issue, state, and time frame of
the questions. And given the sparse content and lack of objectivity
of media advertising, the gap between the two sets of voters may be
wide indeed.

My next task is to assess the implications of these findings about
campaigns and voters for competing theories of democracy, most
notably the Progressive participatory model and the more recent
pluralist or polyarchic model set forth by Robert Dahl and others.

Implications for Competing Models of Democracy

Not everyone applauds the new level of public participation. To
some, the referenda and initiative process is representative democracy working as it should . . . that such affairs have taken on a new
complexity is no reason to doubt people's ability to cope with them.
Others are not so sure. They see most members of the citizenry
as too uninformed to make such momentous choices, and, at the
extreme, recommend limiting participation. (Kuklinski, 1982)

Put in the simplest terms, the major argument for the initiative
and referendum, as well as other mechanisms of direct democracy

advocated by the Progressives, was an almost boundless faith in decision-making by a citizenry unhampered by the filtering effect of representation. Progressives not only mistrusted legislatures; they also objected to the organized interests and party organizations that had captured those bodies. Given an opportunity to legislate for themselves, and left to their own devices, citizens might form ad hoc groupings around specific issues, but the presumption was that they would seek the general good, in contrast to the self-seeking behavior of existing representative bodies and private organizations.

The task expected of citizens was in fact great, since they would need to inform themselves without reliance on what modern scholars would call reference groups or party cues. The hope was, however, that most citizens would be eager to do so, if taking such responsibilities enabled them to reclaim their heritage from a corrupt, debauched, no longer independent set of representatives.

Austin Ranney (1978), in an important comparative study of the use of referenda, summarizes the anticipated benefits. Among the most important are:

(1) The threat that voters will accomplish what a legislature refuses to handle, thus either forcing action or facilitating citizen action through the initiative;
(2) The inclusion of *all* issues on the public agenda, rather than an agenda that only benefits special interests;
(3) The expression of the popular will without filtering or distortion by the representational process;
(4) An end to alienation or apathy about government, since voters will now view government as their own;
(5) The maximization of the full human potential of citizens, as they come to realize that civic participation is part of what it means to be human.

These expectations constitute an enormous load to place on a set of procedural mechanisms; they can be, of course, an even greater load on the citizens in the 22 states where both the direct initiative and referendum were adopted. One wonders at the hope that the expression of economic self-interest would miraculously disappear, and the mind boggles at the self-education on political issues expected of a presumably lone individual.

There are yet other problems with the reform premises. The most important concerns activities normally undertaken by legislatures:

weighing the *intensity* of beliefs, protecting the rights of minorities, and negotiating compromises that may partially accommodate both sides, rather than dealing with simple yes-or-no dichotomies. Government by petition, it has been argued, would simply count yeses and nos and would deal with extremes, with no chance for amendment. This argument, of course, can be answered, as can the points about intensity and minority rights, by pointing out that initiative petitions seldom reach the ballot without the sort of consultation and compromise among supporters that will assure a possibility of the widespread support needed both for signature collection and ultimate victory at the polls. The fact remains, however, that the Progressives did not applaud or even recognize the necessity for bargaining and compromise on political issues; such bargaining—especially between legislators and affected interests—was in fact the very process that the mechanisms of direct democracy were intended to circumvent.

WERE PROGRESSIVE REFORM HOPES FULFILLED?

If present-day campaigns on ballot questions are appraised by the original Progressive standards, current practice would seem to be woefully lacking on several counts. The first and most obvious is the key role played by traditional interest groups on almost all but the least controversial proposals. Far from *replacing* group lobbying efforts vis-à-vis the legislature, the initiative and referenda campaigns seem to *provide an alternate channel* for the very group activities the reformers denounced. Worse yet, the extraordinary emphasis on group-financed media campaigns, and the success of these efforts, would probably cause the likes of Hiram Johnson to turn in his grave.

This of course leads to related points about levels of voter knowledgeability and participation. While I have noted one instance (the property tax cap in California) where the citizenry clearly was drawn to the polls by the issue rather than by candidates, and many cases where the number of blanks in key candidate races (even in a presidential primary) was higher than it was on some ballot questions, the fact remains that the opportunity for direct participation on major issues does not seem to have galvanized large numbers of voters. If it had one would expect, for example, to find significantly higher turnout in states that allow the initiative and referenda or a much lower number of "undecided" voters in polls on controversial issues. A markedly lower number of blanks on citizen initiatives and referenda should also occur, in contrast to legislative proposals for state constitutional amendments and/or proposed bond issues. Neither difference was found.

And of course the most damning of all my findings, from the Progressive reform perspective, is the obvious success of the well-financed media campaigns in defeating so many proposals initiated by ad hoc groupings of concerned citizens. While it might be argued that passage of a property tax cap in Massachusetts or California helped lessen the anger or alienation of many homeowners, by the same token the defeat of bottle bill or gun control proposals by vested interests has probably angered or alienated at least as many others among those who strongly supported the initiatives. Furthermore, high-spending sloganeering campaigns at the level of "D is dumb" seem to be aimed far below the level of the maximization of the full human potential envisioned by reformers, and worse yet, many of these low-level campaigns are successful.

The two hopes of the reformers (as summarized above) that do seem supported by my observations are, first, that of markedly broadening the public agenda, and second, that of forcing action on a topic ignored by the state legislature. The first point can be established by scanning the list of 72 ballot questions considered here, which include many topics not previously on the state legislative agenda, the nuclear freeze, nuclear power, and bottle bills being the most prominent examples. In regard to the second hope, property tax relief (whatever the merits of Proposition 13 and its equivalents) is a clear case in point. Other more complex examples include nuclear safety in California and utility rate increases in Michigan, where extreme ballot measures brought forth moderate statutory change from the legislature itself.

I do not argue that every cause that reaches the ballot ultimately bears legislative fruit—fluoridation in Oregon, the graduated income tax in Massachusetts, and Jarvis's post-1978 efforts for an income tax cap or a limitation on rent control are obvious counterexamples—but there is considerable evidence in both the 1976-82 period and in the earlier years in many initiative states to justify the reformers' hopes for both an enlarged agenda and the possibility of action on issues brought to that agenda by citizen petitions.

BALLOT QUESTIONS AND THE PLURALIST MODEL

If my findings are generally pessimistic in regard to Progressive hopes (with the exceptions just noted), what of their relevance to a less demanding model of democracy—namely, modern pluralist thought? Let me hasten to state at the outset that Robert Dahl's classic formulations, in *A Preface to Democratic Theory* (1956) and in *Who Governs?* (1951), do not include a discussion of the mechanisms of initiative and referenda. In fact, Dahl's rejection of "populist democracy," on both ethical and empirical grounds, would lead me to infer that these ballot mechanisms, enthroning the twin principles of absolute majority rule and political equality, would most especially be rejected as well.

Let me also be very clear about my present purpose. I have no wish at this point to critique Dahl's (or other pluralist) thought or to add to old debates about pluralism. I simply intend to hold my findings up to the light of at least one version of the pluralist model, and Dahl's work was chosen as one of the earliest and clearest formulations of that model. My major query follows from the preceding discussion: if the current operation of campaigns and voting on ballot questions fails to fulfill the democratic expectations of the progressive reform movement, does it at least meet the conditions of the pluralist model?

The core effort in the conclusion to Dahl's *Preface* is essentially a transformation of eight utopian conditions for the operation of polyarchical democracy into social norms that concern individual *opportunities* for political participation.[7] Thus insistence that every member of the polity participate in voting becomes the norm that all members have the opportunity to do so; similarly, the requirement that all individuals possess identical information about policy alternatives becomes an opportunity to acquire such information (Dahl, 1956: chap. 3). In the end, Dahl (1956: 137) describes the "normal American political process" as "a political system in which all the active and legitimate groups in the population *can make themselves heard at some crucial stage in the process of decision*" (emphasis added).

It is clear from Dahl's earlier discussion of the principle of majority rule that he recognizes the implications of the common disparity of campaign resources. His description of the problem during the "prevoting" state of decision-making (1956: 66) could, in fact, have been based on observations of some of the high-spending media campaigns encountered in the present study:

> . . . many influences, including those of superior wealth and control over organizational resources, so greatly exaggerate the power of the few as compared with the many that the social processes leading up to the process of voting may properly be spoken of as highly inegalitarian and undemocratic, though less so than in a dictatorship.

This disparity apparently is not troublesome, however, given Dahl's acceptance of the norm that the opportunity for participation "at some crucial stage in the process" will suffice. The point is made even more clearly in the concluding section of *Who Governs?* when he suggests (1961: 324) that "the beliefs of the ordinary citizen become relevant only when professionals engage in an intensive appeal to the populace." This is because Dahl describes (and, by implication, endorses) a process of bargaining, negotiation, and compromise among "professionals" in which general public intervention and active participation is relatively rare. He subsequently argues, in fact, that this limited participation (or "slack"—the gap between the potential and actual mobilization of political resources) contributes to the flexibility and stability of the system.

For Dahl the glue that holds the polity together is a widespread consensus on "the democratic creed" (beliefs about democracy and political equality) which operates in two crucial ways: first, "to make an occasional appeal" to the populace inevitable in cases where professionals disagree on policy, but second, to limit "the character and course of an appeal" to alternatives consistent with the general consensus. The citizen's role in such a pluralist system is thus limited or encouraged by two general factors: whether or not he or she *chooses* to become part of the active or professional sectors (and Dahl argues [1961: 276-281] that most citizens choose to be interested rather than active in politics) and whether/how often the professionals find it necessary or expedient to appeal to the general citizenry. As long as no insurmountable barriers exist in regard to that first choice (to become active), then indeed the general polyarchical rule that people "can make themselves heard at some crucial stage" will hold.

A closer examination of Dahl's eight conditions for polyarchy (transformed into norms about opportunity) indicates that four of the first six are generally met by the campaigns considered in this study. (I shall not consider the seventh and eighth, which deal with implementation and the question of whether elections are controlling until the next opportunity for a decision arises.) The first three and the sixth deal with the voting process and the counting of votes for alternatives; the only problem, as far as my findings are concerned, centers on those rare occasions when overlapping or conflicting propositions are approved by voters. (An example of this was found in regard to Michigan utility rates in 1982.)

The fifth condition—an opportunity for all individuals to obtain identical information about alternatives—is problematic, not simply because of the complex, technical nature of many proposals, making information difficult for nonspecialists to process and apply to the voting choice, but because of the extensive use of simplification and deception in media campaigns. Thus some of the unwary nonprofessional citizens may refrain from seeking supplementary information in the mistaken belief that they understand a proposal. In addition, I have found (at least in Massachusetts) that it is almost impossible to obtain much information beyond the Voters Information Pamphlet about some of the less-publicized questions (aid to parochial schools in 1982, the 1976 advisory question on a deep water refinery.) If this is true for a scholar-activist, it must be even more difficult for nonspecialists. A rejoinder that all citizens may be equally ignorant simply will not do, given the fact that the initiators and major opponents of such proposals surely must possess some information not generally available.

Finally, the initiative process by its very nature makes the fulfillment of Dahl's fourth norm very unlikely. Dahl's initial statement of this norm (1956: 70) as a condition for polyarchy is:

> Any member who perceives a set of alternatives, at least one of which he regards as preferable to any of the alternatives presently scheduled, can insert his preferred alternative(s) among those scheduled for voting.

I have touched on this norm when discussing the charge, cited by Ranney and others, that referenda voting only provides a yes-no choice for the voter, and answered the criticism by pointing out that early negotiation and compromise were undoubtedly essential if supporters hoped to obtain petition signatures and later put together an electoral majority. Yet this doesn't quite answer the problem of the fourth norm. I can envision, for example, many different stances (and implied alternatives) on the 1982 Peripheral Canal proposal in California, including:

1. opposition because more effort should be made to find and render affordable alternative water sources for southern Californians (desalination of salt water, solar collectors, etc.);
2. opposition because southern Californians should be forced to lower water usage (by propaganda campaigns, prohibitive surcharges on high consumption, a ban on outdoor use, etc.);
3. opposition because the only way to deal with north-south tensions on this and other problems is to form two separate states and let those crazy people go their own way;
4. opposition because the government should not be in the business of water diversion at all.

I do not pretend that these alternatives were feasible or widely supported. My point is simply that the lengthy, technical negotiations that took place for some years both inside and outside the legislature and the bureaucracy modified the canal plan itself in order to placate various interests who were concerned about costs, environmental impact, abutters' rights, etc. For Dahl's condition to be met properly, some means—at some stage in the negotiation process—necessary for the hypothetical opponents who favored entirely different alternatives (including no canal at all but efforts to meet the problem) to feed their proposals into the *voting* process should have existed. By the time the campaign itself began, the options were indeed narrowed to a simple yes-no.

As a practical matter, obtaining the signatures for even one initiative that proposes an alternative to a ballot question is no mean feat; this is why we have yet to see more than two alternative ballot questions (possibly three in the case of the Michigan tax proposals in 1978). And one shudders to think of the resulting length of the ballot and confusion of voters if even two ballot questions were available on all issues.

My conclusions about the implications of these findings for pluralistic democracy are, nevertheless, somewhat more positive on the whole than they were in regard to the progressive reform model. As stated, the pluralist model expects less of citizens than did the Progressives. They need not be universally informed, interested,

and active on all things political. They need not act in splendid isolation from organized interests or parties, since the model assumes
shifting coalitions of such groupings to function as a continuous
part of the polity. All that is indeed required is the *opportunity* for
civic participation (and the lack of barriers, except for categories
of people reasonably excluded from voting—prisoners, children,
aliens) by those who *are* interested or who *do* wish to take an active
part. The ordinary citizen who regularly seeks such opportunities
will of course join the ranks of the active and perhaps—if politics
becomes a vocation for this person—of the professionals. It is further assumed in Dahl's writings that the ordinary citizen will most
frequently become active if called upon to do so by dissident elites.

I have seen a modest number of citizens-turned-activists and even
citizens-turned-professionals in the campaigns considered in this
study. Barbara Anderson and Howard Jarvis continue an active
watchdog role on Massachusetts and California tax issues. Tom
Hayden (a national student activist before moving to California)
moved from the ranks of a local activist in Santa Monica to that of
state representative in part through his leadership in fighting various Jarvis proposals. At a less prominent level, hundreds of ordinary citizens who became involved in the bottle bill and nuclear
freeze efforts in several states (without much prior experience) have
remained active participants in allied causes. My argument is that
campaigns on ballot questions have provided an increasingly common channel for the transformation of interested citizens into activists, perhaps even more frequently than is the case with participants
in partisan campaigns for state and national office.

I have also found innumerable examples of disagreements among
elites that result in appeals to, and activation of, ordinary citizens.
Tax policy is again a prominent example. All of the controversial
referenda placed on the ballot by dissenting professionals are further evidence of the point: for example, reapportionment and the
Peripheral Canal in California, the bottle bill in Massachusetts, the
proposed repeal of the Oregon Land Use Act. In fact, an appeal to
the electorate through ballot questions seems to be an increasingly
common way for elites to handle problems where irreconcilable differences (or a lack of political courage) exist. Thus while Dahl never
discussed the mechanisms of direct democracy, I suspect that he
would find this particular practice quite consistent with the pluralist model, although perhaps overemployed.

The one major use of such devices that seems contrary to the spirit of pluralist thought is the tendency (especially in California) of some dissident nonelites to use the initiative process to broaden the agenda and occasionally to move into areas outside of or contrary to the democratic creed. Proposals involving curtailment of civil liberties would seem to fit this category (for example, the initiatives on homosexual teachers and parts of the Victims' Bill of Rights).[8] Schemes for confiscatory taxation and/or sweeping economic redistribution may also fall under this heading. (None of the 1976-82 proposals was as extreme as the famous "Ham and Eggs" initiative in the 1930s, but opponents of the graduated income tax, the flat electric rate, or of vouchers for education might well see these proposals as pushing at the boundaries of the existing consensus.)

My present purpose is not to pass judgment on the specifics of such proposals but to point out that the flip side of the coin of enlarging the public agenda, and thus decreasing alienation among some voters (two achievements that might cause rejoicing in the camp of the progressive reformers), is the occasional challenge to the democratic creed itself and certainly a shrinkage in the amount of "slack" that Dahl and others believe facilitates bargaining and compromise among elites. Put baldly, the initiative process occasionally allows a bunch of outcasts to upset the careful elite compromises and thus perhaps to threaten the stability so prized by pluralists. This turn of events is not likely to meet with approval from one (Dahl, 1956: 51) who characterized the messy decision process of "the American hybrid" as "a relatively efficient system for reinforcing agreement, encouraging moderation, and maintaining social peace in a restless and immoderate people."

PROPOSALS FOR REFORM

This study of ballot question campaigns leads me to a cautiously optimistic appraisal of the practice *and potential* of those devices from the dual perspective of the aspirations of activist citizens (who want to make a difference) and the desirability of a democratic polity that can be both innovative and stable. On the plus side there is little question that the public agenda has been enlarged for better or worse; that balky state legislatures have been either circumvented or forced to deal with issues like property tax reduction or nuclear safety after years of inaction; that hundreds of citizens, many of whom ignore partisan or "normal" politics except by voting, have become involved and sometimes remained as long-term activists or professionals in movements or interest groups through these campaigns on the issues. In short, the political process has been enriched and broadened, on balance, in several states where the initiative and referenda are available.

At the same time, the preceding analysis leads to some rather grim conclusions. The signature-gathering and campaign processes have become expensive and, in some states, highly professional operations dominated by media consultants who run deceptive or simplistic operations. Successful grass-roots efforts are beginning to require a high degree of professionalism as well. Traditional interest groups have become as potent in the referenda process as in lobbying, at least on issues on which they have something to gain or lose. The majority of citizens participate in the act of voting on the issues with about the same frequency (sometimes higher) that they vote for state officials and U.S. congressmen, but usually without the party cues that might assist that choice. There has not been, except in rare cases, the surge of citizen interest, awareness, and activism envisioned by reformers. There is even considerable question about the number of voters who make competent or informed choices on complex issues, given the key role of money and advertising in these campaigns. And finally, there is one point we have not heretofore emphasized: there seem to have been some hastily or poorly drawn statutes or amendments that might have benefited from professional drafting or legal advice. And there have been too many cases of citizens concerned about civil rights or civil liberties implications of some proposals forced to assume that, as a last resort, a measure would be declared unconstitutional by the state supreme court.[9]

Some of these problems probably cannot be solved without infringing on basic rights of petition or free speech. Others await a transformation of "civic man" into "political man" that procedural changes alone will not provide and that may be either a utopian or undesirable hope (or both). But a fair volume of current reform literature now addresses direct democracy, and most concrete proposals have realistically addressed some of these problems. The objects of reform can be divided into four rough, partially overlapping categories: (1) drafting of proposals, (2) collection of signatures, (3) campaign finances, and (4) equity and honesty in advertising.[10]

DRAFTING OF PROPOSALS

Most suggestions for reform at the drafting stage are concerned with problems of unclear or careless writing by amateurs, whose ideas may either confuse voters or raise constitutional problems. Thus Shockley (1980: 40) notes (with apparent approval) that after 1976, Colorado began requiring that sponsors of initiatives meet with the director of the legislative council for an initial review of the proposal, and that the attorney general, secretary of state, and director of the legislative drafting service would form a board to prepare the official summary and title of a proposal. Nick Brestoff (1975: 922), after a sweeping indictment of the California initiative process, advocates what amounts to a return to the indirect initiative (with public hearings and legislative input) in part to correct drafting defects in advance.

I do not see poor drafting as such to be a major problem for most initiatives. While some ballot questions indeed show evidence of hasty drafting, obscure or complex language, or of dubious constitutionality (especially on civil liberties issues), the most hastily drawn measures have been eleventh-hour compromise alternatives to property tax caps, nuclear regulation proposals, utility regulation, and the like *offered by the state legislature itself.* Complex language usually results from complexity of issues, as in the Chavez amendment or the nuclear proposals, rather than from the efforts of misguided amateurs. Ambiguity, especially via use of very simple language, is a strategic device sometimes used in initiatives as it is by legislatures to gain the widest possible support. While my own policy preferences have led me to denounce ambiguous (probably unconstitutional) proposals on civil liberties issues, I acknowledge similar ambiguity in proposals I like—for example, the nuclear freeze resolution. Drafting assistance is not the answer.

While I would endorse the availability, in all initiative states, of drafting assistance and prior advice on constitutionality, like the new Colorado arrangements (which are nonbinding), I am wary of anything that looks like advance censorship—for example, mandatory assistance. A case in point is Massachusetts, where the attorney general is empowered to reject proposals that he judges beyond the proper scope of the initiative process. In 1984, in fact, he refused to approve a widely discussed ballot proposal dealing with legislative rules reform, arguing that this would have interfered with internal processes of the legislature.

Granted, a lack of concern about the niceties of wording, subject matter, or constitutionality may mean some waste of time, energy, and taxpayers' money. At the same time, until similar standards are applied to efforts of the legislature, advance censorship or even insistence upon absolute clarity seems to be a subversion of the initiative process itself. While I cannot claim to have read the texts of a large number of statutes emanating from the four state legislatures, as I have the texts of initiatives, I am inclined to accept the judgment of Crouch (1950) and La Palombara (1950) that laws originating by initiative have been neither better nor worse in language and clarity than their legislative counterparts.

THE COLLECTION OF SIGNATURES

Another set of reform proposals concerns the process of collecting signatures to qualify ballot questions. One problem relates to the collectors themselves; another has to do with misrepresentation (to potential signers) of the purpose of the question. Oregon laws were modified in 1935 to prohibit paid signature collection because of fear that wealthy interests were beginning to subvert the initiative process. While La Palombara speculated (1950: 106-110) that some paid circulation probably continued to exist, the low precampaign costs in Oregon, especially in contrast to California, would seem to indicate that either the laws or the norms supporting the laws are relatively effective.

California voters took a somewhat different tack by placing a limit of $10,000 on the amount that could be spent in the early part of the campaign in the sweeping Political Reform Act of 1974 (itself passed as an initiative). Most of the financial limitations of the act, however, were subsequently declared unconstitutional, as has been the case with restrictions on corporate spending in some states.

The prohibition of several abusive practices in regard to signature collection, however, remains in effect in California as a result of this act. Among political activities are the use of "dodger cards" held over the official explanation of the proposal. This restriction was a response to the finding that voters had been misled, in some campaigns, about the purpose of petitions they had signed.

Shockley (1980) is one of many to discuss another frequent bone of contention about signatures, namely, the question of requiring some geographic dispersion of signatures (for example, requiring a minimum percentage from each county). The hope behind this sort of requirement is to prevent a dominant metropolitan area, or a few areas where colleges are located, from placing on the ballot measures which have little potential support in other parts of the state.

These are only a sampling of the many proposals that deal with some aspect of the petition process, but probably enough to give a sense of the problems addressed. One approach concerns itself with the inherent advantage of financial resources and attempts to equalize disparities by limiting expenditures on signature collection. The dilemma, which also arises in the later campaign for voters, is that financial limitations, whether on spending for advertising or signature collection, are also a limit on the exercise of First Amendment rights no matter how laudable the goal or reprehensible the high spender. In contrast, the concern over deceptive explanations, whether through dodger cards or by word of mouth, is certainly an important and legitimate one, though I am surprised at the assumption of many writers that signatures do or should come exclusively from those who agree with a petition. (I know many voters who sign both candidate papers and petitions simply to help assure a hearing for the person or issue at stake.)

The requirement for geographical diversity of signatures, on the other hand, arises partially from a desire to keep "frivolous" or lost causes off the ballot and almost always seems to be aimed at a segment of the population seen as radical, transient, or irresponsible, such as city people or students. Even if the political preferences of such categories of voters were repeatedly vetoed by the rest of the state over several elections (as they were, for example, on the Michigan drinking age), the idea of denying a hearing for issues simply because they are typed by some as lost causes seems (to put it mildly) repugnant. As a practical matter as well, today's urban or student crusade may become tomorrow's statewide majority preference.

Thus, while I can readily agree that a minimal level of support should be demonstrated by signatures before a measure is placed on the ballot, I am not convinced that geographical balance (with an obvious eye to counterbalancing a mistrusted group) is any more desirable in this instance then it was in the days when legislatures were dominated by rural counties. Given the extremely sparse population in many of the hinterland counties in three of the states studied here, such a requirement may also place an impossible burden on a grass-roots, shoestring effort, even in cases where potential support from the sparse areas actually exists.

In sum, I am wary about two sets of limitations on the petition process—those designed to equalize financial resources via limits on spending and those aimed at weeding out "frivolous" proposals—despite my sympathy with the first goal. My concern is the same as that of the courts—rights of petition and free speech—and also stems from a willingness to tolerate some degree of both economic disparity and frivolity in return for an initiative process that is open to debate and experimentation.

CAMPAIGN FINANCES

The present analysis points to two major problems in the area of campaign finance: the escalation of costs in general (especially in California, but to an increasing degree in other states too) and the one-sided nature of far too many campaigns. This would not be of such profound concern if I had not found that in fully 78% of 72 cases the high-spending side won, frequently (when spending was over $500,000) as a result of an elaborate media campaign managed by political consultants. Obviously a modest grass-roots effort is at a tremendous disadvantage unless it can somehow raise the funds for an effective countercampaign.

One approach to the problem of heavy spending, used by all four states in this study and currently in effect in a total of 21 states, has been the requirement for public disclosure of campaign finances, including a list of contributors of sums in excess of a specified minimum. The theory behind disclosure requirements is that knowledge about massive spending by vested interests will arouse the voters to defeat the purposes of the spenders. One problem with this solution is that some of the heaviest spending is not reported until just before or just after the election, too late to have much impact. A larger problem is that considerable "educational" activity, especially if it involves released time by corporate personnel, may not be reported. But most problematic of all, even when extremely high levels of spending have been publicized, as in the multimillion dollar campaigns involving tobacco, bottling, or gun manufacturing interests, there seem to be only a few instances of such campaigns backfiring at the polls.

An alternative approach to both the problems of high spending per se and one-sided campaigns was the effort in California to place ceilings on both the total spent and the balance of spending between the two sides. This 1974 law, as mentioned, was declared partially unconstitutional, as was an earlier effort by Massachusetts to limit corporate spending. (*First National Bank of Boston v. Bellotti*, 435 U.S. 765 [1978]. The Supreme Court ruled that the *potential* for undue influence did not justify the restriction.)

If the "club" is an unconstitutional means to control finances because of its implications for free speech, perhaps—in the eyes of some reformers—a "carrot" technique could be used. Shockley (1980: part IV), for example, advocates a voucher system whereby the government allocates a specified amount to all registered voters for use on whatever issues or candidates they choose. Lowenstein (1982: 570 ff.) favors public financing in a way analogous to current practice in presidential campaigns. The hope is that referendum committees could be limited both in their acceptance of private funds and in the ways those funds are used as a condition for public financing. One practical problem with this approach, however, is determining which claimant is entitled to be named the official referendum committee. Obviously another problem would be finding the public support needed for enacting and financing such proposals.

My own skeptical view about the curative value of procedural reforms for problems of inequity and abuse leads me to doubt the probable effectiveness of such measures, even assuming that public financing (for example) could gain general approval. I suspect that in the long run disclosure laws hold the most promise, despite what seems to be current indifference, except for sporadic outcries during particularly excessive campaigns. There was, perhaps, one ray of hope in the 1984 Massachusetts congressional campaigns, where public pressure forced almost all major candidates to forego PAC funding. It is unfortunately much easier to bring pressure on a candidate than on the sometimes obscure heads of referenda committees. It is for this reason, as well as the importance of the First Amendment, that other approaches than those involving financial limits may be preferable. One of the most widely discussed concerns the FCC Fairness Doctrine.

EQUITY AND HONESTY IN ADVERTISING

The most troublesome findings of this study relate less to the escalation and one-sided nature of spending in ballot campaigns than they do to the media advertising that is purchased with that money. Time after time I have noted the initially favorable attitudes of voters shift to negativism, in large part as a result of advertising that is at best simplistic, coming as it does in 30-second spots, and at its worse deceptive. Some of the extremes in deception have been found in California, on rent control (where initial ads implied the proposal would *strengthen* existing local controls) and on the Clean Water Act (where opponents implied the disappearance of the school milk program). But misleading statements were also present on the workings of the Michigan and Massachusetts bottle bill proposals, the Oregon self-service gas proposal, and all three West Coast efforts to regulate nuclear power. And both sides in the Michigan utility rate controversy of 1982 deserve an award for the "D is dandy"/"D is dumb" entry into the competition for most simplistic slogans.

There are really two issues. One concerns the underdog's lack of exposure and an opportunity to reply in a timely fashion to opposition claims in a one-sided campaign. The other, extensively discussed above, has to do with the use to which both parties in a two-sided controversy put their funds and other efforts. Let us consider these issues one by one.

Randy Mastro and colleagues concluded (1980), after an intensive study of both the spending and advertising content in the 1976 Colorado campaigns, that the FCC Fairness Doctrine provided inadequate protection for the low-spending side of campaigns. They found in all ten campaigns that the high-spending side, dominated by corporate funding, won over the grass-roots competition. More important for present purposes, they report that even when citizens' groups attempted to gain exposure by invoking the Fairness Doctrine, broadcasters' responses were usually negative and were clearly "too little and too late." (I use the term in two senses: late in the campaign and late in the viewing day.)

Among their many proposals, two are particularly interesting:

(1) That citizens groups organize media campaigns well in advance of their funding; that they also contact local broadcasters in time to learn about scheduled advertisements, and that they be prepared to file a complaint with the FCC *early enough to matter,* if it turns out that they will need free time in the absence of funds;

(2) That the FCC should treat referenda campaigns in the same way as candidates, using the "equal opportunities rule" rather than the "reasonableness" standard. (At present, ballot questions are lumped with "issues" instead; a "reasonable balance" does not mean "equal time", and usually varies from $1/3$ to $1/10$ of the time purchased by the other side.) (1980: 329)

Broadcasters and the FCC are likely to oppose the second proposal, despite its merits, in an era when deregulation is favored by the federal administration and its appointees. More hope thus rests for the present on the public-regardingness of broadcasters. Here it would seem that there is great room for improvement. My impression in Massachusetts, for example, has been that while a great deal of referenda coverage is provided on radio talk shows, the major television networks try to avoid the complex ballot questions, except for a few local editorials. Two of the three Boston network stations in fact refuse paid advertisements on the grounds that 30-second or 60-second spots are inevitably superficial and misleading. They do not seem to feel an obligation, however, to provide much of their own analysis in lieu of such advertising.

The proposal for early planning and action on the part of citizens groups thus seems imperative, though probably not feasible for many of those organized on a shoestring, ad hoc basis. (Such planning seems highly appropriate and realistic for ongoing semiprofessional groups like the state PIRGs.) My major concern, however, relates to the second issue mentioned above: assuming reasonable amounts of broadcast time available, either through the FCC or because the campaign is two-sided, *how will that time be utilized?*

It is doubtful that Chavez or the gun control advocates in California used scare tactics, or that the opponents of automatic utility rate increases in Michigan resorted to the "D is dandy" level of argument, out of sheer contempt for the voter. At least in the case of gun control, the advertising strategy was based on market research about the relative effectiveness of campaign arguments. It is also likely that the advocates of nuclear regulation in the early California and Oregon campaigns failed in part because they refused to mimic the opposition's use of scientific experts and the implied pressure of prestige suggestion on the voter. In the best of all political worlds (and in the world envisioned by the Progressives), campaigns might be won by the provision of solid, nondeceptive, and low-keyed information. If the object is winning rather than making a purist point at all costs, this may not be the case. Thus the low level of most two-sided advertising is no surprise, and by extension, miracles are unlikely to result from even a broadened use of the Fairness Doctrine.

The Future of Direct Democracy

How good it would be to write that political man (and woman) is alive and well in California . . . or Oregon, Michigan, and Massachusetts! If I cannot say this about the Progressives' dreams, however—because those dreams overestimated the degree to which politics is, or can be, central to the lives of all of us—I can at least assert that *some* citizen-democrats flourish because of opportunities provided by that dream. The list of flaws is a long one: the dominant role of money, the continuing apathy and ignorance of many voters, the lopsided and simplistic nature of campaigns, and on and on. Accepting the fact, however, that too much was expected, both of the citizen and of the magical mechanisms, leads to two different lines of defense for the initiative and referendum.

First, as La Palombara (1950) and Crouch (1950) assert, the content and wording of statutes and amendments approved via the ballot are probably neither better nor worse than the equivalent products of the state legislatures. In fact, many new ideas have reached the public agenda through the ballot, and even when defeated, have often opened up discussion that led to later adoption of part or all of some proposals. This is especially true of those venturesome proposals that take time to gain public support: for example, labor legislation and pension plans in the past and comprehensive tax or environmental measures in the present. An analagous point could probably be made about the role of lobbying money, the level of debate, and the degree to which those who vote are well informed, if I had comparable information about legislatures. Lydenberg (1979: 10-11), in fact, suggests that we should not decry the role of corporate spending on ballot question campaigns without analyzing lobbying expenditures on similar issues.

The campaigns and outcomes on issues that take the ballot route, in short, probably compare favorably to those that travel the more familiar roads through the legislature. Unfortunately, this is one of the many intriguing questions on which I have no firm data. Among the questions I would like to see answered, comparing the legislative and ballot question outcomes and processes, are:

(1) The number and kind of statutes declared unconstitutional in whole or in part;
(2) The number and kind of innovative proposals that never reached a vote because of failure to amass early or strategic support;
(3) The number and kind of proposals passed or defeated by heavy expenditures of interested parties;
(4) The amount of deception or simplistic debate in legislatures as well as in ballot question campaigns;
(5) The degree to which confused legislators vote "no," especially when dealing with a long agenda.

Some of this information is available, at least in principle. Scholars should be able to answer questions about constitutionality, for example, with relative ease. Other questions on deception, simplistic debate, or confusion call for extreme care in defining the criteria for judgment. And in still other cases, especially on spending, the amount of *accurate* information available may be problematic. The questions, however, cry out for research.

A second and far more affirmative line of defense, however, moves beyond beyond the "no better, no worse" level of argument. There is no doubt that campaigns over ballot questions have sometimes had an expansive and invigorating effect on the political process. The agenda has been expanded, for better or worse. New people have become and remained activists, and sometimes professionals, as a result of their involvement with initiative campaigns. Probably some of them and even some voters are less alienated as a result, although one would need to survey a great many losers as well as winners to be sure of this. With the growing campaign experience of several public interest groups, there may even be a future increase in the proportion of grass-roots victories over moneyed interests.

Although "the heavenly chorus [still] sings with a strong upper-class accent," even Schattschneider (1960: 35) would probably be pleased at the emerging clout of groups like Mass Fair Share and ACORN as well. Given the prominence in 1982 of several relatively young decentralized networks of ballot campaign organizations (both the PIRGs and the nuclear freeze groups), I see every reason for a continuation of the trend toward a more open process. (My impression is that the trend continued, in some states, in 1984 as well.) Thus, while these mechanisms for direct democracy are hardly the universal panacea that some past reformers have claimed, they have helped to open up new pathways for participation, for political communication and even for policy innovation. This is no mean accomplishment for a simple set of procedural devices!

Notes

1. My efforts to learn more about the location and political activities of evangelical churches in Oregon, given their occasional surfacing on three ballot questions, met with stone walls erected by Massachusetts evangelican contacts. I thus decided it was pointless to pursue the same kind of information in California.

2. I understand that ACORN in Michigan and Fair Shares organized in other states have a similar working-class base, but I have no first-hand knowledge of such groups outside of Massachusetts.

3. On some issues all legally required financial reports on contributions were made by one or two organizations with names like "Yes on 2 Committee"; in many other instances, however, literally dozens of local or regional groups submit separate reports on contributions and expenditures.

4. The 1982 measures in this category were the Oregon property tax cap and four California proposals: the peripheral canal, water resources plan, gun control, and the bottle bill. I also reported on two additional cases in the 1976-80 period where opinion changed in the high-spending direction by margins just short of victory.

5. I cannot provide exact figures because of my necessary reliance on newspaper accounts on two Michigan and two Massachusetts elections, and because it is not always possible to identify all expenditures *by function,* since reporting is done by names of recipients. I thus make inferences from both the amount of advertising that surfaced in the media and from the reports of names of political consulting firms I was able to identify as such.

6. The 1982 campaign was the most sparsely covered, by all but the *Detroit Free Press,* of any of the campaigns studied, in spite of the presence of major issues in every state and the absence of competition with a presidential race.

7. The eight characteristics of polyarchy, formally stated in Dahl (1956: 84) are: That during the voting period, "1. Every member of the organization performs the acts we assume to constitute an expression of preference among the scheduled alternatives, e.g., voting. 2. In tabulating these expressions (votes), the weight assigned to the choice of each citizen is identical. 3. The alternative with the greatest number of votes is declared the winning choice. During the pre-voting period: 4. Any member who perceives a set of alternatives presently scheduled, can insert his preferred alternative(s) among those scheduled for voting. 5. All individuals possess identical information about the alternatives. During the postvoting period: 6. Alternatives (leaders or policies) with the greatest number of votes displace any alternatives (leaders or policies) with fewer votes. 7. The orders of elected officials are executed. During the interelection stage: 8.1 Either all interelection decisions are subordinate or executory to those arrived at during the election state, i.e., elections are in a sense controlling, 8.2 or new decisions during the interelection period are governed by the preceding seven conditions, operating, however, under rather different institutional circumstances, 8.3 or both."

8. Scholars disagree about the number and implications of racist or antilibertarian proposals that reach the ballot. Allen (1979) is quite sanguine, in contrast to the sweeping indictment of Bell (1978), who cites (among others) two pre-Civil War referenda to establish the case.

9. This line of reasoning is followed by Lee (1978). I also encountered it in 1964 among fellow activists working against California's Proposition 14 (the ban on open housing, subsequently declared unconstitutional) and in the 1982 death penalty campaign in Massachusetts.

10. I have omitted, among other topics, a discussion of ballot pamphlets and the dissemination of official information on issues both because it is discussed above and because I have too little information on states that do not provide this information.

REFERENCES

Books and Articles

Adamany, D. (1977) "Money, Politics and Democracy: A Review Essay." American Political Science Review 71 (March): 289-304.
—— (1969) Financing Politics: Recent Wisconsin Elections. Madison: University of Wisconsin Press.
Alexander, H. E. (1979) Financing the 1976 Election. Washington, D.C.: Congressional Quarterly Press.
—— (1972) Money in Politics. Washington D.C.: Public Affairs Press.
Allen, R. J. (1979) "The National Initiative Proposal: A Preliminary Analysis." Nebraska Law Review 58: 965-1052.
Attiyeh, R. and R. F. Engle (1979) "Testing Some Propositions about Proposition 13." National Tax Journal 32 (June): 131-141.
Baus, H. M. and W. B. Ross (1968) Politics Battle Plan. New York: Macmillan.
Beck, P. and T. Dye (1982) "Sources of Public Opinion on Taxes: the Florida Case." Journal of Politics 44 (February): 182-192.
Bell, D. A. (1978) "The Referendum: Democracy's Barrier to Racial Equality." Washington Law Review 54: 1-29.
Benedict, R., H. Bone, W. Leavel, and R. Rice (1980) "The Voters and Attitudes toward Nuclear Power: A Comparative Study of 'Nuclear Moratorium' Initiatives." Western Political Quarterly 33 (March): 7-23.
Berelson, P., P. F. Lazarsfeld, and W. N. McPhee (1954) Voting: A Study of Opinion Formation in a Presidential Election. Chicago: University of Chicago Press.
Berry, J. M. (1977) Lobbying for the People. Princeton: Princeton University Press.
Bone, H. A. and R. C. Benedict (1975) "Perspectives on Direct Legislation—Washington State's Experience 1914-1973." Western Political Quarterly 28 (June): 330-351.
Brestoff, N. (1975) "The California Initiative Process: A Suggestion for Reform." Southern California Law Review 48 (March): 922-958.
Buchanan, J. M. (1979) "The Potential for Taxpayer Revolt in American Democracy." Social Science Quarterly 59 (March): 691-696.
Buchanan, W. and A. Bird (1966) Money as a Campaign Resource: Tennessee Democratic Senatorial Primaries, 1948-64. Princeton: Citizens' Research Foundation.
Butler, D. and A. Ranney, (eds.) (1978) Referendums: A Comparative Study of Practice and Theory. Washington, D.C.: American Enterprise Institute.
Campbell, A. (1966) "Surge and Decline: A Study of Electoral Change," pp. 40-62 in A. Campbell, P. Converse, W. E. Miller, and D. Stokes (eds.) Elections and the Political Order. New York: Wiley.

Carmines, E. G. and J. A. Stimson (1980) "The Two Faces of Issue Voting." American Political Science Review 74 (March): 78-91.

Citrin, J. (1979) "Do People Want Something for Nothing: Public Opinion on Taxes and Government Spending." National Tax Journal 32 (June): 113-129.

Conrad, T. (1970) "Rationality and Political Science: A Critical Analysis of the Consumer Choice Model." Polity 2 (Summer): 479-493.

Crouch, W. W. (1950) The Initiative and Referendum in California. Los Angeles: The Haynes Foundation.

Dahl, R. (1961) Who Governs? Democracy and Power in an American City. New Haven: Yale University Press.

——— (1956) Preface to Democratic Theory. Chicago: University of Chicago Press.

DeCanio, S. J. (1979) "Proposition 13 and the Failure of Economic Politics." National Tax Journal 32 (June): 55-66.

Diamond, R. J., P. R. di Donato, P. J. Manley, and P. V. Tubert (1975) "California's Political Reform Act: Greater Access to the Initiative Process." Southwestern University Law Review 7 (Fall): 453-602.

Downs, A. (1957) An Economic Theory of Democracy. New York: Harper and Row.

Edelman, M. (1971) Politics as Symbolic Action. Chicago: Markham.

Everson, D. H. (1981) "The Effects of Initiatives on Voter Turnout: A Comparative State Analysis." Western Political Quarterly 34 (September): 415-425.

Feldman, S. (1982) "Economic Self-Interest and Political Behavior." American Journal of Political Science 26 (August): 446-466.

Freeman, J. (1983) Social Movements of the Sixties and Seventies. New York: Longman.

Gafke, R. and D. Leuthold (1979) "The Effect on Voters of Misleading Ballot Titles." Public Opinion Quarterly 43 (Fall): 394-401.

Gamson, W. (1975) The Strategy of Social Protest. Homewood, Ill.: Dorsey.

Gerlach, L. P. and V. Hine (1970) People, Power, Change: Movements of Social Transformation. Indianapolis: Bobbs-Merrill.

Goldman, E. F. (1952) Rendezvous with Destiny. New York: Knopf.

Greenberg, D. S. (1966) "The Scope of the Initiative and Referendum in California." California Law Review 54 (October): 1717-1748.

Hamilton, H. D. (1970) "Direct Legislation: Some Implications of Open Housing Referenda." American Political Science Review 64 (March): 124-137.

Heard, A. (1960) The Costs of Democracy. Chapel Hill: University of North Carolina Press.

Hensler, D. and C. P. Hensler (1979) Evaluating Nuclear Power: Voter Choice on the California Nuclear Energy Initiative. Santa Monica, CA.: Rand.

Hinckley, B. (1976) "Issues, Information Costs, and Congressional Elections." American Politics Quarterly 4 (April): 131-152.

Hofstadter, R. (1960) The Age of Reform. New York: Vintage.

Kelley, S., Jr. (1960) Political Campaigning: Problems in Creating an Informed Electorate. Washington, D. C.: Brookings Institute.

Kuklinski, J. H., D. Metlay, and W. D. Kay (1982) "Citizen Knowledge and Choices on the Complex Issue of Nuclear Energy." American Journal of Political Science 26 (November): 615-642.

La Palombara, J. G. (1950) The Initiative and Referendum in Oregon: 1938-1948. Corvallis, OR: Oregon State College Press.

Lee, E. (1978) "California," pp. 87-122 in D. Butler and A. Ranney (eds.) Referendums: A Comparative Study of Practice and Theory. Washington, D.C.: American Enterprise Institute.

Levy, F. (1979) "On Understanding Proposition 13." The Public Interest 56 (Summer): 66-89.

Lippmann, W. (1922) Public Opinion. New York: Harcourt, Brace, and World.

Lowenstein, D. H. (1982) "Campaign Spending and Ballot Propositions: Recent Experience, Public Choice Theory and the First Amendment." U.C.L.A. Law Review 29 (March): 505-641.

Lowery, D. and L. Sigelman (1981) "Understanding the Tax Revolt: Eight Explanations." American Political Science Review 75 (December): 963-974.

Lutrin, C. E. and Settle, A. K. (1975) "The Public and Ecology: The Role of Initiatives in California's Environmental Politics." Western Political Quarterly 28 (June): 352-371.

Lydenberg, S. D. (1979) Bankrolling Ballots: The Role of Business in Financing State Ballot Question Campaigns. New York: Council on Economic Priorities.

Magleby, D. (1984) Direct Legislation: Voting on Ballot Propositions in the United States. Baltimore: Johns Hopkins University Press.

Mariotti, S. (1978) "An Economic Analysis of the Voting on Michigan's Tax and Expenditure Limitation Amendment." Public Choice 33 (January): 15-26.

Mastro, R. M., D. C. Costlow, and H. P. Sanchez (1980) "Taking the Initiative: Corporate Control of the Referendum Process through Media Spending and What to Do about It." Federal Communications Law Journal 32 (Summer): 315-369.

Mueller, J. (1969) "Voting on the Propositions: Ballot Patterns and Historical Trends in California." American Political Science Review 63 (December): 1197-1212.

Musgrave, R. (1979) "The Tax Revolt: Causes and Cures." Social Science Quarterly 59 (March): 697-703.

Owens, J. R. and E. C. Olson (1977) "Campaign Spending and the Electoral Process in California, 1966-1974." Western Political Quarterly 30 (December): 493-512.

Patterson, S. (1982) "Campaign Spending in Contests for Governor." Western Political Quarterly 35 (December): 457-477.

Patterson, T. E. and R. D. McClure (1976) The Unseeing Eye: The Myth of Television Power in National Politics. New York: Putnam.

Price, C. M. (1975) "The Initiative: A Comparative State Analysis and Reassessment of a Western Phenomenon." Western Political Quarterly 28 (June): 243-262.

Ranney, A. (1978) "Practice," pp. 3-21, and "The United States of America," pp. 67-86 in D. Butler and A. Ranney (eds.) Referendums: A Comparative Study of Practice and Theory. Washington, D.C.: American Enterprise Institute.

Riker, W. and G. Ordeshook (1968) "A Theory of the Calculus of Voting." American Political Science Review 62 (March): 25-42.

Rogin, M. P. and J. L. Shover (1969) Political Change in California: Critical Elections and Social Movements 1890-1966. Westport, Conn.: Greenwood.

Sapolsky, H. (1969) "The Fluoridation Controversy: An Alternative Explanation." Public Opinion Quarterly 33 (Summer): 240-248.

Schattschneider, E. E. (1960) The Semi-Sovereign People. New York: Holt.

Scott, W., H. G. Grasmick, and C. M. Eckert (1978) "Dimensions of the Tax Revolt: Uncovering Strange Bedfellows." American Politics Quarterly 9 (January): 71-87.

Sears, D. O. and J. Citrin (1982) Tax Revolt: Something for Nothing in California. Cambridge, MA.: Harvard University Press.

Shockley, J. S. (1980) The Initiative Process in Colorado Politics: An Assessment. Boulder: Bureau of Governmental Research and Service, University of Colorado.

Stedman, M. and S. Stedman (1950) Discontent at the Polls. New York: Columbia University Press.

Stipok, B. and C. Hensler (1982) "Statistical Inference in Contextual Analysis." American Journal of Political Science 26 (February): 151-175.

Thomas, N. (1968) "The Electorate and State Constitutional Revision: An Analysis of Four Michigan Referenda." Midwest Journal of Political Science (February): 115-129.

Useem, M. (1975) Protest Movements in America. Indianapolis: Bobbs-Merrill.

Walker, J. (1966) "A Critique of the Elitist Theory of Democracy." American Political Science Review 60 (June): 285-295.

Weatherford, M. S. (1983) "Economic Voting and the 'Symbolic' Politics Argument: A Reinterpretation and Synthesis." American Political Science Review 77 (March): 158-174.

Wilkinson, P. (1971) Social Movements. New York: Praeger.

Wolfinger, R. and F. Greenstein (1969) "Comparing Political Regions: The Case of California." American Political Science Review 63 (March): 74-85.

—— (1968) "The Repeal of Fair Housing in California: An Analysis of Referenda Voting." American Political Science Review 62 (September): 753-769.

Wolfinger, R., S. J. Rosenstone, and R. A. McIntosh (1981) "Presidential and Congressional Voters Compared." American Politics Quarterly 9 (April): 245-256.

Newspapers

Boston Globe, September 1-November 10, 1976; September 1-November 10, 1978; September 1-November 10, 1980; September 1-November 10, 1982. Boston, Massachusetts.

The Chronicle, April 1-June 10, and September 1-November 10, 1976; April 1-June 10, and September 1-November 10, 1978; April 1-June 10, and September 1-November 10, 1980; April 1-June 10, and September 1-November 10, 1982. San Francisco, California.

Detroit Free Press, September 1-November 1, 1976; September 1-November 10, 1978; September 1-November 10, 1980; September 1-November 10, 1982. Detroit, Michigan.

Los Angeles Times, April 1-June 10, and September 1-November 10, 1976; April 1-June 10, and September 1-November 10, 1978; April 1-June 10, and

September 1-November 10, 1980; April 1-June 10, and September 1-November 10, 1982. Los Angeles, California.
The Oregonian, September 1-November 1, 1976; September 1-November 10, 1978; September 1-November 10, 1980; September 1-November 10, 1982. Portland, Oregon.

Supreme Court Cases

First National Bank of Boston v. Bellotti, 435 U.S. 765 (1978).
Buckley v. Valeo, 424 U.S. 1 (1976).

State Publications

California Fair Political Practices Commission (1982) Statewide Ballot Measures, November 2, 1982 General Election, Summary of Receipts and Expenditures. Sacramento: (mimeo).
——— (1982a) Statewide Ballot Measures, June 8, 1982 Primary Election, Summary of Receipts and Expenditures. Sacramento: (mimeo).
——— (The same document for November 4, 1980 General Election; June 3, 1980 Primary Election; November 7, 1978 General Election; June 6, 1978 Primary Election; November 2, 1976 General Election; and June 8, 1976 Primary Election.)
California Secretary of State (1982) California Voters Pamphlet, General Election. Sacramento.
——— (1982b) Statement of Vote, General Election, November 2, 1982. Sacramento.
——— (1982c) California Voters Pamphlet, Primary Election. Sacramento.
——— (1982d) Statement of Vote, Primary Election, June 8, 1982. Sacramento.
——— (The same documents for general and primary elections in 1980, 1978, 1976.)
Massachusetts, Department of the State Secretary (1982) Massachusetts Election Statistics 1982 (Public Document 43). Boston.
Massachusetts, Secretary of the Commonwealth (1982) Massachusetts Information for Voters. Boston.
——— (The same two documents each year for 1980, 1978, 1976.)
Michigan Department of State (1982) Official Canvass of Votes, General Election, November 2, 1982. Lansing.
——— (1982a) Overall Expenditures on Statewide Ballot Questions. Lansing: (mimeo).
——— (The same two documents for 1980; Official Canvass of Votes for 1978. For 1976, xeroxed copies of voting returns, n. d., no title.)
Oregon Secretary of State, Elections Division (1983) Official Abstract of Votes, General Election, November 2, 1982. Portland.
——— (1982) Voters Pamphlet. Portland.
——— (The same documents for 1980, 1978, and 1976 General Elections.)
——— (Mimeographed copies of reports on election expenditures, for 1982, 1980, 1978, 1976 General Elections. No title.)

INDEX

ABOUT THE AUTHORS

Betty H. Zisk, a Professor of Political Science at Boston University, was educated at Swarthmore, Haverford, and Stanford. She has authored four earlier books, including two on political interest groups and one on research methods, as well as articles on a range of topics in the American field. She has been a political activist since 1952, in California, New England, and Washington, D.C. Her interest in state ballot issues began in 1964, during the California campaign on fair housing, and continues to be relevant to her research, which is now focused on the peace and environmental movements.

NOTES